COLLECTING NATURE

DEVELOPMENT OF WESTERN RESOURCES

The Development of Western Resources is an interdisciplinary series focusing on the use and misuse of resources in the American West. Written for a broad readership of humanists, social scientists, and resource specialists, the books in this series emphasize both historical and contemporary perspectives as they explore the interplay between resource exploitation and economic, social, and political experiences.

John G. Clark, University of Kansas, Founding Editor
Hal K. Rothman, University of Nevada, Las Vegas, Series Editor

COLLECTING NATURE

The American Environmental Movement
and the Conservation Library

Andrew Glenn Kirk

 University Press of Kansas

Published by the University Press of Kansas (Lawrence, Kansas 66049), which was
organized by the Kansas Board of Regents and is operated and funded by Emporia State
University, Fort Hays State University, Kansas State University, Pittsburg State University,
the University of Kansas, and Wichita State University.

Library of Congress Cataloging-in-Publication Data

Kirk, Andrew G., 1964–
    Collecting nature : the American environmental movement and the
Conservation Library / Andrew Glenn Kirk.
        p. cm. — (Development of western resources)
Includes bibliographical references and index.
    ISBN 0-7006-1123-1 (cloth : alk. paper)
    1. Environmentalism—United States—History—20th century. 2.
Environmental policy—United States—History—20th century. 3. Denver
Public Library. Conservation Library—History. I. Title. II. Series.
    GE197.K57 2001
    333.7'2'0973—dc21
                            2001002314

British Library Cataloguing in Publication Data is available.

Printed in the United States of America
10 9 8 7 6 5 4 3 2 1

The paper used in this publication meets the minimum requirements of the American
National Standard for Permanence of Paper for Printed Library Materials Z39.48-1984.

For Lisa and Harrison

CONTENTS

PREFACE

An endless series of fragments, bone, cloth, wood, metal, glass and phials with dark powders, one of which I learned contained the charred remains of the city of Sodom, and another some mortar from the walls of Jericho. All things, even the humblest, for which an emperor would have given more than a castle . . . which represented a hoard . . . of immense prestige.

Umberto Eco, *The Name of the Rose*

This book began with a simple question. How does an environmental library created by an older generation of technophobic men evolve, in fifteen short years, into a cutting-edge laboratory for alternative technology research run by young women? This is precisely what happened between 1960 and 1975, when the Conservation Library in Denver, Colorado, was transformed from a museum for the trophies of Progressive conservation into a federal government–sponsored clearinghouse for alternative technology information and a test site for new information technologies.[1] This transformation at the Conservation Library is just one of many examples of environmental activism becoming enmeshed in a set of shifting social politics, generational and gendered definitions of what conservation or environmentalism should mean, and dramatically changing ideas about the proper role of technology in an environmentally viable future.

The Conservation Library illustrates in microcosm the deep changes in definitions of environmental problems and their solutions. A microhistory of this unusual attempt to reify a particular set of environmental ideals in physical space and artifacts and the subsequent reinterpretation of the place and the things by a new generation of activists provides an opportunity to rethink American environmentalism during a period of startling change. There is much evidence that during the 1960s and 1970s environmental activism shifted away from the wilderness-versus-civilization trope and toward a more direct engagement with the complex social issues of the era and an acceptance of the obvious connections between environmental degradation and human social problems. To understand environmentalism during this time, historians must turn away from John Muir and Gifford Pinchot and look more closely at E. F. Schumacher, Stewart Brand, and the generation of environmentalists who struggled to craft a philosophy that recognized how humans and the products of their labor

ix

were part of, not apart from, nature. In the first edition of the *Whole Earth Catalog* (1968), editor Stewart Brand captured the spirit of a new postscarcity environmentalism with his opening statement, "We are as gods and might as well get good at it." At a time when a retiring generation of conservationists and wilderness activists felt confident that their legacy was secured, Brand and the new leaders of the Conservation Library, among others, had already abandoned the old paradigm and many of the most cherished assumptions of their forebears in the movement.

Interpretations of environmental politics in the 1960s and 1970s often focus on changes in philosophy and direction as Progressive conservation evolved into environmentalism. New environmentalists, in the standard interpretation, inspired by the work of Rachel Carson and by ecology in general, embraced environmental holism and rejected the utilitarianism and technological optimism of Progressive conservation. Renewed scarcity fears coupled with this new sense of environmental holism inspired the wilderness preservation movement and led to the passage of the Wilderness Act in 1964. Following the victory of the Wilderness Act, a significant split developed between local, grassroots activists and national, beltway-based organizations that practiced the cautious politics of bureaucratic maneuvering. This split led to a fragmentation of the new environmental alliance and a period of confusing stagnation lasting until the present day. To a certain extent the Conservation Library story supports this view. As the 1960s progressed, a significant change in the composition and methodology of the environmental movement occurred as environmental organizations moved away from their grass roots. As conservation became environmentalism, new factions formed as old coalitions realigned or dissolved. The shift from Arthur Carhart's grassroots library toward a federally funded information clearinghouse under the direction of Kay Collins reflects this transition.

There are, however, several problems with standard explanations of changes in environmental advocacy in the twentieth century. First, how can one explain the significant numbers of conservationists who, throughout the twentieth century, used Progressive modernist means to act on decidedly antimodernist fears of technological progress? What do you do, for instance, with someone like Arthur Carhart, whose career touches on almost every aspect of conservation, preservation, and environmentalism but defies categorization under current models of historical environmental activism? Second, how can this generally accepted model of change account for the strange cohabitation, in the 1960s, of back-to-nature primitivism and renewed technological enthusiasm among a younger generation of environmental advocates? What place is there in existing historical models for individuals and organizations that defy easy classification, such as Stewart Brand and his *Whole Earth Cata-*

log or Kay Collins and her Regional Energy/Environment Information Center? Finally, what role do social and cultural factors play in the changing landscape of environmentalism in the 1960s and 1970s? The shift from conservation/preservation to environmentalism does not seem to provide an adequate explanation for the diverse crowd of individuals and organizations that claimed the movement in the 1970s.

So, I have often been asked, you write about libraries and environmentalism? Frequently this question is accompanied by the kind of look usually reserved for small children or the insane, especially if I'm talking to environmental historians. Aside from the ones given earlier, there are many compelling reasons to look to libraries as historical subjects. I grew up in Denver, not far from the main branch of the Denver Public Library. As a child I was fascinated with this cavernous and mysterious place, but because of a learning disability I learned to read late. Then, for many years I tore through books at a furious pace, trying to make up for lost time. Reading was a hard-won privilege that I never took for granted. Hence, libraries have always held a special attraction for me. Over the years I've wandered the halls of libraries in many places, but something always drew me back to the more pedestrian Denver Public Library, where among the books dwell the ghosts of my past and this story. I recall lazy Saturday afternoons spent perusing the books in the children's section. As I got older, I often explored other areas of the library. I am quite sure that on several occasions I walked through the Conservation Library as I aimlessly meandered through the stacks; I may have even bumped into Arthur Carhart, John Eastlick, Kay Collins, or the other characters in this story. But I would not have known them, and they never would have guessed that this young patron would someday feel compelled to write a history about their lives and efforts.

I never would have thought to write this story had it not been for a series of accidents of time and place. At first the Conservation Library interested me only as part of a larger study of grassroots environmentalism in the American West. During my research on that project, I discovered the surprisingly vast collections of the Conservation Library and became intrigued by the history of this strange little place. It was not only a vast and essentially untapped resource on the history of environmentalism but also a case study of changing environmental politics in and of itself. Early on I realized that the history of the Conservation Library offered important lessons in the dynamics and changes in American culture and environmental ideology in the twentieth century.

The microhistory of the Conservation Library revealed an intricate web of personal and social issues that weave their way through American discourse about nature, wilderness, and the environment. Likewise, the records of the library disclosed connections between the gentle sciences of librarianship and conservation, connections previously over-looked or ignored. Contrary to prevailing assumptions, libraries are hardly the quiet and dusty resting places of passive records and retiring people. They are often vibrant centers of social and political advocacy. Women, for instance, used libraries throughout the twentieth century to gain access to the public sphere and to pursue their personal and social agendas. In addition, men of a variety of social, economic, and racial backgrounds used libraries to support their work in social causes such as civil rights, labor organization, and environmentalism.

What follows is the story of a mentor, Arthur Carhart, and a student, Kay Collins, and all the conflict, angst, and soul-searching that follow the passing of the torch. The story begins in chapter 1 with a tour of the Denver Public Library and the collections and artifacts of the Conservation Library as they exist today. This chapter serves as an introduction to the space and artifacts of the library and explores the historiography and interdisciplinary work that influenced and shaped this study.

Chapter 2 investigates the life, career, and environmental philosophy of Arthur Hawthorne Carhart. Throughout his life, Carhart struggled with issues that still confound environmental activists and scholars. He grappled with complex problems such as the tensions between modernism and antimodernism, masculinity and nature, false hierarchies of "naturalness," and reconciling public access to wildlands with the need to maintain a level of seclusion. At each stage of his career, culminating with the creation of the Conservation Library Center (CLC), he strove to reform land use policies and educate the public about the complexity of managing America's wildlands. With a few notable exceptions, historians have ignored Carhart's significant career. One of my goals in this chapter is to provide a much-needed critical reevaluation of his influence on the evolution of environmental thought in America.

Chapter 3 raises and tries to answer questions about the motivations and goals of the founders of the Conservation Library. Initially Carhart conceived the library for two reasons: as a monument to conservation and as a center for continued advocacy. Before either of these goals could become reality, he had to do some collecting on his own, assembling financial and institutional support, advisers, experts, advocates, and well-connected allies. More than simply a collection of things, the library also became a collection of people. Hundreds of people, famous and not, came together at the Conservation Library to foster something called "conservation." In the long run, defining and delineating an environmental ideology upon which they could all agree proved far more difficult than anyone initially imagined. The first, and most complex, task facing all those involved in the project was to establish the terms of the conservation debate: Was conservation concerned primarily with renewable or nonrenewable resources? Should the movement openly acknowledge an anthropocentric position, or should it move toward biocentrism? Most important, what were the reasons for, and purposes of, conservation? What would be included in and excluded from the collection process? These questions and the debate over the meaning of conservation reflected a broad and shifting spectrum of opinion in a fast-growing social movement.

Chapter 4 focuses on a set of questions about how the history of the Conservation Library reveals aspects of gender and generational tensions within the developing environmental movement. For example, in what ways did the evolving policies and financial exploits of the CLC in the mid-1960s reflect larger changes in environmental ideas and politics? And how does the library's history fit into the larger story of grassroots environmental advocacy in the battleground state of Colorado during the period from 1960 to the late 1970s?

Chapter 5 explores Kay Collins's life and career and the implications of the shift in leadership at the CLC from an older, more politically and ideologically conservative generation of conservationists to a younger, more radical generation of environmentalists. This generational shift entailed significant changes in the ideological foundations for political action on behalf of nature. This chapter also explores how, during the middle period of the Conservation Library's history, advocacy on behalf of the nonhuman world became a vehicle for changes in the way that humans dealt with other humans. How, in other words, did environmental advocacy entail social change, and to what extent? In addition, this chapter focuses on the conflict between male-dominated management and subordinate female labor in public libraries.

Finally, chapter 6 moves through the final stages of this history and explores changes in direction at the CLC during the late 1970s. For a brief time, because of a new relationship with several federal environmental agencies, the library grew larger and more influential than ever before, becoming one of the largest environmental advocacy organizations in the nation. Interestingly, the union of the Conservation Library and the federal government came at the exact moment when millions of Americans were questioning the role of government and bureaucracy in daily life. The reincarnation of the CLC as the Regional Energy/Environment Information Center proved to be short-lived, a final burst of energy before the big Reagan surprise halted the dream. Although this last stage of the CLC's story is brief, it raises significant questions about subtle changes in American environmental philosophy during the 1970s. In particular, the reincarnation of the CLC as the Regional Energy/Environment Information Center demonstrates how a new generation of environmentalists began to question the antimodernist leanings of their predecessors and to move toward a new postscarcity environmental philosophy that openly embraced evolving ideas of "appropriate technology" and "soft-path" solutions to the energy crisis. This ideological reorientation led to what appears to be the most spectacular irony of the CLC story. The younger generation, in order to save a floundering institution, embraced the Department of Energy, the manager of America's nuclear establishment, and became a direct heir to the Manhattan Project and "that fearful brightness of the atomic bomb" that had terrified and inspired the previous generation to build the CLC in the first place.[2] Why was the younger generation so willing to engineer such a complete about-face? Was this embrace of technology as ironic as it appears at first glance?

Few environmental historians have acknowledged this rapid and fundamental ideological shift from antimodernist fear to postscarcity acceptance, concentrating instead on the transformation of the movement from a primarily amateur and grassroots phenomenon to a bureaucratic and national movement. The metamorphosis of the Conservation Library, however, presents a different picture of changing ideology during the 1960s and 1970s. The changing perception of technology at the library highlights the most dramatic shift in environmental thinking in the twentieth century and provides a model for understanding environmentalism as the movement advances into the new millennium.

In addition to furnishing information on changing environmental ideas, the Conservation Library's brief history provides insights into the nature and growth of environmental advocacy in postwar America and highlights social tensions within that movement. In the process of collecting and assembling material artifacts to represent their ideology, the founders of the library, in some small yet significant ways, helped shape attitudes and perceptions of the relationship between humans and the nonhuman world and the relationship of humans to other humans. This microhistory affords the luxury of looking closely at specific individuals and organizations over a short period of time so as to understand how evolving trends in society influenced those who dedicated their lives and labor to the protection of the environment.

The example of the Conservation Library obviously cannot fully explain the myriad contradictions of environmental advocacy in America. There are limitations in using a microhistory such as this to reach conclusions about such a large, diverse, and complex movement as environmentalism. Still, a close look at the evidence from the Conservation Library raises intriguing questions and provides some insights toward a more complex explanation of what happened to environmentalism as a social and political force in the late 1960s and 1970s. Additionally, it reintroduces us to Arthur Carhart and other influential figures who have been mysteriously ignored or glossed over in previous histories of environmental activism.

What follows is an account of the shifting landscape of environmentalism in the late twentieth century told through the lens of the Conservation Library. It is a story of perseverance, dedication, and lasting success. At the same time it is a cautionary tale that demonstrates that in social and environmental advocacy everything gained comes with a loss. More than anything else, the story of the Conservation Library demonstrates that we cannot understand the history of environmentalism apart from the social context that drove the movement and shaped its history. By erasing false boundaries and moving beyond simple dichotomies, we can begin to understand the subtle and shifting relationships between human culture and ecology that will shape our common future in the decades to come.

ACKNOWLEDGMENTS

The characters in this story were ordinary people, not towering historical figures. Still, I felt the weight of their expectations as I wrote. Many of the characters are alive and well, and I earnestly hope they find this story to their liking, although I realize that some may not. Others are, unfortunately, gone. Of these, it is to Arthur Carhart that I feel the most indebted. As the architect of the Conservation Library, he realized the importance of preserving this unusual historical record for future research. He was so convinced of the importance of his life's work and the story of the CLC that he left specific instructions for future use. Over the years I discovered a series of notes that Carhart had addressed "to a future historian" or "for my biographer." With these notes, he spoke from beyond the grave, admonishing the researcher not to forget a particular incident or the role of an obscure character in the saga of American conservation. For Carhart, the meaning of his existence was encapsulated in the papers and artifacts he so carefully collected and organized. And he wanted to ensure that no detail was overlooked. I realized early on that I had inadvertently become that "future historian," and by claiming the story of the Conservation Library, I became the unwitting foster parent for Carhart's ghost. Among the living characters of this book, it is to Kay Collins that I owe a most sincere thank-you but also an apology for my pesky questions and dredging up of her past.

So many people helped me with this project over the years that it is difficult to remember them all. I undoubtedly will forget some who deserve thanks, and for this I apologize in advance. Where to start the list is easy. This project would not have been possible without the long-term support of my mentor, Virginia Scharff. She not only pushed me in new directions but also enabled me to see my own points with a clarity I was unable to achieve alone. Over the years and through many revisions of this book, I have made free use of her plentiful ideas and trenchant insights about this topic. Anyone who has had the pleasure of working with Virginia knows her contagious enthusiasm. There were many times during the research and writing of this book that I relied on her energy when mine had ebbed; I never would have finished without her. Her generosity with her time when working with students sets a high standard that I have tried to emulate but may never fully achieve in my own career.

Many other friends and advisers at the University of New Mexico were equally supportive. Richard Etulain read several versions of the manuscript when it was a dissertation and provided invaluable comments, sage advice, and much-needed encouragement. Ferenc Szasz inspired me to use biography as a vehicle for exploring larger issues in American culture. Timothy Moy and Vera Norwood were also thoughtful early readers who encouraged my eclectic interdisciplinary approach.

Over the years I benefited from several readers' comments on evolving versions of this book. Mark Harvey provided encouragement and excellent comments on an early exploratory essay on the CLC and again on this book. Anne Hyde also offered suggestions for revision that substantially contributed to the final shape of the manuscript. Bill Cronon was kind enough to make time on several occasions over the years to discuss this project with me and point out strengths and weaknesses. William Rorabaugh, Michael Doyle, and Peter Braunstein were indispensable in helping me refine my thinking on counterculture environmental politics. Thanks also to my wonderful editor at the University Press of Kansas, Nancy Scott Jackson, who provided insightful suggestions for revisions and shepherded this manuscript through the publication process. My colleagues at the University of Nevada, Las Vegas, provided me with an amazingly collegial atmosphere in which to complete this project. Thanks especially to David Wrobel, Hal Rothman, who both read large sections of the manuscript, and to the participants of the faculty seminar, David Tanehaus, Chris Rasmussen, Paul Werth, Elizabeth White, and Andy Fry, who also read sections and provided insightful comments. My colleagues at Syracuse University, especially Dennis Ramano, Roger Sharp, Fred Marquardt, Norman Kutcher, and Donald Meinig, gave me a wonderful year while I worked on this project. I am especially grateful to Dennis, who made me feel very at home in the great Northeast and provided a hospitable place to welcome my son into the world. I started my Conservation Library research while completing a master's degree at the University of Colorado at Denver. I am forever grateful to Tom Noel, Mark Foster, and Dick Allen for taking me under their collective wings. I never would have thought to begin this project without Tom Noel, who introduced me to Arthur Carhart and the Conservation Library. He also introduced me to the late Eleanor Gehres and Barbara Walton, who hired me to write an administrative history of the library, which the Denver Public Library published as *The Gentle Science*. This little book provided a starting point and narrative line for the present book and sparked many of the questions that drive the following story. Over the years the staff of the Denver Public Library have been amazingly helpful. Barbara Walton, an unsung hero of the field of western history, was my strongest supporter, a good friend, and an astute adviser. She almost single-handedly rescued the Conservation Library from oblivion and deserves a thank-you from all environmental historians for watching over the CLC when no one else cared. Joy Hilliard deserves thanks for her visionary gift to the CLC and her willingness to share her thoughts and personal memories about life as an environmental activist. Ted Swem was also a willing victim of my questioning and a supporter of the library and my efforts to tell its story. Special thanks also to Elizabeth Happy, Lori Swingle, Linda Cumming, Phil Panem, and all the fantastic staff of the Western History Collection at the Denver Public Library.

I am not sure how I can ever thank my Denver friends and family: Rob, Mary, Henry, and Charlie Valuck and Gayle Weatherman, who donated their basements during my research trips and provided food, drink, and a home away from home for me over a period of many years. My deepest appreciation goes to my family. My parents, Glenn and Margaret Kirk, and my sister, Kristen, have always been my strongest supporters. My parents taught me to look with wonder at the world and provided a model of lifelong learning. They are an inspiration to me. I am indebted to my feisty grandmother, Irene Kirk, who died at ninety-five just as I wrote this, for a lifetime of love and friendship and a magical trip to the Austrian Alps that saved my soul. Finally, thanks most of all to my wife and best friend, Lisa, and to our beautiful little boy, Harrison, to whom I dedicate this book.

PROLOGUE

When I first took charge of the Agassiz Museum, I found one big glass jar filled with chicken heads, another with burned matches. . . . The chicken heads were potential material for dissection, and the fact that a dollar's worth of heads filled a twenty-dollar jar never occurred to the man who ate those chickens, who was no other than Louis Agassiz himself.

Dillion Ripley, The Sacred Grove

On December 12, 1968, the sixty-nine-year-old actor James Cagney stepped out of his car and faced the freezing wind that swept through the high-rise canyons of downtown Denver. The weather out on the streets that day might have reminded Cagney of the cold days of his youth on the streets of New York City. In many ways the lecture he was about to deliver at the American Motors Conservation Awards (AMCA) banquet brought him full circle from prodigal son to preacher at the podium. It was a crucial moment for both Cagney and the Conservation Library Center (CLC) of North America he came to honor. Like many prominent conservationists of his generation, Cagney believed that the Conservation Library held the key to the future health of America's environment, and he was hopeful that his celebrity status would help more people realize the importance of this unusual little place.[1] For the directors of this unique environmental library, Cagney's appearance and the national award he was about to bestow seemed to guarantee that their dream of a national center for environmental advocacy was finally secure.

Cagney's personal story rivaled the movie scripts that made him famous. The streets of Cagney's boyhood home, New York's Upper East Side, teemed with life in 1910. At any given moment, thousands of people crowded onto city blocks, jostling for space on sidewalks filled with shouting vendors, hurried workers, and piles of merchandise. A cacophony of voices and street noises echoed up the sides of the tenements, so loud that only voices raised to the level of a shout survived. Down in the streets children ran haphazardly through the crowds, dodging streetcars and horse carts. In the midst of this chaos, the East Side Settlement House on Seventy-sixth Street provided a safe place for working-class women and children to educate themselves with lectures, readings, and talks or to escape the noise and confusion of the street for a moment or two.

1

Carolyn Cagney was an Irish-American immigrant mother who worried about the influence of the streets on her young sons and worked hard to ensure that despite the chaos around them, they would grow up as well behaved and well educated as possible. More often than not, the Cagney boys returned from an afternoon on the streets bloodied from a fight, with clothes torn or precious school supplies lost. Carolyn recognized that her children needed safe diversions away from the rowdy gangs of street toughs who peopled the alleys and stoops of their neighborhood. The settlement house became their refuge.[2]

Lectures were often the main fare of the settlement house. Progressive settlement house workers served a steady diet of paternalistic reform to the working-class mothers and children. The restless Cagney boys squirmed in their seats while stern matrons and professorial gentlemen admonished them to avoid the saloons, attend to their personal hygiene, and stay in school. Not all the lectures, however, were boring or condescending. Young James in particular relished talks on the new ideas of conservation and resource preservation. Tales of the heroes of Gifford Pinchot's Forest Service inspired young Cagney to learn more about the state of America's natural resources.[3] The settlement workers would have been proud to know that for the rest of his life James Cagney dedicated his spare time and money to the Progressive conservation crusade.

By 1936, the street kid from Manhattan had become one of America's most famous and well-paid movie stars. The stumpy little man with the New York accent rode to stardom on the force of his portrayals of hardboiled gangsters in such memorable films as *The Public Enemy* (1931), and *Angels with Dirty Faces* (1938). His screen persona was indistinguishable from the man himself; at least that's what most thought. Underneath the rough exterior, Cagney was a thoughtful, contemplative man who disdained Hollywood and loathed talking about the movie industry.[4]

What he did enjoy discussing was conservation. And talk he did. Whenever he was asked to make a public appearance, he used the opportunity, much to the disgust of gossip-hungry reporters, to sell his audience on the idea of conservation. He was particularly concerned about population, pollution, and erosion. When asked by a Hollywood reporter if all this talk about conservation was really serious, Cagney did not hesitate. "Sweetheart," he said, "do you realize that only a layer of topsoil lies between you and oblivion?"[5] Yet Cagney was far more than simply a celebrity spokesman for the conservation movement. He also dedicated his personal life to the preservation of the environment.

In 1936, about the same time that Aldo Leopold was beginning to restore his Sand County farm, famously recounted in his classic book *A Sand County Almanac*, Cagney bought a similarly run-down farm on Martha's Vineyard, off the coast of Massachusetts.[6] Like Leopold, Cagney had searched for a particularly worn out piece of land that he could work into a showplace of the conservation ethic. Cagney's retreat was clearly more luxurious than the "shack" on Leopold's farm, but the land and house were in comparable shape when Cagney found them. He, too, made the land, not the house, his main priority. A few years later, he purchased another run-down farm in California. For the rest of his life, he split his time between the two places and focused most of his attention on the restoration of the land. As time passed, Cagney's personal environmental philosophy became increasingly radical. He shocked 1950s audiences with strong language about American land use. His relentless attacks on "man's malignant stupidity" and the failure of the American system to provide for the health of the environment were bold and uncompromising. In fact, Cagney's politics placed him in a dangerous position during the 1950s when many of his Hollywood friends became targets of Senator Joseph McCarthy and the House Un-American Activities Committee. Nevertheless, he refused to tone down his rhetoric to please his public relations men. "Unfortunately," he said to an audience at Florida's Rollins College, "our forefathers were one of the most destructive groups of human beings that ever raped the earth. They moved into one of the richest treasure houses ever opened to man and in a few decades turned millions of acres of it into a shambles."[7] By the early 1960s, Cagney was one of America's strongest, and most visible, advocates for environmental protection. His celebrity status gave him an audience that most conservationists could only dream of and made him a natural candidate to promote the Conservation Library.

Cagney was a voracious reader of conservation books. One of his favorite authors was conservationist and Conservation Library founder Arthur Hawthorne Carhart.[8] The two began corresponding in the early 1950s and eventually became friends. Cagney was one of the first people Carhart asked to join the Conservation Library counselors when he and librarian John Eastlick of the Denver Public Library (DPL) founded their archive in 1961. Cagney quickly became a valuable ally. His presence at an event virtually guaranteed a large press turnout, regardless of the subject. Carhart was not unknown to Denver audiences and did a pretty good job of drawing a crowd himself. When the two friends met in Denver that December, Carhart was hardly as famous as his movie star friend, but he was well known in the American West as a conservationist, author, and pioneering landscape architect and land planner. By 1968, Cagney's place in the history of American popular culture was assured. Carhart, on the other hand, a tremendously influential figure in his day, had already begun a slow slide into obscurity. Most readers will know of Cagney, but not of his conservation work; few will know of Arthur Carhart at all, much less of his protégés. On that December day it was

Edward Zern from American Motors, actor James Cagney, and Conservation Library founder Arthur Carhart, December 1968. Denver Public Library, Western History Collection, Conservation Library Collection photos.

Cagney the reporters came to interview. This was precisely what Arthur Carhart had in mind when he drafted Cagney to be the featured speaker at the special Conservation Library banquet that marked an important turning point in the history of the eight-year-old library.

The AMCA banquet was a major public relations coup for the directors of the Conservation Library. The room was filled to capacity, with many local dignitaries, including Denver's mayor, in attendance. Television cameras and lights cluttered the area around the front table, and throughout the afternoon flashbulbs exploded around the guests as eager newspaper reporters recorded the event. Not surprisingly, Cagney's presence as the keynote speaker ensured that this was the best-covered event the library directors had ever staged. They were aided in their promotion by the directors of the AMCA program, who made sure that information about the award was well distributed to America's national press.[9] In the days leading up to and immediately following the event, the Conservation Library gained unprecedented national attention, at the same time that its reputation was elevated to new heights locally. The annual AMCA banquet was always a major media event.

Started in 1953 by the Nash Motor Car Company before it became a part of American Motors, the AMCA program was surely one of the more interesting awards of its time. The program was the brainchild of company president, George W. Mason, an avid outdoorsman who extolled the connections between the automobile and the preservation of America's natural resources to anyone willing to listen.[10] In the early days of the program, few questioned the linkage of a large automobile corporation with the conservation movement. Strange bedfellows were common in the conservation movement. For many, still comfortable with the Progressive ideal, it seemed perfectly in keeping with the times, and it was. "The automobile industry has a stake in conservation," one Nash executive said, "because so much of the enjoyment of the outdoors depends on the automobile."[11] This was a statement that many Americans who spent their weekends cruising through national parks or car camping in the national forests could easily appreciate. The motor car, Mason said, was a "recreational necessity—a means for men and women to get away from crowded urban areas into mountains and forests . . . where they can literally re-create their bodies and perhaps more importantly, their minds and souls."[12] For wilderness advocates the relationship between American Motors and the conservation community was more uncomfortable, but most seemed willing to accept the association because of the favorable press the awards generated for groups desperately in need of recognition. According to American Motors, the awards were designed to recognize "the dedicated people whose work is not ordinarily in the public eye, but who typify the best traditions of those who work in the front lines of the conservation movement."[13] In coming years, many younger environmentalists came to question the politics of the award in the face of increasing concerns about air pollution and auto emissions, but in 1968 it was still viewed as a feather in the cap of the individual or organization that received it.

In many respects the 1968 AMCA banquet represented a turning point in the history of the Conservation Library. It was the last event at which the older generation of conservationists still controlled the library. At the very moment when the Conservation Library was basking in the glory of its initial accomplishments and successful first decade, a new era was about to begin. Cagney, well aware of the change, made the passing of the torch the theme of his address.[14] "In spite of all the pessimism," he said, referring to America's youth, "you people are the answer."[15]

On that blustery December afternoon of the AMC luncheon, James Cagney may have been the only one of his generation present who grasped the extent of the changes to come. "I do have the distinct feeling," he wrote after criticizing the old guard, "I was a little too down-beat for Art Carhart's tastes."[16] Cagney realized that while at that moment things looked good for the Conservation Library and the conservation movement as a whole, the future was uncertain. He looked forward to the complex challenges facing the environmental movement and the next generation of environmental activists, while Carhart and the library founders were still looking back to a simpler time when environmental problems were obvious, and friends and enemies were easy to tell apart. Environmentalism was about to become a lot more complicated than Carhart or any of his contemporaries had ever imagined.

CHAPTER ONE

Collecting History

The reasons for many of the physical characteristics of the pencil are as lost
. . . as are the origins of the sizes and shapes of many a common object, but
the relatively recent origin and short history of the modern pencil also
makes it a manageable artifact to twirl about in the fingers and reflect upon
in the mind. When we do this we also realize that for all its commonness and
apparent cheapness, the pencil is a product of immense complexity and sophistication.

Henry Petroski, The Pencil

If you look at the city of Denver from the air, you cannot help noticing the
clean lines and swaths of green radiating out from the center of the metropolis. From the brown prairie, wide parkways lead visitors to the
"Queen City of the Plains," an oasis on the edge of the Rocky Mountains.
All spokes take you toward the crowning glory of Denver's "City Beautiful" movement—Civic Center Park. Its lavish flower beds, towering trees,
and classical statuary announce your arrival into a "natural" space carved
out of the heart of downtown. Businessmen, weary state politicians, and
office workers find solace from the vicissitudes of the white-collar jungle
in this peaceful garden. Surrounding this well-ordered landscape stands
a collection of massive neoclassic buildings that house the offices of government for the city and the state. The theme of the architecture is unmis-
takable—progress and enlightenment. Amid these hulking replicas of
ancient splendor, two singular structures catch the modern observer's
eye. The Denver Museum of Art is a towering monument to modernism,
with gray ceramic tiles that reflect the sun and highlight a profusion of
seemingly random windows. No less startling is the whimsical facade of
the Denver Public Library, completed in 1995 at a cost to the taxpayers of
$70 million. Composed of towers of native stone crowned by an unlikely
copper mortarboard, large enough to land a helicopter, the library
screams for attention. Like the neoclassic buildings that surround it, the
library is a product of its time—a postmodern dream, or nightmare depending on who you talk to, embodying the idea of organized chaos.[1]

In the spring of 1995, the DPL opened its newly constructed main
branch in downtown Denver. The library was designed by Michael
Graves, an architect known for creating buildings that never fail to gen-

Denver's Civic Center as seen from the air in the early 1950s. Denver Public Library, Western History Collection, Conservation Library Collection photos.

erate interest and controversy.[2] Denver's new library building was no exception. The local press closely covered the construction, and the grand opening was front-page news. Immediately upon my arrival in Denver in 1995, to spend the summer doing research in the Conservation Library Collection, I was besieged with requests from people eager to tour the $70 million structure. About twice a week throughout the summer, I led friends or acquaintances through the building and became so familiar with the architecture, art, and history of the place that I began to feel like a docent.

My tour of this iconoclastic structure began, quite naturally, at the main entrance on the corner of Broadway and Thirteenth Avenue. I often met my visitors next to the steamy hot dog stand run by recent Russian immigrants, who shout to their customers above the noise of speeding cars. Just beyond the hot dog vendor, a towering portico led Lilliputian visitors from the noise and confusion of downtown streets into the quiet grandeur of the entrance hall. The library is at once an ordinary place, where homeless people, trying to stay warm, methodically flip through the pages of magazines and a mysterious place full of remarkable relics and forgotten stories. The soaring entry hall ushers visitors toward a bank of stainless steel elevators. On any given day one might encounter groups of rowdy second graders who spill out over each other as the elevator empties in preparation for a trip from the public space of the lobby to the rarefied atmosphere of the upper research floors. Walking through the library, one encounters haggard college students jostling with lawyers and businessmen for space on computer terminals, while other patrons sit on the floor of the stacks, lost to the world, deep in books they seem unable to put down. Regardless of the time of day or the day of the week, the library always buzzes with activity.

In the months I spent in the library, I worked out a system for leading tours. First we walked through the large public space of the main floors. During this portion of the tour, I focused on the unique architecture of the building and the history of the library in Denver. Next we moved to the middle floors, which house the standard fare of public libraries, such as fiction, periodicals, and reference services. We walked quickly through these areas as I pointed out notable architectural details, such as carefully crafted ergonomic desks with matching chairs, designed to be comfortable enough to study in but not overly so for the sleepy homeless. The final phase of the tour took us to the upper research floors, where we lingered the longest.

Stepping out of the elevator onto the fifth floor—home of the renowned Western History Collection—library patrons find themselves suddenly and unexpectedly in a "sacred space." The cold steel and high ceilings of the main lobby give way to warm woods, dim lights, and rooms on a more human scale. The first thing one notices as the elevators doors slide closed is Albert Bierstadt's monumental painting *Estes Park— The Rocky Mountains* (1877). The juxtaposition of late twentieth-century modern architecture and grand nineteenth-century romantic landscape painting never fails to startle the unsuspecting visitor. A window on the wilderness, the painting provides the entry point into a sanctuary of preserved nature, where visitors can view the relics of the conservation movement and, in so doing, reevaluate their culture of consumption and reconstruct their view of nature in the heart of the city.

Just beyond the painting lies a vast array of material objects representing the dream of preserving the romantic wilderness world depicted on Bierstadt's canvas. Gradually, as the visitor walks through the rooms of the fifth floor, a story unfolds. The history of the American West and the effort to preserve it take physical form in stately rows of books, stacks of manuscripts, paintings, and jumbles of artifacts. Restoration of the human spirit through contact with wilderness, the central ideal of the conservation movement until the 1960s, is embodied in Arthur Carhart's Conservation Library Collection, the once beloved, but now forlorn, stepchild of the Western History Collection. Growing out of the seed of

Carhart's personal collections—gathered over a forty-year career as a Forest Service land planner and conservation author—the Conservation Library came to represent an attempt, in the 1950s and 1960s, to preserve a particular vision of the American environment and to educate a new generation of environmental advocates. This vision initially encompassed fears about dwindling natural resources, overpopulation, human nature, and technocracy in a postatomic world.

By the end of my fourth month on this floor of the library, I knew every painting, sculpture, architectural detail, and shelf of books. As the tour progressed slowly through the various rooms, I told the story of the rise and fall of the Conservation Library and the people who built it, carefully explaining how this little story related to the larger history of the rise of the American environmental movement. The rooms became like chapters of a book, each representing a different part of the story, each punctuated by material artifacts, carefully preserved relics, yellowed and dusty documents, and crisp black-and-white photographs of long-dead conservation heroes. During the course of the tour, many questions arose. Seemingly simple questions often led to complicated and incomplete answers. Why did this unusual place come into being when and where it did? Why were some things collected and others ignored? What was the relationship between the artifacts and the cultural politics of the environmental movement? Why, in the 1960s, did many of the leaders of the American environmental movement work so diligently to create a physical space to house their ideas? What happened to the library when the older men who built it were forced by illness and age to turn it over to a younger generation? Why are all the older pictures of middle-aged men and the more recent pictures of young women? Often our tour ended back at the Russian hot dog stand, where I would attempt to answer these questions over lunch.

THE VAULT

To many, the story of this compact place and short moment in time may seem too small a vehicle for reaching broad conclusions about the complicated development of the American environmental movement, with all its political, social, and intellectual subtleties. There are, of course, limits to how far one can generalize from the specific, especially when dealing with messy human history and events that arose out of particular national and regional contingencies. Still, just as Henry Petroski uses the lowly pencil as a paradigm for the complexities of the design process, I think that the CLC provides a useful metaphor for understanding the evolution of environmental thinking in postwar America.[3]

In many respects, the history of the Conservation Library mirrors changes in American culture and social movements from the 1950s through the 1970s. During these years the library became a center for environmental advocacy and a national clearinghouse of environmental information. Its history is a case study of the changing ideologies and evolving philosophies of the American environmental movement. Many significant environmentalists, from David Brower and Howard Zahniser, to Rosalie Edge and William Vogt, along with hundreds of grassroots groups and local individuals, participated in the creation of this remarkable archive. By the 1960s, the library had become a meeting place for individuals from diverse political, economic, and ideological backgrounds. For a brief time, hunters and hikers, lumber company executives and lawyers, mountaineers and ornithologists, library commissioners and senators came together to support the programs of the Conservation Library. This convergence of previously diverse interests fostered a fragile and fleeting sense of community among the users and protectors of the environment, and it provided a unique opportunity for cooperation on a variety of environmental issues. At the same time, the CLC opened up avenues for individual empowerment and reflected contemporary social changes.

Within the archives of the Conservation Library, one finds a wealth of introspective records chronicling the rise and fall of various environmental movements and philosophies. This material constitutes one of the largest collections of conservation material in the nation, one that covers a wide range of environmental topics. Researchers of wildlife management, land planning, wilderness, water, reclamation, grassroots advocacy, organizational history, population, energy policy, and many other topics can find rich material in the library's holdings. In all, there are today approximately eleven hundred linear feet of manuscripts, along with about ten thousand related volumes, plus a host of unusual artifacts and items in the collection.

For many years, much of this material, the most sacred artifacts of the conservation movement, was kept in "the vault," a temperature-controlled cement-encased tomb for the icons of environmentalism. For the few researchers who gained entry to this inner sanctum, an unexpected treasure of conservation lore waited, dusty and untouched. Boxes of reel-to-reel tapes contained interviews with hundreds of pioneer Forest Rangers and conservationists. Beautifully crafted wooden boxes held copies of leather-bound photo albums from early American forests. Heavier wooden boxes contained thousands of glass lantern slides depicting forest conditions from the Civil War era. Leafing through one of the smaller, leather-bound books, such as W. C. Muenscher's *Keys to Woody Plants* (1936), you might find tiny limbs from a far-off shrub falling into your hands, neatly snipped off generations ago by some unknown

DPL maintenance worker checks the humidity in the vault, which was beginning to fill with conservation artifacts by the summer of 1961. Denver Public Library, Western History Collection, Conservation Library Collection photos.

forester—maybe Muenscher himself? The jumble of artifacts, manuscripts, and folios was so dense in the vault that it was barely possible to walk through the space without dislodging some treasure.

The manuscript collections form the heart of the CLC Archive. They include the letters and papers of a number of leading environmentalists, such as wilderness bill author Howard Zahniser; conservationist Arthur Carhart; Hugh Bennett, "the father of soil conservation"; wildlife expert Lois Crisler; pioneer ornithologist Rosalie Edge; as well as prominent conservationists such as Olaus Murie, Sigurd Olson, and Charles Lathrop Pack, to name only a few. In addition to the papers of individuals, the collection contains the records of a variety of national and local environmental organizations, such as the Wilderness Society, the Outdoor Writers Association of America, the Colorado Open Space Council, the National Association of State Foresters, and the Rocky Mountain Center on Environment. These manuscripts, along with rare conservation books and a wide variety of unusual artifacts, once occupied a distinct physical space within the Denver Public Library system, especially designed to represent a particular set of ideas about nature and conservation. This physical space became known as the Conservation Library.

During the first thirty years of its history, the Conservation Library experienced remarkable highs and dismal lows. Established in 1960, the library quickly rose to national prominence. During the next twenty years, the center played a small, yet meaningful, role in the development of the American environmental movement. The ideology of its founders and administrators changed and developed along with larger trends in environmental thinking and the social movements of the 1960s and 1970s. The library gained a reputation as a resource for the resolution of environmental disputes and as a treasure chest of environmental information. In addition, the unique collection became a model for cutting-edge information systems and library management. In 1979, President Jimmy Carter hailed the Conservation Library as a "prototype of future information services."[4] By the late 1970s, the collection had surpassed the most optimistic hopes of its founders. To all involved, it seemed that the future of the CLC was secure.

In many respects early success fostered an overconfidence in the public's willingness to support the library. Sometimes blinded by their ambition and accomplishments, the directors of the library embarked on a dramatic expansion of the collection. To fund this expansion, they turned to the federal government. Ultimately the library became dependent on federal money, and between 1975 and 1980 the U.S. government, primarily through the Department of Energy, provided nearly all of the institution's funding. In 1980, however, the collection fell victim to the Reagan revolution. Energy Department appropriations were slashed, and funding for the

CLC dried up. Unable to recover from the loss of the federal funds, the overextended collection closed its doors for an extended period, beginning in the fall of 1982. Although the CLC officially ceased to exist as an autonomous place, the archives and collections remained intact. Everything was stored in an immense warehouse in lower downtown Denver, where the heart of the CLC remained, virtually untouched, for the next fourteen years. From an archival point of view, the CLC collections were simply subsumed into the larger manuscript division of the DPL. Although limited access to the collection remained available to qualified researchers, the CLC soon faded from public memory. Few environmentalists or historians of the 1990s knew that the collection existed.[5]

For fourteen years, the collections of the Conservation Library remained dormant. Most environmental historians, unaware of its existence, ignored its role in the history of the American environmental movement and the development of modern environmental philosophy.[6] This failure to acknowledge the CLC's part in the rise of environmentalism in the 1960s and 1970s left a gap in the story of American environmentalism. The significance of this topic, however, goes far beyond simply uncovering a good story previously untold. The history of the Conservation Library also provides new insights into current interdisciplinary debates over the intellectual roots and social significance of the environmental movement.

CULTURAL CONSTRUCTION

The building of the Conservation Library was an exercise in cultural construction, with the architects of this unusual archive embodying their ideology in physical space and material collections. The institution they created speaks to the challenges and struggles of building an environmental movement within the confines of an inherently materialistic and acquisitive industrial culture. In the Conservation Library, ideas and philosophies assumed physical form, in published pamphlets, press releases, artifacts collected and displayed, and in the books and manuscripts assembled and cataloged. Past successes of the environmental movement were quantified in linear feet, numbered artifacts, and floor space.

Between 1950 and 1980, scholars working from a number of different perspectives generated a large body of literature focusing on the history of the American environmental movement and the development of an American environmental philosophy. Few of these works, however, addressed the role of archival collecting and cultural representation in this process. In some ironic ways, material culture, the products of humanity, and the process of collecting material things can reveal deep-seated ideas about nature and the nonhuman world.[7] As historian Donna Haraway demonstrates, for instance, the artifacts and physical space of the New York Museum of Natural History perfectly expressed early twentieth-century ideas of nature and gender.[8] From a different perspective, cultural historian James Clifford looks at the way "collecting has long been a strategy for the deployment of a possessive self, culture, and authenticity."[9] Still another perspective on the issue of nature and culture may be found in the literature of museology.[10] This work is of great value for the study of changing environmental ideas and environmental politics. Still, few histories of the environmental movement use these sources.

All this is not to say that environmental historians have failed to analyze environmental ideas. On the contrary, studies of the rise of environmentalism and environmental philosophy in American life have long been a staple of environmental history. Many of the classics of the field deal with the evolution of environmental thinking. Works such as Roderick Nash's *Wilderness and the American Mind,* Samuel P. Hays's *Conservation and the Gospel of Efficiency,* and Donald Worster's *Nature's Economy* exemplify this trend.[11] The following history of the Conservation Library is, to a certain degree, also an intellectual history, particularly when I focus on the development of environmental ideas, ideologies, and philosophies in the middle to late twentieth century. On the other hand, while continuing a tradition of environmental history writing, I hope to add a new dimension to the story. Many early histories of environmental ideas depicted sharply dichotomous relationships among various environmental philosophies. In this regard, conservationism, preservationism, and environmentalism appear as separate and ultimately irreconcilable modes of thinking. In some of these studies, environmentalism becomes the logical outcome of a linear evolutionary process, from wise use to deep ecology. For the student of environmental thinking, linear evolutionary models of this type present many problems. First, they tend to reduce complex processes into a neatly taxonomized course of progressive thinking, leaving little room for individual agency and historical contingency. Additionally, they often emphasize large-scale change at the expense of careful analysis of local variation and individual difference. I argue instead that environmental ideas arise out of particular circumstances and particular times and rarely fit into neat models of large-scale cultural change. Environmental politics are inspired by multiple and constantly shifting layerings of sometimes compatible, sometimes contradictory goals, motives, and imperatives. Attempts to uncover the "American mind" or other such transhistorical constructs do little to illuminate the motivations, achievements, or failures of the people involved in engineering social change in very specific local settings.[12] A microhistory of the Conservation Library, by carefully illuminating the development of this crossroads of environmental ideology, can contribute to the ongoing effort to provide a more balanced and complex picture of environmentalism.

Over the past few years, scholars from a variety of disciplines have focused on the poetics and politics of environmental language.[13] In fact, questioning the language and assumptions of American environmental thinking has long been a goal of environmental ethicists, philosophers, and environmental historians. Following in this tradition, the Conservation Library project required a remarkable amount of introspection. Those involved constantly questioned the project of environmentalism and wrote extensively about their struggles to define the terms of the debate. For example, in the early 1960s the founders of the CLC were questioning terms like "nature," "wilderness," and "human nature." The second generation of CLC directors thought hard about ideas like "gender," "appropriate technology," "soft tech," "modernism," and "antimodernism." Because of this explicit focus on rhetoric and language, the history of the CLC makes a significant contribution to the ongoing study of environmental discourse.

Another trend in recent historical analysis of environmentalism is the attempt to use methods from women's history and feminist theory to deconstruct environmental language. Too often feminist influences are absent from intellectual histories of environmentalism in America. Although partially remedied by a recent surge in studies of environmentalism from a feminist and "ecofeminist" perspective, the problem nonetheless persists.[14] Like other postwar social movements, the rise of environmentalism brought gender tensions to the surface and created avenues for personal empowerment for thousands of women involved in the movement. The story of the Conservation Library illustrates changing gender politics in the environmental movement and library and museum systems, traditionally viewed as havens for educated women. Over time, political, professional, and social relations among those who worked in the library changed, reflecting developing and contested power configurations in the larger society.[15] As the institution evolved, women increasingly moved through the ranks, thus changing the social dynamic within the library and the environmental movement.[16]

Gender was not the only significant difference between the CLC founders and the young women who ran the library in the 1970s. To a certain extent this new generation of leaders also rejected the antimodernism and wilderness trope of their elders. Antimodernist fears of technocracy and the environmentally devastating power of atomic science led Arthur Carhart to found the CLC as an antidote to what he viewed as a decline of American society into an "unnatural" modernism. Carhart's antimodernist philosophy was perfectly in tune with American conservation of his day. Environmental advocates from Henry Thoreau and John Muir to Robert Marshall and David Brower expressed similar antimodernist views. This antimodernist trend in environmental thinking created a sharp dichotomy between "nature" and "civilization" for those working in the conservation movement.

In the late 1960s, a new group of young environmentalists began to question this bipolar configuration and to propose new ideas for reconciling modern technology and environmental philosophies. In the 1970s, environmentalism began to cope with contingency and complexity in a typically modern American way by turning to specialization and professionalization in newly invented methods of data gathering and generation, through new environmental sciences and policy studies, and by continuing to generate innovative local projects. At the Conservation Library, Carhart's protégé, Kay Collins, and a new generation of professional environmental advocates began to understand that from a social and ecological point of view, everyone in the late twentieth century was paradoxically situated. They realized that the modern world of technology had become so woven into the fabric of the "natural" world that it was inescapable. Further, they realized that escape from technology was not even desirable. Instead, they began to think about ways to use new advances in technology to further the cause of environmentalism. This shift in thinking was perfectly embodied in the transformation of the Conservation Library into the Regional Energy/Environment Information Center in the mid-1970s. A primary thesis of this book is that this shift in thinking about technology was one of the most significant and least understood changes in environmentalism after the 1960s.

CONCLUSION

In the fall of 1995, after fourteen years in limbo, the Conservation Library was reborn as a part of the new Denver Public Library main branch in downtown Denver. The CLC has a home in the new central library building, near the back of the fifth floor, appropriately overlooking the Denver Museum of Art. Joy Hilliard, an outdoor enthusiast and reluctant actor in the history of the CLC, engineered this rebirth. In 1994, she gave the Denver Public library a significant gift to rebuild the Conservation Library as a part of the new central building, with a small room as a memorial to her late husband, conservationist Edward Hilliard. The Hilliard room is tucked away from view in a corner of the new fifth floor of the DPL. Only a small sign marks the border between the genealogy department and what remains of the Conservation Library. On any given morning, one can find a group of elderly genealogists waiting impatiently outside the library for the doors to open. Soon they rush up to the fifth floor, grabbing favorite microfilm machines and tables. Some have staked a claim to the sunny little room at the back of the building. There they sit, quietly reading weighty volumes of family history and tracing bloodlines back through the centuries. Most of these relative detectives do not realize that they sit among the ruins of a once-proud and vital center of environmental advocacy. As they search for their roots, they are literally surrounded by an intellectual family tree of the American environmental movement.

CHAPTER TWO

A Clean-Cut Outdoor Man

His clean-shaven, determined jaw, steady brown eye, and hair that tried to curl, were those of a clean cut outdoor man.

Arthur Carhart, Through the Red Dusk

The connection, as I learned by degrees, between a person's collection and their life's actions was inexorable.

Nick Bantock, The Museum at Purgatory

In the early years, the Conservation Library sometimes seemed to be, in the words of Ralph Waldo Emerson, "the lengthened shadow of one man." That shadow belonged to Arthur Hawthorne Carhart, the founder of the Conservation Library and the driving force behind its early growth and success, whose personal odyssey plays a large role in the story of the CLC.[1] Even a brief review of the literature of the environmental movement shows Carhart's influence on conservation history; yet to many environmentalists and environmental historians he remains a controversial, enigmatic, or inconsequential figure.[2] A master of hyperbolic self-promotion, Carhart sometimes inspired dedicated admirers to inflate his role in key events and processes.[3] While some exaggerated his importance, others ignored him altogether. Carhart rarely receives more than a passing reference in the literature of environmental history. When he does make an appearance, it is usually only for the year 1919, when he worked with Aldo Leopold to develop a wilderness plan for the national forests. The narrow snapshot provided by most historians does little justice to a long life of environmental advocacy marked by a remarkable variety of significant experiences, accomplishments, and failures.[4] His life provides the context for the gender and generational issues that arose as the library evolved.[5]

Carhart was, like all of us, a product of his time. Unlike some of his contemporaries in the environmental movement, such as Aldo Leopold and Bob Marshall, Carhart never transcended his time. He never moved beyond his era's anthropocentric environmental ethic, and he never advocated a radical reorganization of human society to accommodate other living things. From a twenty-first-century environmental point of view, many of his conservation writings and arguments seem conservative. Carhart's unwillingness to support the Wilderness Act is viewed by those few historians who have studied him as a tragic flaw. In fact, his perceived failures in the area of wilderness preservation have been the one area of his career examined and highlighted by historians and environmentalists over the years.

The discourse of environmentalism and environmental history is driven by the wilderness trope. Historical actors in the drama of twentieth-century environmental advocacy are often rated on a sliding scale according to the purity of their wilderness vision. Using this system, most environmental historians have ranked Carhart low on the scale, far below wilderness heroes like Muir, Leopold, or Brower. This focus on perceived flaws in Carhart's wilderness philosophy, however, has led historians to ignore his crucial contributions to American environmental thinking and, more important, the representative character of his environmental ambivalence. Carhart's constant personal and professional struggle to reconcile conflicting ideas of environment, culture, and gender can tell us more about the evolution of environmental thinking in America than we can learn from the study of those purists who stood alone against the tide of popular opinion.

Throughout his life Carhart wrestled with issues that still resonate with environmentally aware Americans. He grappled with complex problems such as the tensions between modernism and antimodernism, the problem of defining and delineating something called "wilderness," the false hierarchies of "naturalness," and issues of free public access to nature versus seclusion and restriction. In a more oblique fashion, he and his contemporaries in the conservation movement dealt with the social issues inexorably tied to environmental politics. During his career Carhart helped perpetuate class-based perceptions of human nature and gender while simultaneously working to create a more inclusive type of environmental advocacy that circumvented the elitism of the wilderness trope. At each stage of his career, culminating with the creation of the Conservation Library, Carhart strove to reform land use policies and educate the public about the complexity of managing America's wildlands while attempting to reconcile these reforms with the ever-changing social and cultural landscape of the twentieth century. Of the social issues he and his generation of conservation advocates confronted, gender proved one of the most complex.

From its earliest manifestations in the Progressive Era, American conservationism was a gendered discussion.[6] Crafting conservation coalitions required the male leaders of the movement to reach out to women's organizations and ultimately allow women to move into leadership positions. As conservationists worked to change American opinions about the proper relationship between man and nature, they often faced troubling questions about the proper relationship between men and women. Conservation advocacy also, on the private and federal levels, became a meeting place for seemingly contradictory ideals of American masculinity. Virtually all the male leaders of the Progressive conservation movement struggled to reconcile "civilized" masculine virtues such as "strength, altruism, self-restraint, and chastity" with a more violent strain of masculinity closely associated with hunting and other "intense experiences" in nature.[7] Theodore Roosevelt, Aldo Leopold, Arthur Carhart, and others defined their masculinity through both civilized advocacy on behalf of nature and violent conflict with nature.[8] In Carhart's case the juxtaposition of civilization and savagery was often startling. His life story reads like a textbook of conflicting ideals of American manhood. Throughout his life he reveled in blood sports and wrote graphic stories of death and dismemberment for a male readership. During the same time he produced lovingly crafted landscape and flower-arranging publications for women's magazines and garden clubs and wrote about hygiene and other social virtues for a primarily female audience. One motivation for analyzing Carhart's life is to reveal some of the subtle ways that gender assumptions lurked behind many conservation debates and influenced antimodernist critiques of twentieth-century America.

Arthur Carhart's life story, his work in the U.S. Forest Service, his career as an environmental author, and his eighteen-year experience with the Conservation Library provide an excellent example of the subtle ways that gender assumptions shaped environmental discourse throughout the twentieth century. Carhart framed his conservation advocacy and participation in outdoor sports in terms of masculinity and manhood consistent with his generation of American men. Carhart's conservation novels and short stories reveal his deeply ingrained notions about gender and nature and raise some interesting questions about the problems of linking environmental advocacy to masculinity while simultaneously attempting to move one's message into the mainstream of American political discourse where women form a key constituency.

One of the ironies of Carhart's career centered on the question of audience. While his writings often revealed ambivalence about women in conservation, he consistently depended on women and women's groups to read and listen to his viewpoints and ultimately build coalitions to achieve his conservation goals. This "clean-cut outdoor man" who was known as somewhat of a swaggering "man's man" spent the last decades of his life surrounded by women in a culturally feminized indoor world, dependent on female expertise and financial largesse to achieve his dream of an environmental library. For some of his male colleagues in conservation, his buddies in the Denver Westerners (a group of writers, historians, and history enthusiasts), and his legions of outdoor sports readers, the transformation of Carhart from a buckskin-wearing outdoor man to a well-groomed librarian surrounded by society ladies might have seemed a startling and even disturbing emasculation. To understand Carhart's seemingly strange transformation from hunter to librarian, which I argue is representative of larger transformations of the American environmental movement, one must look at his early life. Many of Carhart's ideas about the proper relationship between humans and the nonhuman environment grew out of his experiences growing up in the rural Midwest.

ROOTS

Arthur Hawthorne Carhart was born on September 18, 1892, in Mapleton, Iowa. The only child of older parents, he spent his youth tramping through the woods and fields around a family farm homesteaded under the Tree Claim Act by one of his grandfathers, David Thomas Hawthorne.[9] Later in life Carhart relished memories of his early years of solitary wanderings through the countryside, fishing the Maple River, hunting muskrats and other small game, and carefully studying the local flora, all of which became keys to his later career and conservation philosophy. Speaking about the farm fields of his youth, Carhart remembered the captivating profusion of life they contained: "Bloodroots, dutchman's breeches, blue, white, yellow violets, ferns, jack in the pulpits, grapes after the first frost, thorne apples red and mellow," and "crows flying to their nightly roosts, squirrels hoarding against the winter. . . . Coyotes coming to within a hundred yards to steal lambs."[10] The diverse and plentiful animal and plant life of the farm and surrounding countryside left an indelible impression on young Art.

Long winters at school in Mapleton inevitably followed the freedom of the summer on the farm. Although not a particularly strong student, Carhart displayed an early talent for writing, at the age of twelve publishing his first article, a study of the downy woodpecker, in the *Women's Home Companion* in 1904. The young Carhart was consumed with a love for botany, music, and writing. But these desires were placed on hold because of Carhart's father's wish that his son spend his time on more manly and practical subjects.[11] Carhart's studies reflected the pragmatic outlook of his father, who pushed him to concentrate on business and accounting, hoping that young Arthur would succeed him in running the family hardware store.

After graduation from high school in Mapleton, Carhart left for business school in Sioux City. For the boy from Mapleton, Sioux City seemed like a metropolis, with infinite possibilities for entertaining oneself away from mind-numbing bookkeeping classes. Like many ambivalent college students, before and since, Carhart rebelled against his father's wishes and spent his time playing drums with a series of bands in dance halls and bars around the Sioux City area. One of his steadiest jobs was as the sound effects man for silent movies at the Majestic Theater. Late into the night, Carhart sat beneath the screen, improvising footsteps and gunshots with his drums.[12]

In the spring of his second fruitless year of business school, the late nights and hard living of a bandleader left Carhart in bed with a serious case of pneumonia. Returning home to convalesce, he renewed his connection with the land, spending the summer cultivating a flower garden that became "locally famous."[13] About this same time he found and carefully read a copy of *The Tree Doctor*, by pioneer tree surgeon John Davey.[14] The book struck a chord and inspired Carhart to write to Iowa State College to inquire about programs in landscape architecture. By the beginning of the fall semester, despite strong opposition from his father, Carhart was living in Ames, enrolled as a full-time student and hoping to follow in the footsteps of the venerable Davey.

Under the direction of Frank Hamilton Culley, Carhart began his program of study, which was loosely organized and afforded plenty of leeway for exploration in related fields. Drawing on personal experience, Carhart focused his attention on landscape and outdoor recreation. His senior research paper was a study of the plant species of rural Iowa, a subject he knew very well. In addition to landscape architecture, Carhart also studied bacteriology and veterinary science; meanwhile, he continued his sideline as a club musician and student manager of the school band. Gradually, the once-quiet farm boy had grown into a sociable and popular student leader with a talent for promoting causes. Eventually he joined a fraternity and a number of student groups.[15] His degree in landscape architecture, awarded in 1917, was the first ever given by Iowa State in that field.[16] After a brief stint with a Chicago architecture firm and an unsuccessful job hunt, a frustrated Carhart enlisted as a musician with the U.S. Army band.

During Carhart's basic training in Georgia, a medical officer asked the new recruits if any had prior experience with the natural sciences or an interest in biological work. Carhart responded in the positive, and after the army "found out [he] knew which end of a microscope to look through," he was sent to Washington to train as a medical officer, still maintaining his position as bandleader.[17] In the months that followed, several rapid promotions, "illogical except in the Army of World War I," left a somewhat bewildered Carhart in charge of an eleven-man laboratory responsible for the safety of the water supply of Camp Mead, Maryland, and the surrounding communities.[18] First Lieutenant Carhart spent the remainder of the war stationed at Camp Mead, carefully analyzing local rivers and milk and food supplies, as well as performing bacteriological tests on the soldiers of the camp. During World War I, massive outbreaks of food poisoning and digestive disorders were regular occurrences at army camps, with serious illness and even death resulting from polluted food and water supplies. One of the most serious incidents to occur during Carhart's tenure as hygiene officer was attributed to sabotage. A night watch officer shot and killed a man attempting to dump a bag of poison into a large water tank on the outskirts of the camp. By the time security officers discovered the plot, seven thousand soldiers lay ill in the field hospital, and four were dead.[19] The incident dramatically demonstrated to Carhart that environmental contaminants could be as deadly as any weapon. During his two years at Camp Mead, Carhart worked diligently to understand the causes of pollution and educate his fellow soldiers about the environmental links between the camps and communities and their surrounding hinterlands. Drawing on these experiences, Carhart later wrote about industries and individuals responsible for polluting, damming, and diverting America's waterways as a force more malicious and dangerous than the "enemy agent" dumping poison into the water supply at the army camp.[20]

Like many other young hygiene officers imbued with the Progressive spirit of reform and management, Carhart became obsessed with cleanliness as a social and environmental issue. Dirty water, he thought, endangered not only the soldiers who had to drink it but also the very fiber of American society. World War I catalyzed middle-class ideas about hygiene and cleanliness.[21] Just as a dirty face (once the symbol of a good day's work) became associated with disease and social decay, so did dirty rivers (formerly a sign of progress and growth) come to represent dangerous levels of environmental decay. The army hygiene training reinforced Carhart's growing belief that the health of the rivers and wild areas reflected the health of American society.

In many ways this early experience in the army helped solidify Carhart's environmental attitude. The lessons learned as a sanitary officer especially reinforced his experiences as a boy in Mapleton. In Iowa, Carhart had watched the fishing streams of his youth become increasingly cloudy and eventually unfishable because of unregulated dumping, soil erosion, and excessive use of chemical fertilizers and insecticides. By the time he left for college, his beloved Maple River had become "a great muddy storm sewer of intensive agriculture."[22] Later, long summer days observing the interconnections of the local environment of the Maple River enabled Carhart to understand the cause-and-effect relationship between environmental degradation, unregulated human habitation, explosive population growth, and unregulated modern life. In Mapleton the victims of thoughtless environmental exploitation were the trout and muskrats; at Camp

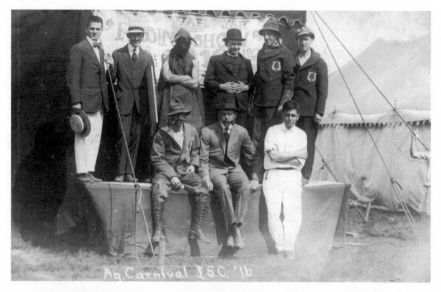

Carhart, in white, and fellow foresters at an Iowa Agricultural Carnival, 1916. Denver Public Library, Western History Collection, Conservation Library Collection photos.

Mead the victims were the soldiers and the people of the surrounding community. For the rest of Carhart's life, understanding connections between local environments and human communities was a primary focus.

The year 1919 brought many changes for young Carhart. He married his college sweetheart, Vera Van Sickle, and after an honorable discharge from the army, he was once again on the job market. At first he sought opportunities for an aspiring landscape architect with a special interest in outdoor recreation. Then, a letter from his mentor, Frank Culley, encouraged him to take advantage of his proximity to Washington and search for employment at the newly formed National Park Service. The Park Service was recruiting landscape architects and other outdoor experts to help develop and manage a growing system of national parks. An ardent supporter of the Park Service and an acquaintance of the newly appointed director, Stephen Mather, Culley was aware of these new opportunities and thought that Carhart stood a good chance of getting in on these new government jobs. Armed with a letter of recommendation, Carhart went to the Park Service offices to meet with Mather. But Mather was out of town, and his personal assistant was not very encouraging, telling the disappointed Carhart that he might try the Forest Service office to see if it needed someone with his background. In the following years, Mather came to regret this assistant's advice.

FOREST SERVICE

Carhart's arrival at the office of U.S. Forest Service chief forester E. A. Sherman's could not have been more perfectly timed. Earlier that same month, Sherman had decided to hire a landscape architect to help direct the recreation efforts of a large western forest district. In the larger context, Carhart was fortunate as well. Competition between the Forest Service and the Park Service for American's expanding interest in outdoor recreation opened up new opportunities for employment in both agencies. Sherman took an instant liking to the young Carhart. Like Carhart, Sherman was a graduate of the Iowa State University forestry program, and the two men shared a love of hunting and fishing. After some wrangling with the civil service requirements, Carhart was hired as the Forest Service's first landscape architect. In February 1919, he left for the District 2 headquarters in Denver.

The hiring of a landscape architect represented a major departure for the Forest Service. Residents living near the nation's forests had traditionally used forest lands for recreational and noncommodity purposes such as hunting, camping, fishing, and picnicking. But prior to 1919, the Forest Service Administration did not consider recreation one of its mandates, allowing the Park Service to promote outdoor recreation in the public domain.[23] In addition, the Park Service and the Forest Service maintained different environmental philosophies and land use policies. In 1919, the Forest Service still embraced Gifford Pinchot's strict utilitarian philosophy of maximum yields and sustained commodity production through scientific management. In keeping with this utilitarian scientific bent, Carhart's official title, as he began his new career, was "recreational engineer."

What recreational engineering actually meant was land planning, using comprehensive regional evaluations of public lands to maximize all aspects of use, from commodity extraction to recreation. Land planners argued that wilderness recreation areas needed to be managed just like trees and crops to ensure sustained yield and to avoid waste. In time, preservation of wilderness areas became a central goal for land planners.[24] Vast areas of land were surveyed and evaluated for their potential as recreation areas, with greater interest paid to especially scenic areas. Overall, the job of the wilderness land planner was to ensure access without seriously damaging the existing environment. On the East Coast, visionary land planner Benton MacKaye, architect of the Appalachian Trail, pioneered this type of regional recreation management.[25] Carhart was hired as a part of the Forest Service's effort to expand recreation land planning and to incorporate MacKaye's ideas into its management scheme.

Although the chief forester hired Carhart, his welcome in Denver

The "Beauty Engineer" prepares to enter the backcountry of Superior National Forest, 1921. Denver Public Library, Western History Collection, Conservation Library Collection photos.

could not be called warm. In fact, some forest rangers and Forest Service bureaucrats fought the idea of recreation in the nation's forests. In his first months, Carhart often met with stiff resistance and snubs. Skeptical fellow foresters in Denver dubbed Carhart the "beauty doctor" or "beauty engineer," laughing at his notion that hundreds of thousands of Americans might like to tromp into the forests for fun. Carhart was already sensitive to questions about his masculinity because of his love of flowers, gardening, and music, and the comments of the foresters rankled. He realized that he would need to work hard to demonstrate that landscaping and aesthetics could be as masculine as any other forest work.[26] Others in the Denver office, including Carhart's new supervisor, C. J. Stahl, welcomed the opportunity to begin serious recreational planning in their district. Throughout his short and tumultuous career with the Forest Service, Carhart received strong support from the influential Stahl. But Carhart virtually created his own job, so new was the concept of recreation planning in a Forest Service hitherto concerned chiefly with timber management, grazing allocations, and watershed administration.[27] District 2 of the Forest Service included Wyoming, Colorado, Nebraska, South Dakota, Minnesota, and Michigan and contained a total area of nearly twenty-three million acres. Although Stahl supported Carhart's appointment, he gave little direction to the young architect. The plans they developed for the position seemed grandiose and frightening to the young Carhart, "far beyond what I would have thought my own capacity could handle at that time."[28]

After a not-so-productive first winter, Carhart was assigned to spend the summer of 1919 laying out plans for summer cabins around the spectacular and secluded Trapper's Lake, nestled at the base of the Flat Tops in the White River National Forest.[29] Access to the lake, which is remote even today, required a circuitous train or auto trip followed by a strenuous hike or horse trip. During his days working out of a sportsmen's camp, Carhart was impressed with the pristine beauty of the location.[30] Later he waxed romantic about his first vision of the place: "The winds whispered and sang, sunlight danced on little waves."[31] During his two weeks surveying the shores of the lake, Carhart pondered the beauty and serenity of the spot but kept on with his work, carefully plotting cabin sites and roadways. Although he was immediately impressed with the setting of Trapper's Lake, a transformation in his thinking about the management of the lake, and areas like it, did not come to him in a flash of inspiration. They emerged only after a verbal bludgeoning from local sportsmen who had already staked a claim to the area.

One evening, after a long day of surveying, as the story goes, Carhart sat by the fire outside the tent of Paul J. Rainey, a well-known outdoorsman who ran the camp where he was staying. Then William McFadden, an Oklahoma oil man and avid hunter, joined them. The two men spent their summers at Trapper's Lake and enjoyed the remote, secluded setting. As the sole purveyor of accommodations and supplies to the area, Rainey had a vested interest in keeping others out. After several diplomatic attempts to ascertain Carhart's goal in surveying the lake, the two men finally decided to speak their minds. "Do you have to circle every lake with a road?" they asked. "Can't you bureaucrats keep one superb mountain lake as God made it?"[32]

Carhart listened to what the two men had to say and realized that their argument confirmed his own feelings about his mission. Convinced that the plan to build a road and cabins should be abandoned, Carhart returned to Denver with a new perspective on managing wildlands. Why, he wondered, should a few people who were lucky enough to obtain a lease be able to usurp the public's right to enjoy beautiful places? The plan that he placed on Stahl's desk argued that Trapper's Lake had more value without the private cabins. In fact, he argued that the Forest Service should preserve the area without any development whatsoever.[33] Impressed by Carhart's reasoning, Stahl accepted the plan and agreed to leave Trapper's Lake as it was.

Although clearly a departure from standard Forest Service policy, the plan for Trapper's Lake represented only a tentative and cautious advance for the wilderness movement. The area under study was a mere 300 acres, already invaded by sportsmen, that showed the signs of years of occupation. Several other more significant assignments, including much larger areas of land, followed the work at Trapper's Lake. These included surveys and comprehensive recreation plans for the Mount Evans area, the 650,000-acre San Isabel National Forest, and a 3.5-million-acre tract of southwestern Colorado.[34]

Carhart's land-planning work for the Forest Service culminated with an evaluation and recreation plan for the Superior National Forest on the Canada-Minnesota border. The Superior National Forest consisted of a remarkable series of rivers and lakes covering thousands of acres and connected to an even larger system of waterways on the Canadian side of the border. Carhart spent weeks canoeing through the area and listening to both sides of a local debate over how the region could best be used for recreational purposes. The main point of disagreement concerned access. Local developers wanted to build an extensive series of roads through the region to enable car traffic to reach the most desirable areas. In addition, cabins and lodges would be built along the shores of Lake Superior to facilitate tourism. As with the work on Trapper's Lake, Carhart's plan once again proved controversial, if not radical, for the conservative and utilitarian Forest Service. He recommended that the money to build roads be pulled and that the region remain accessible only by boat.[35]

Prior to the Superior trips, on December 6, 1919, Aldo Leopold visited the Denver regional office of the Forest Service. The two men talked for many hours about their ideas for wilderness preservation and wilderness recreation. The older Leopold impressed Carhart with his deep thinking on the subject.[36] Years later, Carhart readily admitted that he was uncertain about his own stance on the wilderness issue and acknowledged Leopold as the more sophisticated philosopher: "I guess I get stirred up when someone comes at me . . . asking if I discovered . . .

wilderness. I didn't."[37] Although Leopold clearly was the more influential of the two, the exchange was not merely one-way. Even though his philosophy was immature in comparison to Leopold's insightful and far-reaching criticisms, Carhart nonetheless contributed his knowledge as a landscape architect and land planner to the discussion.

Modern environmental purists often find fault with Carhart's early wilderness thinking. His was a pragmatic and often instrumentalist view, and yet his insights into the uses and psychological value of outdoor recreation remain perceptive and important. More than many, Carhart recognized the zeitgeist. He realized that Americans had a paradoxical relationship with the modern world, tearing down and building at a desperate pace while simultaneously dreaming of vacations in the forests and on the shores of quiet lakes. He understood, as he wrote to Leopold, that in time "scenic spots, where nature has been allowed to remain unmarred, will be some of the most highly prized . . . features of the country, and unless the Forest Service has thoroughly exerted all influences possible to preserve these areas, severe criticism will some day be meted out by the collective owners of this territory, the public."[38]

Early on, Carhart maintained strong views on the social value of wilderness and outdoor recreation. Therefore, his arguments for the protection of wild lands and the development of recreation policies in the national forests focused on moral issues rather than utilitarian concerns. Carhart's definition of recreation changed over the years and according to his audience, but it always stayed close to the literal definition of the word: "refreshment of one's mind or body."[39] Moreover, recreation was, in Carhart's view, an outdoor activity that centered on the individual and the nonhuman environment, with fishing and hunting as primary activities. Hiking, exploring, camping, picnicking, bird-watching, and other less strenuous outdoor activities also counted as recreation. More than mere sport, recreation meant spiritual rejuvenation. Through recreation, Carhart wrote, people learned "the individual in relation to Creation, the strength of self-reliance, that only earthy harmony with the outdoors can build."[40] This type of "re-creation of the sprit" could not be replicated through organized sports or other urban activities.[41] Commenting on the spread of organized sports during his lifetime, Carhart lamented the growing American obsession with spectator recreation: "We have had a considerable substitution of athletic games and contests to take the place of outdoor activities . . . but that type of play . . . does not offer the same thing as an individual gets hunting and fishing."[42]

Based on his belief that outdoor recreation played a crucial role in individual and social stability and growth, Carhart argued consistently that recreation, not commodity production, was the best and most important use of the public domain. He wrote, "Perhaps the rebuilding of body and spirit is the greatest service derivable from our forests, for of what worth are material things if we lose the character and quality of people that are the soul of America?"[43] Carhart's motivation for recreation planning went beyond fulfilling the duties of his job with the Forest Service. He felt compelled to help ensure that the recreation that had played such a crucial role in his early life would be available to shape the character of the youth of the future.

Like other pioneer regional planners and landscape architects, Carhart had the ability to look beyond political boundaries and view the land in the context of large natural systems. His ideas about land planning and regional development usually eclipsed his thinking on wilderness in the abstract. Working on the practical level and constructing a plan for a particular region, Carhart produced his most insightful work.[44] In many respects Carhart's ideas about regional planning foreshadow, in their respect for large ecosystems and ecoregional boundaries, current ideas of bioregionalism. Reflecting on his weeks of surveying in the Colorado backcountry, he remarked, "The artificial straight line boundaries . . . were of no actual consequence. The wildlands continued as such, extending unbroken either side of sections or township lines on a map."[45]

Early on in his career as a conservationist, Carhart recognized the inherent problems with restrictive delineations of value and hierarchy in land use. Instead of viewing a forest region in terms of a hierarchy, with wilderness at the top and heavily developed areas at the bottom, Carhart viewed the regions he studied as a whole made up of different, yet equally valuable, parts. The terrain he surveyed in Colorado, and later in Minnesota, was not all pristine wilderness. Many of these areas had been occupied and abandoned, logged, mined, and crisscrossed with roads. Carhart did not see this evidence of human presence as a problem; instead, he viewed it as a challenge. The job of the careful land planner was to uncover the value in all the public lands without concentrating on one type or ideal. In this regard, Carhart's strategy for wilderness was different from Aldo Leopold's, but in some respects his pragmatic idea of compromise and accommodation was a more practical blueprint for preservation planning. The main difference between Leopold and Carhart stems from their definitions of wilderness. Like Robert Marshall and the other core founders of the Wilderness Society, Leopold was more of a wilderness purist, defining wilderness as a primarily undeveloped area large enough to absorb a two-week pack trip. Carhart, on the other hand, was less of a purist, willing to accept limited development and overlook past use. The ambivalence in Carhart's early proposals reflected the general ambivalence of Americans toward preservation and development during these early years. "I suppose I am a typical American," he once wrote, a statement supported by the pull he felt between the modern world he lived in and enjoyed and the wilderness world he worked in and loved.[46]

By 1921, Carhart had produced a remarkable quantity of work and had gained the respect of his peers and supervisors in the Forest Service. Yet his few years with the service were marred by controversy and conflict. The most damaging of these arguments arose out of an inadvertent confrontation with National Park Service director Steven Mather. In the winter of 1921, Carhart traveled to Des Moines, Iowa, to attend a national parks conference. During the meeting, he "made a few extemporaneous remarks about Forest Service recreation programs."[47] After Carhart finished his comments on his recreation work, Mather "rose and fiercely denounced the idea of recreation uses in the forests." He later elaborated to members of the media, explaining that he thought "the national forests were to grow wood, protect watersheds, [and] furnish grazing for domestic livestock," and were not to be used as recreation sites.[48] The story was picked up by the national press and presented to the public as an example of the ongoing fight between the two competing agencies. Arguments between the two services had recently been exacerbated by congressional attempts to have the Park Service administer Forest Service recreation. Both organizations were defensive and spoiling for a fight at the exact moment that young Carhart decided to make his unfortunate public remarks.[49]

The Carhart-Mather incident concluded without any serious repercussions for either the Park Service or the Forest Service, but the confrontation left another black mark on Carhart's record. There was little danger that he would be relieved of his duties, however, because most of his supervisors strongly supported him and his ideas about recreation. They only wished he had used a little more diplomacy and restraint in his public remarks. Although support for his plans remained strong at the regional level, recreation as a part of the Forest Service's multiple-use mission continued to be a source of controversy on the national level. Since the bureaucracy of the Forest Service moved slowly, Carhart began to worry about the lack of action on any of his land-planning efforts. For Carhart, the work of endlessly explaining his ideas and dealing with the cumbersome hierarchy of the service began to seem "deadly slow" and hedged with "civil service politics" that made success seem impossible.[50]

In December 1922, Carhart resigned his position with the Forest Service. Frustrated and disillusioned, he left the Denver regional office after only four years. As he revealed in his autobiographical notes, he had little patience for an "organization primarily made up of technical foresters and cowmen, most of them set in viewpoint through years of bureaucratic conformity to precedent."[51] The restrictive confines of the federal bureaucracy proved too small for his ambition, and so he moved on. The parting was bitter, and his constant battles with the men he viewed as "mindless bureaucrats" became fodder for his fiction in the coming years. In contrast, the older and more patient Aldo Leopold stayed within the system, working for wilderness. In partnership with the irrepressible Bob Marshall, Leopold made great strides toward changing the ideological orientation of the Forest Service in the succeeding decades, pushing far beyond Carhart's tentative early plans.[52]

In the decades after Carhart's departure, the Forest Service gave Leopold sole credit for the origination of the wilderness concept within the service. After Donald Baldwin's publication of a revisionist history of Forest Service wilderness policy, which gave Carhart full credit for the wilderness concept, the Forest Service wrote Carhart back into its story, on March 14, 1973, even bringing the aging Carhart to Washington for a special ceremony honoring him as "America's pioneer wilderness planner."[53] The top Forest Service officials were on hand to praise Carhart, including two former chiefs of the service and the current chief, John McGuire. All the comments that day indicated that the Forest Service had uncritically accepted Baldwin's reinterpretation.[54] After 1973, the service continued to support the addition of Carhart to the canon of Forest Service wilderness heroes, alongside Leopold and Bob Marshall; eventually it founded the Arthur Carhart Wilderness Training Center to coordinate interagency wilderness planning and training.[55]

Although the Forest Service was ready to anoint Carhart as a wilderness hero, recent critics of Carhart's wilderness work question this interpretation of his career. The main argument against Carhart seems to revolve around his qualifications as a "real" preservationist. Using his 1922 plan for the Superior National Forest as an example of how greatly his wilderness vision differed from Aldo Leopold's and those of other founders of the Wilderness Society, historian David Backes argues that Carhart does not deserve credit as the originator of the wilderness ideal. Backes correctly asserts that rather than viewing wilderness as a pristine area of land simply left alone and unchanged, Carhart saw it as a "relatively natural landscape where one could withdraw from civilization's complexity without having to sacrifice too much of civilization's comforts."[56] Many of the criticisms of Carhart's Forest Service career ring true. Unfortunately, most historians base their conclusions on this one small phase of Carhart's life.

As an architect, Carhart did not shy away from building even within a wilderness area.[57] In the complicated semantics of environmentalism, wilderness is one of the most slippery terms. Often viewed simply as the place where we are not, wilderness has always been a human construct. As historian William Cronon recently wrote, "Far from being the one place on earth that stands apart from humanity, it is quite profoundly a human creation."[58] For some, Carhart's wilderness vision seemed "impure" because it included areas obviously modified by human contact. Such a vision offended those who believed there was such a thing as "pristine wilderness" devoid of human history. They further believed that the only type of wilderness preservation that really counted was the one preached by Aldo Leopold, Bob Marshall, and the other founders of the Wilderness Society.

Unlike some of his peers, Carhart did not have a personal vision of wilderness as a wholly "natural" environment devoid of overt human presence. Rather, the cornerstone of Carhart's land-planning ideal was direct human management and control, with an emphasis on different types of "wildlands," ranging from urban parks to high-mountain wilderness sanctuaries. As David Backes explains, "The political complexity of managing this international wilderness seems to confirm at least one of Carhart's fundamental ideas: wilderness management cannot be purely 'natural,' but must instead consist of a set of social and environmental compromises."[59] The hallmark of Carhart's environmental career was compromise. He realized early on that the best "wilderness," like the best parks, required careful planning and design.

After four years of tramping through vast remote regions and returning to his Denver office to map and delineate uses, Carhart concluded that wilderness was more a way of thinking about the world than an actual place. As he later wrote, "Wilderness is not entirely made up of unscaled pinnacles, faint, little-trodden trails, great solitude, vast spaces surrounding. . . . *Your* wilderness is what you glean in sensory treasures . . . living as a part of the geo-ecological habitat."[60] Although Carhart officially left the nascent wilderness movement when he resigned from the Forest Service, he continued to think and write about the subject for the remainder of his professional life. Over the years his philosophy evolved in complexity while maintaining elements of ambivalence and compromise.

Carhart's accomplishments in the Forest Service are remarkable, especially considering the short time he spent there. Employed for only four years as a junior officer with little power, a tiny budget, and almost no experience in large-scale land planning, Carhart nonetheless contributed in a significant way to major changes in Forest Service policy.

NATURE STORIES

Carhart's departure from the Forest Service left him again searching for a job. Within a few weeks he received good news from his old adviser, Frank Culley, who was leaving Iowa State to form a landscape architecture firm in the Denver area and wanted Carhart to join him. Carhart

signed on as a partner in the venture and spent the next six years working with Culley and Irvin McCrary. The firm became an instant success,
garnering choice city and state contracts around the West and providing
Carhart with a considerable increase in personal income.[61] At about the
same time he joined the firm, Carhart began, in his spare time, to pound
out short stories, articles for outdoor sports magazines, and landscaping
advice columns. Throughout his career in the army and the Forest Service, Carhart never gave up his avocation of writing.[62] The relative freedom of private life left him with plenty of time to write on a variety of
subjects. Beginning in the mid-1920s, he regularly published articles in
magazines as diverse as *American Forestry, Sunset, Outdoor Life, Better
Homes and Gardens, House and Garden,* and *Blue Book Magazine.* By December 1931, he had published more than two hundred articles and three
books in his "spare time."[63]

Carhart's notoriety as an author of fictional stories expanded nationally, and in 1928 he sold his first novel, *The Ordeal of Brad Ogden.*[64] It was,
fittingly, a highly romanticized tale of a young conservation-minded forest ranger battling a stubborn bureaucracy. The pioneer forest ranger,
Brad Ogden, embodied the young Carhart, an idealistic conservationist
willing to risk his career to support his environmental principles. Using
standard western plot lines and characters, descendants of Cooper's
Leatherstocking and Owen Wister's Virginian, Carhart spiced his story
with conservation wisdom. Throughout the 1920s, he sold a number of
short stories with this theme to western pulp fiction magazines such as
Blue Book, Two Gun Western, and *Five Novels Monthly.* Most of Carhart's
fiction dealt with conservation themes thinly glossed by weak and repet-
itive plot lines that often bordered on the ridiculous. Although the quality of his prose was weak, he likely reached more people with his
conservation novels than with all his official endeavors in the conservation field or his later more serious publications.

Under titles like "The Sacrifice of Centipede Ranch," "The Race of the
Forest Men," "Black Treasure," and "Through the Red Dusk," Carhart's
pulp fiction spun familiar tales of rugged individualism on the western
frontier.[65] Virtuous lone heroes battled monolithic forces of evil in a quest
to live simply on the land. Philosophers of primitivism and spearheads of
empire, Carhart's protagonists embodied his fundamental ambivalence
about the relationship between modern civilization and wilderness
virtues. They also provided some striking insights into Carhart's vision of
masculinity and the conservation crusade. Virtually all of Carhart's fiction
featured a relationship between men and women that grew as they faced
an environmental crisis. In his companion novels, *Son of the Forest* and *The
Ordeal of Brad Ogden,* Carhart contrasted a masculine version of action-ori-
ented conservation advocacy with a more docile feminine love of natural

EVERY STORY COMPLETE

Five-Novels

25¢ Monthly

June, 1931

FIVE-NOVELS MONTHLY

25 cents
IN CANADA 30c

Five Novels for June

The Sacrifice of Centipede Ranch
A Colorful Romance of the Range Country
By *Arthur Hawthorne Carhart*

Tidal Wave
Love, Adventure and Thrills in Hawaii
By *James W. Bennett*

Tiger Ride
A Brilliant Love Drama of the Foreign Legion
By *Alice M. Williamson*

Peril Island
An Engrossing Love Mystery
By *T. T. Flynn*

Double Hit
A Love Novel of Hearts and Home Runs
By *William Bruner*

Cover of *Five Novels Monthly* featuring Carhart's story, "The Sacrifice of Centipede Ranch," June 1931.

beauty. Carhart's protagonists were always strong male figures willing to risk all for the sake of advocating an unpopular position. Strong willed, but naive, women were the foils for these men. The women loved nature and were a crucial audience for the message, but they required the example of a man to "convert" to the conservation cause.[66] What strikes the reader familiar with Carhart's own experiences is the way he neatly divided the feminine and masculine versions of nature advocacy that were so deeply entwined in his own life. Despite his ongoing attempts to reconcile contrasting views of nature advocacy in the real world, the same type of stark gender division that he fought against when working as a "beauty doctor" characterized Carhart's fiction.

Carhart's depiction of gender roles in his pulp fiction was hardly unique in this medium aimed almost exclusively at a male audience. What made Carhart's pulp different from the thousands of other western pulp stories marketed in the 1920s and 1930s was the environmental message that permeated his plot lines. Even the romances centered on environmental issues, with the main characters linked by their love of the land. Most of his stories, including the archetypal *Ordeal of Brad Ogden*, featured a forest ranger or college-trained agricultural engineer as the hero.[67] After moving into a rough area of a national forest, the hero encountered mobs of greedy ranchers and ignorant developers determined to destroy the local environment through ignorance about overgrazing, erosion, carelessness with fire, or overdevelopment. The protagonist inevitably confronted the villains during an apocalyptic natural disaster, such as a forest fire or flood, and converted his enemies to the conservation cause by sheer willpower: "'Chris,' [the villain] said, his voice shaking, '—my boy, [you have] proved one thing for me. You Forest men play square. I'm through fighting you. I'll go into any court you name and plead guilty to all the stock I have in trespass. . . . Hereafter I'm with you."[68]

Like many pulp magazines and dime novels, Carhart's fiction was aimed at a male audience and focused on male characters.[69] His characters were rugged and masculine, with a disdain for effete bureaucrats and intellectuals. They experienced nature through masculine activities such as hunting, fishing, and arduous pack trips. Confrontations between the men in his stories and the natural world and between the characters were often violent. The standard conclusion to one of his short stories generally involved a bloody fight scene. The same held true for his novels. Clearly, the message of these stories, expressed through violent action, was that conservation is a "manly" pursuit. Women, when they appeared at all, always played a secondary role, never taking a direct part in the action of the story. Carhart considered conservation, like hunting and fishing, as quintessentially male pursuits; this attitude toward women and conservation changed somewhat over the years, but he never renounced it completely.

Although Carhart spent a great deal of time preaching his pro-environmental message to America via the pulp magazines, the message was not always clear. As with his early philosophy on wilderness in the Forest Service, Carhart's environmental fiction displayed considerable ambivalence and contradiction. The most surprising example of this tendency appeared in his second book, *The Last Stand of the Pack* (1929).[70]

Written with the help of Stanley Young, the wildlife expert and principal biologist of the U.S. Biological Survey, this book tells the story of government hunters and the extermination of the last wolves in the western United States. Published about the same time that Aldo Leopold altered his view of ecosystems and wildlife management after watching the "fierce green fire" fade from a wolf's eyes, Young's tales are victorious and vengeful, offering a ringing endorsement of the predatory animal control policies of the Biological Survey.[71] Arranged around stories of individual wolf packs and the hunters who eventually exterminate them, the book provides a glimpse into the contradictory nature of Carhart's early conservation philosophy and the most startling evidence of the differences between Carhart and Leopold.[72]

In *The Last Stand of the Pack,* the extermination of the remaining wolves is portrayed as sad evidence of the fading of the frontier, but it is justified because of the need to protect the new civilization that inherited the West from the rugged mountain men and cowboys. The authors tell a bizarre story to justify the killing and to make the wolf hunters seem heroic and masculine. Wolves were great hunters and a key element of the ecosystem for centuries, the story begins, killing only the weak buffalo and deer. As settlers moved in, however, the "good" wolves died off, unable to compete for a dwindling food supply. The wolves that remain are "evil" predators with "revenge" burning in their hearts. The wolves have become, according to Carhart and Young, "outlaws" and "renegades," no longer a part of the natural world.[73]

Carhart and Young justified the annihilation of one of the greatest symbols of wilderness by anthropomorphizing the wolf, endowing it with all the worst qualities of human outlaws. In these stories the wolf takes the blame for environmental degradation and wanton destruction of "innocent" animals. At the same time the rhetoric used to describe the trapping and killing paints a gruesome picture, indicating the author's ambivalence about the systematic and decidedly unsportsmanlike way the wolves are hunted. As they wrote, "Twisted many times, frayed a little, cut a bit by the sharp edges of the trap, the tendons still refused to give release."[74] The story of the wolves' demise represented a turning point in Carhart's early conservation philosophy and highlighted one of the central paradoxes of Carhart's attitudes. Like many others of his generation, he vacillated between a broadening conception of conservation and continued support for hunting and fishing. In Carhart's case, hunting was the best example of his masculine contact with nature, helping to offset his "beauty engineering" and gardening.[75] Perhaps repentant about his unfortunate portrayal of the wolf slaughter in Last Stand, Carhart never again attempted to justify predatory animal control, arguing later for sharp regulation and containment of animal control policies.

Throughout the remainder of his career as an author and conservationist, Carhart dedicated much of his writing and advocacy work toward reconciling sportsmen and other conservationists. One of the central insights Carhart contributed to the environmental movement over the years was his belief that sportsmen needed to play a role in any successful environmental coalition in the American West.[76] Carhart realized that conservationists united with sportsmen could wield considerable bipartisan political power. His thinking on wilderness and other environmental issues always included this subtle logic and helped shape his career as a writer.

Both of Carhart's first books sold well and received good reviews. Reviewing Last Stand for the Saturday Review of Literature, southwestern writer Mary Austin praised the book's accuracy, although she admitted that her "sympathy [was] almost wholly engaged on behalf of the Pack."[77] Regardless of the writings' lack of literary sophistication, or possibly because of it, the national conservation community and the general public alike generally accepted Carhart's early work.[78] At the same time he continued to receive numerous contracts from pulp magazines and sold many of his freelance stories to national publications.

As writing began to consume more of Carhart's time, he decided, in September 1930, to quit the architecture business, beginning a thirty-year career as a freelance writer.[79] The decision to quit a steady job for the uncertainty of a writing career at the beginning of the Great Depression indicates Carhart's confidence in his ability to produce a steady outpouring of western romance and environmental drama. He later commented, proudly, that he successfully "rode out" the Great Depression on his typewriter.[80]

Carhart and his colleagues in the pulp business produced a remarkable body of work during a relatively short period. During the 1930s, he had two main contracts with pulp magazines, each requiring him to produce two stories a month, one for twenty-five thousand words and one for fifteen thousand at one cent per word.[81] On top of the huge output for the pulp magazines, he also wrote dozens of articles a year on landscaping, forestry, outdoor sports, and even education and writing. In addition to the steady stream of articles, Carhart published six more books during the 1930s, including a very popular guide to his adopted state, entitled simply Colorado.[82] At the end of the 1930s, he estimated that he had produced over one million words of published material each year for more than a decade.[83]

The ability to survive by typewriter alone became a source of lasting pride for Carhart. At a time when America's literary culture joked about popular western writers, Carhart strove to maintain his regional themes in the face of criticisms that deeply wounded him. Popular western literature has always endured sharp criticism from those outside the region— often with good reason. The dime novel and its predecessor, the pulp, depended on stock characters and maudlin plot lines. As a proud resident and western booster, and as someone who made his living by writing, Carhart felt the sting of this criticism and fought to legitimize popular western writing in the eyes of the literary world.[84] In the early 1930s, he founded a western writers group based in Denver, with the goal of promoting popular western literature and polishing the image of local writers. Carhart became a strong advocate of western regional writing, corresponding with Bernard DeVoto and others to encourage the culture of the West through both fiction and nonfiction writing. One of the main themes stressed by the western writers group in Denver was the positive message of their work. "There is something too big, too powerful, too dynamic in this western rhythm to allow him [the western writer] to climb a little ladder of superiority and sling muddy ink at his home folk and homeland," Carhart insisted.[85] For him, writing was a tool for reform; he never really grasped the idea of writing as art.

During the 1940s, Carhart began to move away from fiction and to use his fame to directly promote conservation and outdoor sports issues. The main targets of his ceaseless typewriter during this decade were stockmen attempting to deregulate, and thus gain control of, federally protected lands in the West. His attacks on Colorado stockmen and their bids to gain control of the national forests became both strident and effective.[86] As the protagonist of one of his novels stated, echoing Carhart's own sentiments about the public land, "[I am] powerful jealous of these leagues of mountain and desert."[87] This love of the land led Carhart to begin working to more directly incorporate his environmental ideology into works of nonfiction aimed at outdoor sports enthusiasts.

Outdoor recreation became the primary focus of Carhart's writing during the 1940s. In these works, he emphasized the relationship of hunting and fishing to the welfare of the environment and to the moral health of the nation. "It is the outdoorsman . . . who builds nations," he wrote. He followed this with a warning: "Unless we supply the facilities, the opportunities [for recreation] . . . a force of national decadence will increasingly erode the individuals and therefore the nation."[88]

The growing distrust of hunters and fishermen among many of Carhart's friends in the conservation community convinced him of the need to reconcile the two groups. At the same time he realized that many hunters and fishers did not fully understand the benefits of habitat conservation. Accordingly, in the 1930s through the 1950s, he worked to clear up misunderstandings and forge ties based on mutual interest. With annual sales of hunting and fishing licenses reaching the twenty-five million mark in the 1940s, Carhart saw a vast group of individuals and organizations with a vested interest in wilderness preservation. He made it his personal mission to bring the conservationists and sportsmen together under the banner of conservation.

When Carhart wrote about recreation, his rhetoric tended to highlight some assumptions about gender that influenced his thinking about environmental advocacy. Constant references to "sportsmen" indicate his gendered vision of the environmental community. Only rarely did he mention women outdoor enthusiasts as key players in the coalitions he struggled to create.[89] This was an interesting omission, considering that many of his earlier writings on conservation topics had appeared in women's magazines or in gardening publications aimed at female audiences. Carhart's personal biases illustrated two general tendencies among the leaders of America's nascent environmental movement. The first was to assume that women possessed an innate appreciation for beautiful things and places and therefore required no convincing on aesthetic preservation issues. The second tendency was to assume that women's place was in the home and that there was no need to include them when discussing public policy and conservation issues.[90] Although Carhart toed the line when speaking to male conservation colleagues and writing for his male audience, he never stopped producing conservation pieces aimed at women and women's groups that valued his knowledge of landscape principles and provided important grassroots support for conservation issues.

The 1940s brought more success with the publication of some of Carhart's most popular books and articles. Four books aimed at sportsmen sold well and went through multiple reprintings and editions. The most popular, surprisingly, was *The Outdoorsman's Cookbook,* an unintentionally humorous guide to wilderness cuisine featuring such absurd recipes as "armadillo sausage" and "stewed muskrat."[91] The other three books, *Hunting North American Deer, Fresh Water Fishing,* and *Fishing in the West,* were practical guides for sportsmen, each laced with a strong conservation message.[92] Carhart used careful language and straightforward utilitarian arguments to convince sportsmen that conservation and environmental protection were in their best interests. Chapters such as "Tomorrow's Fishing," "Our Heritage," and "Dust in Your Creels" emphasized the connection between outdoor sports and the large issues facing conservationists, ranging from reclamation, grazing, and pollution to wilderness, recreation, and attempts to sell federal forest lands. The message was repeated in hundreds of articles in sports magazines, reaching hundreds of thousands of readers. One such reader later wrote to Carhart to thank him for his conservation work: "You have done so much for the American Sportsman. . . . No one could have awakened the people to impending dangers as you have."[93] Arguably, Carhart's greatest contribution to the spread of environmental thinking in America came from his carefully crafted writings for the outdoor sports community.

In addition to maintaining his phenomenal output of fiction and nonfiction publications, Carhart also began in the late 1930s to work with various government agencies. Perhaps exhausted by the frantic pace required to survive as a writer in this period, Carhart turned to other sources for financial relief. In 1938, Teller Ammons, then governor of Colorado, asked Carhart to take charge of the newly formed Federal Aid in Wildlife Restoration Program for the state of Colorado.[94] Carhart spent the next five years working on wildlife surveys and coordinating statewide wildlife restoration programs, resigning his post in 1943. Throughout the 1940s, Carhart held other part-time positions with a number of state and national environmental organizations, as information officer and as public relations director. In addition, he served as an adviser or board member for national conservation organizations such as the Izaak Walton League and the American Wildlife Federation. During these same years, Carhart established ties with the timber industry, then trying to improve its image with sportsmen. Carhart gladly cooperated and took home some sizable consulting checks from such companies as Weyerhaeuser, Crown Zellerbach, and Kimberly-Clark.[95]

Around this same time, Carhart also became involved with the dude ranch industry and produced his most unfortunate book, *Hi, Stranger! The Complete Guide to Dude Ranches,* written entirely in a bizarre western lingo. For example, "Hi, Stranger! Lighten and cool yore saddle. I'm proud to make yore acquaintance. Let's hunker down beside th' ol' corral an' make medicine."[96] In addition to the ridiculous language, the ideas represented in the book were regressive when compared with Carhart's other work from the same time. Carhart shamelessly advocated massive tourist assaults on the wilderness. Unlike his other books, not even a hint of a conservation message leaked into this putrid text.

The 1950s found Carhart well established as a national expert on conservation and outdoor recreation. His impassioned and prolific attacks against the "land grab" in conjunction with Bernard DeVoto earned him national respect as a champion of the public lands.[97] The 1950s brought Carhart his greatest success as both a conservationist and an author. During this decade his personal environmental philosophy also grew in both complexity and depth. Issues of land use planning and outdoor recreation continued to dominate Carhart's writings and advocacy work, but he also began to focus on the ecological consequences of postwar industrialism and urban expansion. One event of the decade helped crystallize his new environmental philosophy more than anything else: the attempt to construct a dam across Echo Park.

The proposal to dam the beautiful Echo Park sparked the largest organized effort to date on the part of the American conservation movement. Located within the boundaries of Dinosaur National Monument, Echo Park was an isolated federal area in extreme northwestern Colorado near the Utah border. In the mid-1940s, Congress paved the way for the implementation of the Colorado River Storage Project, including a dam to be built within the boundaries of Dinosaur National Monument that would completely flood a beautiful canyon known as Echo Park. Not surprisingly, national conservation groups strenuously opposed the project. Carhart became a leading local spokesman for the anti-dam movement.[98] Although he was deeply concerned with water scarcity in urban centers such as Denver, he consistently opposed Department of Reclamation projects.[99] He argued that overzealous engineers were part of the problem with western water, not the solution.[100] Although Colorado had a long tradition of grassroots conservation, Carhart was one of the few willing to take a strong stand against the dam.[101]

The national effort to defeat the Echo Park dam was a watershed for the American conservation movement. For Carhart, the respect he gained as a spokesman for Echo Park provided an expanded national audience for his writing, setting the stage for the success of his five most important books on the environment: *Conservation Please! Questions and Answers on Conservation Topics* (1950), *Water or Your Life* (1951), *Timber in Your Life* (1954), *The National Forests* (1959), and *Planning for America's Wildlands* (1961).[102] The style and content of these books owed much to Carhart's experiences as a writer of pulp fiction. His rhetoric was fiery and evangelical, with an emphasis on western idioms and slang. For example, this passage from *Timber in Your Life* is typical of Carhart's rhetoric. "Ray Mason's temper began a slow burn as he left the lumber yard. The man in his office laughed as if anyone asking for a few boards of what old-timers called 'cork pine' was a joke."[103] He used this style self-consciously to distance himself from eastern bureaucrats and conservation intellectuals and to make the books accessible to the general public. Printed in large runs, with most going through multiple reprintings, these books received good notices in the press and praise from the conservation community.[104]

Of all his conservation books, *Conservation Please!* best demonstrates Carhart's evolving environmental philosophy and also foreshadows the formation of the Conservation Library. The book was commissioned by the Garden Club of America to provide a source for members and the general public concerning common conservation questions. It featured answers from well-known experts, as well as commentary on all issues from Carhart. Preparation for the project included extensive research and reading on a variety of subjects ranging from soil erosion to the uses of and problems with DDT. During the research phase of the project, Carhart noticed the scarcity of research facilities dedicated to conservation and environmental advocacy. Simply assembling all the pertinent questions for the book proved so daunting that he commented, "Any volume which would include all questions that must be answered if we are to have reasonably complete conservation achievement in our nation would soon become a library."[105]

Throughout the 1950s, Carhart continue to worry about the availability of conservation information, which he saw as critical to the success of the conservation advocacy movement. One of the key lessons to come out of the Echo Park controversy was the notion that to become a more effective force in American politics, the movement needed some centralized organization to coordinate national environmental advocacy. As Carhart explained, "We lack the basic facilities for all such groups to act in unison in securing fundamental conservation measures which would underwrite the activities of all. We have reached a point when all forces must find some common area of action, greater coordination of effort in that universal area, so the efforts of all in solving basic issues may assist all."[106] Many conservation organizations of the 1950s responded to the need for greater organization by expanding their individual organizational structure to create centers for directing action.

On the other hand, Carhart had more grandiose ideas about how to bring the movement together. His experiences throughout the 1950s reinforced his nascent ideas, eventually driving him to act. The 1950s were also a time of refinement for Carhart's personal environmental philosophy. With the work on *Conservation Please!* he began to move away from his emphasis on recreation and land planning toward a more holistic and ecological vision of conservation. For example, in the introduction to the Garden Club book, he attempted to explain his new vision of human relationships to the nonhuman environment: "It is the truth variously expressed, that we humans are a part of the living world; that we cannot set ourselves apart as outside the realm of natural law, and attempt to impose our will and desires contrary to that law."[107] His more sophisticated vision of environmental protection was integrated into his three major books of the decade: *Timber in Your Life, The National Forests,* and *Planning for America's Wildlands.* Each of these books contributed to Carhart's growing reputation as a leading environmental thinker.

As early as the late 1940s, Carhart became concerned with the overuse and abuse of chemical pesticides. As he stated in a widely circulated pamphlet, "The farmer hears about DDT. He uses it with the one objective of killing one species. Terrific damage to beneficial insects, birds, and ground organisms may result."[108] Twelve years before Rachel Carson warned of the perils of pesticides, Carhart had recognized the extent of the problem from firsthand observation. During his years with the Colorado wildlife agencies, he had noticed alarming dangers to small animals from agricultural use of pesticides. He also saw the effects of overuse of poisons widely deployed to control "pest" animals, warning fellow sportsmen that "your future hunting and fishing are in jeopardy" when ranchers poisoned "varmints" who were then consumed by game animals.[109] The realization of how poisons introduced into a low level of the ecosystem gradually worked their way into all levels helped Carhart broaden his definition of conservation. "Too often," he wrote, "he [the farmer or rancher] breaks one link of the chain, and then tries to repair the damage by smashing other links."[110]

Although Carhart did not rival the visionary Carson in this area, by the early 1950s his environmental thinking had clearly reached a level of sophistication far surpassing his earlier work on wilderness. Carson read Carhart's work on pesticides while conducting her research for *Silent Spring*. The two later corresponded about pollution at the Denver Arsenal and the Lost River in Oregon. During the early 1960s, Carhart was one of the people Carson turned to for help in her effort to "collect as much . . . to counteract the industry campaign to the effect that all untoward happenings related to pesticides occurred some time in the past."[111] Too many historians have treated Carhart as a one-issue person, but his work on pesticides reveals far greater breadth of vision. In addition to his work on poisons, he spent much of the 1940s researching and writing about water and reclamation issues, culminating in the publication of *Water or Your Life* in 1951. Harshly critical of federal reclamation projects, the book generated considerable controversy. Once again Carhart used his folksy rhetoric to carefully usher his readers into the story and make them feel comfortable before shocking them with frightening statistics about the issues. Chapters such as "Have a Swig of Sewage!" utilized muckraking techniques to bring large-scale problems right into the homes of the reading public, hoping they would be converted on larger issues in their communities.

The last, and perhaps the most important, of Carhart's publications was *Planning for America's Wildlands*. One reviewer, the historian Roderick Nash, praised *Wildlands* as the "first systematic statement of philosophy and policy in the nascent field of Wildland management."[112] Overall, the book represented the culmination of more than forty years of thinking about the subject of wilderness and land planning. Its important insight came from the notion that wilderness was only one of many zones of wildland. Carhart forcefully argued that creating a false hierarchy of wilderness values could lead to stagnation and political division. He railed against simple answers and took groups such as the Wilderness Society to task for their rigid definitions of wilderness. What he feared most was that by highlighting pristine wilderness, some environmental advocates limited themselves to preserving only the most inaccessible of places; at the same time they endangered slightly developed or fringe areas with great potential for wilderness-type recreation.[113] Faced with post–wilderness bill gridlock, in the 1990s environmental historians began to question the utility of elevating wilderness as the ultimate goal of the environmental movement.[114] Carhart's work in 1961 presaged this movement by three decades. Early on he recognized that rather than being a clearly definable and mappable place, wilderness was "an experience" profoundly shaped by the particular historical and cultural baggage carried by the people who viewed it.[115] Carhart was often criticized as a waffler and a sellout on the wilderness issue, but his philosophy, as spelled out in *America's Wildlands*, was to a certain extent more sophisticated than those of many of his better known and more respected contemporaries.[116]

By the end of the 1950s, Carhart had gained a reputation in the popular press as the "dean of American conservationists."[117] His steadfast dedication and evangelical fervor won him the respect and admiration of conservationists and resource business organizations alike.[118] His personal environmental philosophy had evolved and become more inclusive and sophisticated. His vast, varied experiences left him positioned to make a unique and significant contribution in the turbulent years that lay ahead.

CONCLUSION

In 1960, Carhart was sixty-nine years old. The intense pace of his writing and advocacy work had taken its toll. Not surprisingly, he began to take stock of his career and started thinking retrospectively about the conservation movement. From the perspective of 1960, the future of the conservation movement looked hopeful, if only the momentum of the previous decades could be sustained. Colorado seemed to be at the center of a major ideological reorientation. Previously irreconcilable groups of business leaders, urban sports enthusiasts, rural ranchers, and others were coming together to support the protection of wild areas in the state. Everywhere environmental issues had moved onto the front burner as political issues.

In this atmosphere Carhart began his search for a conservation archive to house his personal collections. He strongly believed that he and his generation of conservationists needed to build a research and advocacy center for future environmentalists. Likewise, he hoped that this center would become a place where young people could be educated about conservation and trained to fight to save the West from unscrupulous land developers, land-hungry stockmen, and general ignorance about environmental problems.[119] The Conservation Library became more than a convenient means for Carhart to clean out his basement. It became an obsession that dominated the rest of his life.

The development of the Conservation Library came at a particularly important moment in the history of the American environmental movement. The 1960s were a time of unprecedented social upheaval. The conservation movement experienced fundamental change in demographic composition and philosophical direction. During this period gender and generational issues intersected with changing perceptions of technology and environmentalism within the growing environmental movement. As Carhart and John Eastlick perfected their plans for the collection, environmental issues increasingly made their way into the national political discourse. The time seemed right to try to unite the divergent social and political trends of the emergent environmental movement in an entirely new way.

CHAPTER THREE

Collecting Nature

> The collection and preservation of an authentic domain of identity cannot be natural or innocent. It is tied up with nationalistic politics, with restrictive law, and with contested encodings of past and future.
>
> *James Clifford*, The Predicament of Culture

> What is conservation? Can its full scope, its essentiality to life on earth, the goals of the practicing conservationist, all be fitted into a simple, understandable, limited sequence of common words?
>
> *Arthur Carhart*, 1960

One of the inherent problems with the wilderness focus in American environmentalism prior to 1964 was that it required an explanation of specific emotions known only to a select few. In the quest for permanent protection for wilderness, environmental advocates needed to convince the American public, most of whom had not been to a proposed wilderness area, that these remote places were worth preserving. The need to explain a wilderness experience to the uninitiated forced wilderness supporters to use creative means to convey an argument based primarily on personal emotions foreign to most. For those who knew the wilderness from experience, the need for preservation was obvious. The difficulty came when they attempted to explain their faith to nonbelievers. How, for instance, do you describe the feeling of standing alone on the summit of a mountain as the sun sets to someone who has never left the city? How can words capture the mingling of fear and awe inspired by the spectacle of the fading light that ushers in the deadly cold of night? How can one explain the primal joy of locking your sights on a distant mountain goat to city folk used to purchasing their meat in neat little Styrofoam packages?

Generations of pilgrims have tried to preserve their wilderness experiences in words, but they never seem to do justice to the event itself. The emotion and feeling are often lost in the translation into words on a page. How can the intangibles of the experience be captured, replicated, and recorded? How can the people who know in their heart that wild areas matter convey their message? For centuries mountaineers struggled to explain themselves to a bewildered public. Asked about their motivations, many leaned lamely upon the cliché "Because it's there." Explaining their feelings and their reasons for engaging in a seemingly useless but arduous activity often surpasses the difficulty of the act itself. Is that because most people will never find themselves hanging by their fingertips over a yawning abyss or staring through the scope of a high-powered rifle? Or because most people will never go to an area that could be called a wilderness?

Thomas Jefferson once lamented, "It is impossible for the emotions arising from the sublime to be felt beyond what they are. . . . The rapture of the spectator is really indescribable!"[1] Like Jefferson, American environmentalists faced the daunting task of translating the sublime into a reality comprehensible by anyone. Explaining the intangible value of wilderness to a pragmatic and materially oriented public was one of the greatest challenges facing the American environmental movement in the 1950s and early 1960s. The emotional quality of the wilderness appeal made advocates easy targets for critics and was the Achilles' heel of the movement in the 1950s. As the politics of wilderness became more complicated and public action seemed more imperative, some conservationists looked to new media to publicize their cause. The Sierra Club, under the direction of David Brower, launched a successful series of conservation coffee-table books. Lavishly illustrated with photos of endangered wilderness areas, supplemented by nature poems and prose, the books sold by the tens of thousands, raising much-needed funds and, more important, increasing awareness.[2] In addition, the Sierra Club produced a number of films, like those depicting the endangered Echo Park and Grand Canyon, which aired nationally on public television stations. Of course, films with environmental themes were not new. The 1930s classics *The River* and *The Plow That Broke the Plains* began the trend, but slick multimedia productions took on new importance in the 1950s as tools for environmental advocacy. By the 1960s, environmental advocacy groups, large and small, were actively using new methods to reach the American public and to convey the value of wilderness and environmental protection to a broader audience.

Arthur Carhart was among those who attempted to capture a particular view of the wilderness and to distribute it to the widest audience possible. But he also wrote out of self-interest. The economic imperatives of the Great Depression left him virtually chained to his typewriter, a slave to deadlines and word counts. Still, his remarkable output of action-packed pulp fiction conveyed a conservation message, however crude, to readers who might never purchase a slick, expensive Sierra Club publication. By the late 1950s, in the wake of the fight for Echo Park, Carhart realized that something new was needed to educate the public about the virtue and necessity of conservation—something that could transcend the medium of the written word and move beyond coffee-table books and films. The nebulous and ethereal ideas of nature, wilderness, and conservation needed a permanent home, a place where concrete physical artifacts and collections could give form and scale to the intangible.

Drawing on these trends, the founders of the Conservation Library sought to reify their ideology in physical space and to recapture their visions of nature and a simpler, better society in a place open to a potentially unlimited clientele: they would establish a public library. Like a skid row rescue mission with a flickering neon cross, the Conservation Library might stand as a beacon of light in the dark heart of the city. Here in this central location, it was hoped, a generation could be redeemed and returned to the fold, cured of "unnatural" modern behaviors that led to environmental ignorance and, ultimately, to cultural decay. For Carhart and many of his peers in the conservation movement, the surge of emotion inspired by "nature" was so profound that they believed it to be something characteristically human. They were convinced that individuals who did not share their love of the wilderness and the nonhuman world suffered from a false consciousness or, more cynically, were the products of an inferior background. They felt that their own middle-class attitudes toward the natural world were the only legitimate position.[3] Therefore, the mission of the Conservation Library was to enlighten the public, to help ordinary people reawaken their innate connections with the natural world through contact with carefully selected artifacts, books, displays, and, most important, ideas. Conservationists from many different organizations across the country, under the direction of Arthur Carhart, would come together to do the selecting.

This chapter explores the meanings of the effort to create a physical space to house and represent a particular vision of environmental advocacy. We need to understand the explicit and implicit assumptions that motivated Carhart, Eastlick, and the others involved in the founding of the library. Their motives and goals both reflected and shaped the national conservation movement, a site of ideological change throughout the 1960s.

Carhart conceived the library for two reasons: he wanted a monument to conservation, and he wanted a center for continued advocacy. Before either of these goals could become reality, he had to assemble financial and institutional support: advisers, experts, advocates, and well-connected allies. The first, and most difficult, task facing all those involved in the project was to establish the terms of the conservation debate. That is, was conservation concerned primarily with renewable or nonrenewable resources? Should the movement openly acknowledge an anthropocentric position or move toward biocentrism? Most important, what were the reasons for, and purposes of, conservation? What would be included in and excluded from the collection process? These questions and the debate over the meaning of conservation reflected a broad and shifting spectrum of opinion in a fast-growing social movement.

Boxes of manuscripts piling up in the corners of the Western History rare book room, spring 1961. Denver Public Library, Western History Collection, Conservation Library Collection photos.

Ultimately, the Conservation Library project suffered from its founders' and supporters' inability to adequately define their ideology. True, by leaving their definitions vague and open-ended, they maintained a fiction of consensus and ensured a steady flow of contributions from well-meaning supporters, but because they failed to set boundaries, the physical "stuff" they received sometimes did not fit their notions of conservation. Over time, the eclectic mass of material artifacts assembled in the Conservation Library reflected the ballooning boundaries of a new, all-encompassing holism associated with ecology and environmentalism. Supposedly, all the artifacts somehow represented "nature." But artifacts are more than representative abstractions; they also occupy physical space. Ironically, the job of dealing with the material presence of the vast and eclectic holdings ultimately overwhelmed the soul-searching about meaning and significance. At the same time, the vagueness of the meanings of "conservation" was also a strength, enabling the movement to attract diverse adherents who lent support for a variety of reasons.

ALLIES

The Denver Public Library Commission officially sanctioned the Conservation Library on September 20, 1960, telling its head librarian, John Eastlick, to begin receiving materials. It was agreed that Carhart would act as the official "consultant" to the project and that the conservationists who had given their time to help define and encourage the project would be asked to act as a permanent group of "counselors." They would advise the library on questions of scope and mission and aid with fund-raising and acquisitions. Carhart also hoped that this influential group would provide the "good guidance [that] assures the Conservation Library Center will more fully achieve its potential in serving conservation and thereby the community."[4] Most of those asked to become involved agreed to participate, and an impressive who's who of America's organized conservation community came together under the banner of the Conservation Library.

The counselors that Carhart assembled shared certain characteristics, both with Carhart and with each other. They included Horace M. Albright, former director of the National Park Service; Carl W. Buchheister, president, National Audubon Society; James Cagney, Conservation Foundation board of trustees; Robert D. Calkins, president, American Association for Conservation Information; Dr. Clarence Cottam, director, Welder Wildlife Foundation; Dr. Joseph L. Fisher, president, Resources for the Future; Dr. Ira Gabrielson, president, Wildlife Management Institute; Thomas Gill, director, Charles Lathrop Pack Forestry Foundation; Seth Gordon, vice president, North American Wildlife Foundation; C. R. "Pink" Gutermuth, chairman, Natural Resources Council of America; E. Budd Marter III, executive director, The Outdoor Writers Association of America; Richard E. McArdle, chief, U.S. Forest Service; Leslie A. Miller, former chairman, Hoover Task Force on Natural Resources; Dr. Olaus J. Murie, director of the Wilderness Society; Sigurd F. Olson, National Parks Association, Izaak Walton League of America; Bernard L. Orell, president, Forest History Society, and vice president Weyerhaeuser Company; Joseph W. Penfold, conservation director for the Izaak Walton League of America; Daniel A. Poole, editor, Wildlife Management Institute; Dr. Paul B. Sears, former director, Yale University Conservation Project; Richard W. Smith, manager, Natural Resources Department, U.S. Chamber of Commerce; Dr. Robert Stearns, former president of the University of Colorado; Richard H. Stroud, executive vice president, Sport Fishing Institute; Walter P. Taylor, Oklahoma Cooperative Wildlife Research Center; Dr. William Vogt, former executive secretary of Planned Parenthood; Hugh B. Woodward, director of the National Wildlife Federation; and Howard Zahniser, executive secretary, the Wilderness Society.

Conservation Library counselors: unidentified conservationist, Carhart (center), and Ira Gabrielson exploring conservation exhibits on the fourth floor during spring 1961. Denver Public Library, Western History Collection, Conservation Library Collection photos.

The counselors were all men, all white, all successful and powerful in their particular areas of expertise. Most of them were past midlife, and they all shared an interest in outdoor recreation. Many were bird-watchers who had traveled the globe in search of new additions to their life lists; others were hunters, fishermen, and mountaineers. In addition, most of the major environmental advocacy groups of the day appeared on the list of official CLC supporters. The fact that no women were included, despite the large number of women involved in the conservation movement, reflects a shared assumption in U.S. social movements that men led while women staffed the ranks.

Prominent women conservationists, such as biologist Rachel Carson, the sine qua non of the modern environmental movement, bird advocate and researcher Rosalie Edge, and wolf expert Lois Crisler, often worked on their own, outside the mainstream of organized conservation organizations, or were involved in creating their own environmental organizations. This radical amateur tradition of conservation, exemplified by women such as Carson, often ran in different directions from the more conservative institutional brand of male-dominated conservation.[5] For example, women like Edge and Carson made their mark on environmental thinking and advocacy mainly outside the confines of conservation groups, counting instead on support from women's organizations such as the Garden Club of America, the American Association of University Women, and the National Council of Women. Although unquestionably one of the leading voices for environmental protection, Carson often found herself in conflict with the conservation establishment and the powerful men who controlled the movement.[6] The rise of the "conservation sciences"—professional forestry, reclamation engineering, and land planning—in the 1940s and 1950s had pushed women environmental advocates to the periphery: "Women came to be viewed as amateur enthusiasts and propagandists while men carried on the work of wilderness and wildlife administration."[7] In the early years of the CLC, therefore, women conservationists were ignored. As women participated in the social movements of the 1960s, they challenged the assumption of male dominance, and eventually environmental organizations opened their organizational hierarchy to women, whose support they desperately needed. A crucial element of the successful development of the Conservation Library came with the realization of the importance of gender and generational diversity in successful environmental coalitions.

Regardless of early problems of exclusion and elitism, these counselors played a significant role in the development and success of the Conservation Library. The direct link between the library and influential leaders from national and local conservation organizations ensured that the fledgling institution would hold a spot at the center of the conservation movement as it crested a wave of unprecedented popular support in the 1960s. The counselors wasted no time in spreading the word about the newly formed library. It was not long before Ira Gabrielson of the Wildlife Management Institute, William Vogt of Planned Parenthood, and Joseph Penfold, conservation director of the Izaak Walton League of America, sent their personal and organizational papers to the DPL. The counselors also performed the valuable service of recruiting other notable collections from friends and colleagues from around the country.

As a result, significant collections arrived at the doors of the DPL by the truckload. Carhart led the way by donating his extensive and eclectic collection of books, letters, magazines, photos, movies, notebooks, and curios, like the skull of the wolf "Rags," featured in *Last Stand of the Pack.* Impressive piles of boxes, crates, and artifacts began to accumulate on the fourth floor of the main library building. Among the early acquisitions was a large wooden trunk bulging with rare documents chronicling the history of the American Bison Society, one of the first wildlife conserva-tion groups in America, founded in the 1890s; this venerable organization had helped create the National Bison Range in Montana and reestablish the species in the United States. This collection was the gift of Katherine Seymour of New York, the daughter of one of the founders of the group, and a friend of Conservation Library counselor Horace Albright.

In many ways Albright was typical of the conservation counselors. A distinguished former director of the National Park Service, he maintained his stature in the conservation movement, even in his twilight years. Al-bright played a major role in the financing of key conservation efforts during the 1920s and 1930s. As superintendent of Grand Teton National Park, he had convinced John D. Rockefeller to help finance a dramatic ex-pansion of the park through a complex buyout of private land. Over a twenty-year period, Albright worked behind the scenes to help Rocke-feller reshape Jackson Hole and dramatically expand the boundaries of Grand Teton.[8] As a member of the CLC counselors, Albright brought his considerable financial savvy and philanthropic connections to the Con-servation Library, helping Carhart and Eastlick to maneuver their way through the maze of foundation politics. His long experience with the Rockefeller family gave him an intimate knowledge of the machinations needed to gain leisure-class patronage for cultural institutions designed to uplift the plebeian public. Skills such as Albright's helped to alleviate the problems of depending on the lukewarm support of local Denver government.

Although the DPL Commission officially approved the creation of the Conservation Library, it initially allocated no funds or staff for the project. As more and more material arrived, funding quickly became the greatest concern. Soon the library staff was unable to sort the donations, and no provision existed for paying Carhart for the fifty to sixty hours a week he spent on the project. Initially, Carhart and Eastlick had waxed enthusiastic about the response from the nation's conservation leaders and had assumed that the finances would somehow work out. Wealthy donors were happy to contribute materials that bespoke their own historical importance, but they proved less willing to contribute cash. In typical post–New Deal fashion, Carhart thought that money and government support would quickly rise to meet a seemingly imperative cultural and public need. The economy was booming, and the government had been funding increasing numbers of public cultural projects since the 1930s. This faith in the government's desire and ability to continue into the foreseeable future indicated Carhart's economic naïveté during this early period. He never seriously considered the possibility of long-term funding problems. But after a full year with no sign of funding from the Library Commission, Carhart became concerned. In fact, the last months of 1960 and the first months of 1961 were tense times for the Conservation Library. Carhart was beginning to wonder if even after all his trouble, the collection might not receive the full support of the DPL.[9]

Gradually Carhart focused on several, never identified, members of the DPL Commission and city council who maintained strong ideological opposition to conservation in general.[10] Conservation proved a touchy subject in Colorado, with conservation projects never failing to generate political controversy. As conservative political advocates, often with ties to resource business interests, many on the board were less than receptive to the CLC idea. Although deeply concerned about opposition to the project among board members, Carhart displayed his love of a good fight when he compared the political wrangling and backroom deals of the commission with the glory days of the "land grab" fight of the 1940s. "This interlude," he commented in a letter complaining about the board to Denver mayor Richard Batterton, a longtime friend, "reminds me somewhat of certain planning and plotting of 'them good old days!'"[11] Over time, Carhart used his influence with Batterton to "smoke out" opponents to the CLC and to pressure them to approve the project. Because his name was so closely associated with the project and all the early donations of collections came from his personal friends, Carhart thought that his reputation within the conservation community was on the line. In a letter to his friend Paul Sears, former head of Gifford Pinchot's Yale forestry program, he lamented the possibility of failure. "I am deeply concerned," he wrote, "as to the obligation I have personally to my conservationist colleagues, to keep this project directed toward the goals you and I discussed."[12] Adding to the sense of confusion, John Eastlick was too busy managing the DPL system to take an active role in resolving the situation.[13]

One year after the initial meeting that started the project, the official position of the Conservation Library remained unclear. There was still no funding from the DPL. In addition, Carhart was afraid to send out the grant applications he had carefully prepared because he felt that the DPL Commission might abandon the project altogether. This black cloud of uncertainty lifted, however, in the spring of 1961 when Batterton finally turned the tide by convincing the commission that the CLC was not a political organization and that, if funded by the city, it would strive to present all sides of controversial environmental issues to the public. Afterward, the library was allocated $4,500 to cover initial expenses and help support the small staff as they began organizing the collections and handling the administrative duties associated with acquisitions. In addition, the board agreed to work out a payment schedule for Carhart's consulting fees, thus allaying his personal financial concerns.[14] City hall support paved the way for a grant-writing campaign aimed at securing a funding base outside the library system, and immune to Denver city government politics.

Another boost came with the endorsement of the Conservation Library by the Outdoor Writers Association of America (OWAA), which contributed a wealth of records to the library. The OWAA contributed no money, but the support of its twelve hundred members, including columnists, editors, photographers, writers, and sportsmen, ensured that the collection gained an overnight audience among outdoor enthusiasts.

Indeed, the OWAA exercised an influence disproportionate to its numbers. Over the years, the organization counted among its members some of America's most prominent writers, including Bernard DeVoto and Wallace Stegner. Hundreds of other members regularly contributed to almost every publication dealing with outdoor recreation and conservation. The OWAA brought together a diverse group of individuals who spanned the political spectrum. All shared, however, a love for the outdoors and a desire to protect the environment. Over the years the group helped outdoor writers and advocacy groups promote various conservation crusades, ranging from hunting and fishing access to wilderness. The organization likewise influenced millions of politically conservative readers who might never have looked at a conservation publication but who did listen to fellow sportsmen. The OWAA played a key role in reconciling political conflicts between environmentalists and sportsmen. Still, their active participation in coalition building became increasingly difficult as struggles between radical environmentalists, animal rights activists, and hunters and fishers heated up in the 1970s and 1980s.[15]

When E. Budd Marter, the always jovial and supportive executive director of the OWAA, first visited the Conservation Library, he was so impressed with its facilities and possibilities that he sat down and wrote out a personal check for two hundred dollars.[16] Marter looked more like an accountant than the leader of an outdoorsman's organization. Usually dressed in conservative suits and sporting a military haircut, he hardly fit the picture of a rugged sportsman. But beneath his corporate exterior lay a deep love of nature and an abiding devotion to conservation causes. Marter's personal donation and strong endorsement of the CLC marked the beginning of a long, fruitful relationship between the library and the OWAA. As a member of the CLC counselors, Marter worked diligently to promote the CLC to anyone who would listen, especially skeptical members of the OWAA.

To a certain extent, support from groups like the OWAA came fairly easily. Recognition of the CLC by key government agencies, however, required a little more diplomacy. Although the appointment of Horace Albright to the CLC counselors ensured close ties between the library and the National Park Service, to add to federal agency support (one of Eastlick's main goals), the Forest Service had to be enlisted as well. On the first of many trips to the East Coast on behalf of the CLC, Carhart stopped at the office of Richard McArdle, chief of the U.S. Forest Service. Thereafter, McArdle and Carhart corresponded regularly, and, after some convincing McArdle pledged the backing of the Forest Service for the effort. He also offered to join the CLC counselors and to make the Conservation Library a repository for Forest Service records.[17] This cooperative arrangement, although never official Forest Service policy, garnered thousands of documents, manuscripts, and audiotapes for the CLC. Ironically, in the coming years the CLC staff came to regret this agreement as mountains of government documents, many of questionable value or duplicates, flooded the already overflowing storage areas.

By May 1961, the *Denver Post* proclaimed proudly, "World Conservation Center Opening at Denver's Library."[18] Less than a year after its conception, the library was already taking on both local and national importance. Carhart told the *Post* that the scope of environmental materials and subjects available to the library was so vast, he "hardly [knew] where to stop."[19] With the support of the DPL Commission, the mayor, and the local press, the library was off and running. The possibilities for future expansion seemed limitless.

In the fall of 1961, Carhart and Eastlick found themselves wandering through the concrete jungle of New York City, where they had come in search of donations from friendly philanthropic organizations. Acting on advice from Albright, they made their way to the offices of the American Conservation Association (ACA). With the evangelical fire of the newly converted, Eastlick gave a dynamic presentation to the board of the ACA, already warmed to the proposition by Albright. Impressed by the proposal and the support from the city of Denver, the ACA agreed to help the fledgling library with substantial grants. The ACA, well endowed by the Rockefeller family, became one of the CLC's strongest financial allies. The first grant for $15,000 arrived in January 1962; an additional $10,000 was pledged for the next year, with subsequent grants following over the years. The funding from the ACA underwrote a major acquisitions campaign and enabled a newly expanded DPL staff to address the increasingly precarious pile of boxes on the fourth floor in the new home of the CLC.

With the funding situation resolved for the immediate future, the directors and counselors began promoting the CLC and refining goals and policies for later development. Originally the library was to house the papers, articles, books, and artifacts of the American conservation movement. By 1962, however, the original concept broadened and became more complex. The counselors hoped that the library might become a national center for environmental advocacy. Carhart stated the goal succinctly in an early article on the CLC. More than just "a historical collection," he argued, the library was an "instrument to serve constructive action."[20] He hoped that young activists would flock to Denver to learn about the conservation tradition and to study techniques for preserving the environment.[21]

Youth education became a central theme in the development of the CLC. The glue that held the eclectic supporters of the CLC together consisted of a mixture of fear and defensiveness, along with idealism and love of nature. The focus on education derived, in part, from the underlying fears and anxieties that fueled leisure-class social activism in the postwar years. Many of those involved in the CLC project shared antimodernist fears of the rising cultural prominence of hard science and technology in postwar America. Economic prosperity, in the wake of the World War II industrial miracle, brought a renewed emphasis on leisure and recreation. Thousands of new wilderness enthusiasts joined conservation-minded groups and local outdoor organizations between 1945 and 1960. But the industrial miracle also bolstered widespread faith in science, technology, and progress. For many Americans, the prosperity of the 1950s seemed to confirm the notion that science could solve the world's problems. Belief in inexorable linear progress toward technological utopia fueled American politics and culture. But beneath the linoleum of Levittown and the chrome plating on Chevrolets lay fear. Indeed, the politics of the cold war gave a sense of urgency to the push for technological progress at all costs. Individuals who worried about the costs of technological progress found themselves a distinct minority, their cautious attitudes dangerously close to treason.

In 1957, scientists from around the world busily collaborated on projects for the International Geophysical Year (IGY), a multinational celebration of technology and science. The IGY represented a remarkable level of international cooperation aimed at promoting science and technology as the solution to the problems of the modern world. The cooperation and camaraderie of the IGY seemed a harbinger of good times ahead. This positive atmosphere, however, proved fragile. Later that same year, the Soviet Union surprised the world with the launch of *Sputnik*. This shocking technological leap from the supposedly backward Russians caused widespread panic in the United States. In fact, the little beeping space ball set off an explosion of scientific activity unprecedented in world history. In addition, *Sputnik* fundamentally altered the relationship between the federal government and technological research and education. Under intense pressure to overcome the humiliation of *Sputnik*, President Eisenhower launched a program of state-sponsored science education, focused primarily on space and nuclear technology.[22] By the 1960s, education programs emphasizing physics, engineering, and nuclear science were flush with government dollars, and students who pursued a college education in these fields could count on substantial government support in the form of loans and seemingly unlimited research budgets.

In the midst of this hard science and technology love feast, many individuals and organizations involved in the "softer" sciences found themselves suddenly left out in the cold. Conservationists with antimodernist leanings were terrified by the direction the country was moving and deeply concerned about the implications of this new thinking for future environmental science and environmental advocacy. In 1958, Conservation Library counselor Olaus Murie summed up these fears when he stated, "We are in a fever of almost hysterical emphasis on science as a material weapon."[23] Several other CLC counselors echoed this sentiment. Carl Buchheister, a CLC counselor and president of the National Audubon Society, surpassed even Murie in his alarmist rhetoric about the problem. Sounding the tocsin for readers of *Audubon Magazine*, he sternly warned, "The world must be on guard against the myopic technologist who, assuming the aura of 'science,' arrogantly thinks he can play God."[24]

Carhart and Eastlick deplored the glorification of science and technology in popular culture. Instead, they envisioned the Conservation Library as a safe haven in this technocratic storm. By providing a public center for conservation education, the supporters of the CLC hoped to combat the ideas that had America's kids playing Johnny Space Commander instead of Daniel Boone.[25]

Carhart and Eastlick consistently used the rise of nuclear science and the cold war as foils for the Conservation Library. Their prose swelled with melodramatic metaphors and warnings to those who marched in lockstep to the drum of progress. In their most anxious moments they talked about "the public" as if most Americans were no more than glassy-eyed minions genuflecting at the feet of the false god of technology. Although at times their writing was ridiculously melodramatic, genuine fear resonates through their rhetoric. In arguing for conservation education, Carhart once wrote: "Infernos boiling out of nuclear fission have focused attention on the . . . sciences of physics, chemistry and electronics," while "the less spectacular sciences of humble things—soil, water, and the husbandry of green plants . . . have been too generally taken for granted."[26] Anxiousness and a strong sense of purpose drove the founders of the Conservation Library to reach higher and higher as they planned for the future of the collection. For example, Eastlick exulted that "what began as a special collection of the municipal library has become a run-away project destined to serve the Western Hemisphere."[27]

Like many of his generation of conservationists, Arthur Carhart grew up with science as a focal point of his education. He worked throughout his life to bring modern scientific methods to bear on both his hobbies and his career. As a youth he spent the summer months poring over botany and biology books. In college and during World War I, he studied bacteria and disease and praised modern scientific methods that helped humans move toward a brighter future. During the 1950s, however, he and many of the CLC counselors found themselves increasingly alienated from the world of modern atomic science, massive reclamation projects, and postwar technology. Like Henry Adams a generation before, they worried about the growing conflict between the technological and the sublime—the dynamo and the virgin. The counselors and advisers who came together to support the CLC questioned contemporary ideas of progress and modernity and were consumed with fears of imminent scarcity hidden by technological hubris. They worried particularly about the consequences of technocratic thinking for American society and culture.[28]

By the 1950s, many in the conservation movement shared a set of ideas most easily described as "antimodernism." Antimodernism has been defined by historian Jackson Lears as "a feeling of revulsion with the banality and weightlessness of modern post-industrial life."[29] The revulsion of the turn-of-the-century antimodernists evolved into genuine fear after World War II. Fear shaped the antimodernist alienation from the postwar world—fear that the cult of technology, the expansion of the space race, and the explosion of consumerism deemphasized contact with the nonhuman world. Conservationists of the 1950s produced a long stream of popular publications warning Americans of the ominous reality of resource scarcity despite, or in some cases because of, advances in technology.[30]

Ironically, most conservationists of the 1950s, including those who created the CLC, used decidedly modernist means to express and act upon their antimodernist revulsion. Even as their alienation grew, their

Progressive faith in government agencies and protective federal laws continued to be staples of the movement. One of the most interesting aspects of the building of the Conservation Library was the constant tension between modern Progressive methods and hopes, and antimodern ideals and fears.[31]

The Progressives believed that management and efficiency could solve the nation's most pressing problems. For most of its history, the conservation movement embraced organizational principles and actions based on the idea of linear progress through Progressive enlightenment. Antimodernists, on the other hand, tended to view the history of the twentieth century as a steady decline toward chaos and environmental collapse, brought on by rampant population growth and unregulated technological expansion.[32] Although these two ideals seemed to be diametrically opposed and irreconcilable, both were direct responses to the perceived chaos and decline of postindustrial America. By drawing on both traditions, sometimes consciously and sometimes not, CLC supporters attempted to reconcile dreams for reform and competing fears that the system was beyond repair. They hoped, in other words, to bring into balance "the needs of men with the requirements for stability of the natural world."[33]

The Conservation Library was designed as a solution to this disjuncture: a museum that provided a home for nature within the confines of the modern city, a place of instruction where people "blinded by the fearful brightness of the atomic bomb, [and] the winking of traffic lights,"[34] could experience vicariously the wildlands and subdue their innate tendencies toward self-destruction. Collecting physical things became the means for reconciling conflicting ideals. As historian James Clifford explains, "Collecting has long been [used as] a strategy for the deployment of a possessive self, culture, and authenticity."[35] "Heritage is . . . nurtured by technophobia," David Lowenthal has argued; "dismayed by technology, [technophobes] hark back to a simpler past whose virtues they inflate and whose vices they ignore."[36] In assembling the artifacts of the Conservation Library, the leaders of America's conservation movement sought to create a physical sanctuary where familiar objects might provide an antidote to their neo-Malthusian fears and *Dr. Strangelove* nightmares.

Even though the founders of the Conservation Library never intended it to be a museum focused on material artifacts, the place that evolved was more akin to a museum than to a traditional library or archive. Principles of archival management played virtually no role in determining the shape of the collections. Many of the documents and books collected for the CLC were obtained in the hope that their mere physical presence might help illustrate particular conservation principles.

In choosing the medium of collection and display of material culture, the founders of the CLC tapped into a long tradition in Western cultures.

For centuries collectors used the material they assembled to "celebrate the stability of their belief systems" while educating the public about their social and political philosophies.[37] Centuries-long traditions illustrated that collections were, above all, the careful ordering of things in space to create a semblance of order in a chaotic world. The creators of the CLC also assumed that the things they assembled were significant and intrinsically meaningful and that somehow the whole, a collection of conservation-related things, was greater than the sum of its parts. It was, therefore, worth spending time and money to preserve the collection as a distinct body with a distinct physical location. Questions of use were always subservient to the goals of collecting and assembling.

Despite their antimodernist leanings and sharp criticisms of modern industrial life and society, the founders of the CLC shared with most of their middle-class contemporaries an underlying belief in a modernist metanarrative with comprehensible objective truths, indisputable facts, and a patina of scientific legitimacy. In their view, human reason, given time and proper instruction, could define and explain an objective reality. Further, they were convinced that the CLC, as a repository for the primary evidence in the search for truth, could help enlighten the urban public and get society back on track.[38] With these lofty goals in mind, Carhart, Eastlick, and the counselors set about building their center. But before they could begin, they faced the difficult task of mapping out the parameters of their ideology. Before the physical space could be organized, "conservation" had to be defined. More than any other factor, the process of definition shaped the character of the CLC as it evolved during the following decades.

HAZY BOUNDARIES

One of the first assignments for the august coalition of conservationists assembled under the banner of the CLC was to construct a set of guidelines to determine the shape, scope, and location of the collections. Each of the counselors was asked to submit a written response concerning these questions. Most of those surveyed agreed that a critical need existed for a conservation archive and that Denver was a logical place for such an institution. For one thing, Denver was close to the geographic center of the nation, with a good airport and easy access to highways. The Denver metropolitan area also was home to three major universities and colleges with programs in conservation fields such as forestry and wildlife management. In addition, Colorado had a long history of grassroots conservation action in spite of strong resistance. As home to many established grassroots outdoor and conservation organizations, Denver provided a political culture and philanthropic community that were supportive of conservation ac-

The original caption to this publicity photo, ca. 1959, read, "The unusual open plan of the building reflects a freedom from unchanging ideas and preconception." Denver Public Library, Western History Collection, Conservation Library Collection photos.

tion. Most important, perhaps, the city was located in a part of the country that seemed most worth conserving because it was surrounded by mountains, trees, clean water, wide-open spaces, big game, and majestic mountains. Toward the goal of convincing people to support the location, the environmental setting was at least as important as the cultural landscape.

Although not generally known as a conservation-minded state, Colorado had a long history of grassroots environmental advocacy closely linked to a large and prominent group of outdoor sports enthusiasts. Grassroots groups could usually find money and support for conservation action.[39] After World War II, interest in outdoor recreation in the state considerably expanded, bringing new conservation constituents. In addition to this base of support, the Denver Public Library also possessed the physical space and administrative infrastructure to sustain the development of a large archival collection.

The DPL's expansive main building, constructed in 1955, contained all the most modern features. The open, flowing art deco revival architecture conveyed a feeling of forward thinking and prosperity. Carhart raved about the physical layout of the library to his conservation friends, exulting that the "dynamic quality of the Denver Public Library is even expressed in sweeping stairs between the first and second floors."[40] The entire fourth floor was dedicated to the archival collections and artifact storage for the famed Western History Collection. Established in the 1920s, this collection quickly gained a national reputation and brought researchers to Denver from around the country. More important for the CLC, the Western History Collection established a precedent for manuscript collections as a part of the DPL mission.

The answers to the initial queries about the CLC rolled into Denver during 1961. Most respondents, with a few exceptions, strongly approved of the Denver location. The concept of a center for conservation education and a repository for related materials struck a chord with the counselors, most of whom expressed faith in the idea that the collection of conservation materials and artifacts was a powerful new medium for reaching the general public and increasing awareness of environmental problems. An enthusiastic Olaus Murie, director of the Wilderness Society, responded from his cabin in Moose, Wyoming, "It occurs to me that such a project would enhance the concept of conservation and bring it more forcefully to the attention of so many people who are planning for the future of this country."[41] Similarly enthusiastic responses poured in from around the country. Writing from his office in Tacoma, Washington, Bernard Orell, Weyerhaeuser executive and Forest History Society president, wrote, "There is no question . . . the library depository you propose would provide the beginning of a permanent source of knowledge." Nonetheless, as one of the most pragmatic and politically conservative of the CLC counselors, Orell couched his support in cautious rhetoric. He worried about a liberal bias and cautioned, "The most important value of [the CLC] will be the establishment of a collection of work that will make available to the researcher material from all points of view from all sides of a particular controversy."[42] Orell was not alone in his concerns about the politics of the collection. From the start, Richard Smith (a manager of the agriculture and natural resources division of the U.S. Chamber of Commerce of the United States) and Clarence Cottam (Rachel Carson's mentor and former Welder Wildlife Foundation officer) cautioned against overtly politicizing the CLC.[43] Despite strong positive responses and general agreement that the CLC was an idea whose time had come, divergent political viewpoints from the counselors clearly indicated that national consensus building would be harder than anticipated.

The questions of need and location were easy compared with the second task facing the directors and counselors of the CLC. If everyone could agree on the idea of a conservation library, few, even within the movement, could agree on what "conservation" was. How could you build a place to represent an idea if no one could agree about the idea? This problem of definition had long been a stumbling block for the American environmental movement.[44]

True, lumping of groups of individuals into broad categories such as "conservationist" often creates a false aura of consensus where none exists. Yet splitting environmental ideologies into ever finer gradations produces the illusion of division where common interest prevails. The semantics and politics of environmentalism often impose sharp black-and-white boundaries when shades of gray actually predominate. For most of the twentieth century, activists and historians reduced the complex interplay of environmental ideas into a dichotomy between utilitarian "conservation" and aesthetic "preservation." This bipolar configuration, purportedly exemplified by the careers of John Muir and Gifford Pinchot, tended to obscure more than it illuminated. The majority of people who dedicated themselves to the protection of the nonhuman world fit neither the strict utilitarianism of Pinchot nor the evangelical pantheism of Muir. The movement to protect the environment fell primarily to those individuals who found themselves trapped between the comfort and convenience of the modern world and the shocking reality of worldwide environmental degradation. More than any other single element, the American environmental movement was shaped by a profound ambivalence about the proper relationship between humans and the rest of the environment.

Asking a diverse group of environmental proponents to agree on a single definition of their ideology proved difficult, indeed, and for the Conservation Library project, definition was particularly important. Without a clear understanding of what it was they were building a monument to, it would be impossible to define the boundaries of the collection.

In a personal sense, Carhart, the CLC's first major donor, knew exactly what constituted a "conservation collection." It was the material stuff that filled his basement and represented a lifetime of research, thought, and action related to the careful use and preservation of the nonhuman world. But Carhart was more pack rat than archivist. In addition, distinguishing valuable artifacts and records from extraneous material proved a matter of politics, cultural perspective, and personal preference.[45] The question of limits, therefore, bedeviled the early years of the Conservation Library. Defining conservation and assembling physical artifacts to represent the idea forced leaders of the environmental movement to work to create a consensus ideology. To a certain extent, this complex exercise reflected and influenced a significant shift in environmental advocacy in 1960s America.

Bounding the terms of the conservation debate proved far more difficult than simply establishing need and justifying location. Deciding what to collect, defining and explaining conservation, describing the movement, and delineating agreeable standards for environmental ideas proved the crux of the CLC project. During the first year, the CLC counselors raised a number of key content questions in an attempt to define their project. Should the collection focus on the history of the conservation movement? Or perhaps anything related to the conservation of resources? Would renewable resources (trees, range, soil, and game) be the focus, or should the collection include nonrenewable resources (oil, gas, minerals) as well? What about issues surrounding "wilderness" preservation and urban and industrial pollution? The responses varied greatly and demonstrated significant divisions within the conservation community. Defining the boundaries of conservation and the Conservation Library became increasingly difficult, especially as advances in ecology brought a steady stream of discoveries of the interconnectedness of the environment. Rachel Carson's revelations in *Silent Spring* about the far-reaching effects of DDT dramatically expanded popular and professional notions of environmental holism.

By the late 1960s, the question of what should be included within environmentalism had become moot; environmentalism was about "everything." It must be kept in mind that the organization of the Conservation Library paralleled the rise of ecology and environmentalism. Many of the people involved in the project changed or refined their personal philosophies to incorporate new ideas and expanding notions of environmental protection. As a result, the attempt to arrive at one encompassing definition of conservation was like squeezing quicksilver.

For the architects of the Conservation Library, the question of definition caused some deep soul-searching. Carhart and many in his generation identified themselves as conservationists—not necessarily because they lumped themselves with the Progressive utilitarian conservation of Gifford Pinchot and Theodore Roosevelt, although many did. Some wanted to distance themselves from the western stereotype of conservationists as ivory tower eastern elitists and bureaucrats, so often vilified at local stock growers associations and in small-town newspapers. Instead, many conservationists emphasized the practicality and common sense of their prescriptions for saving the land, as in this example from Carhart's *Water or Your Life:* "A water shortage . . . can close a factory where you have a job. It can cause the stock you own . . . to depreciate in value."[46] Even the sometimes rabid and radical CLC counselor William Vogt often resorted to pragmatism to make his point. "Man," he wrote, "quite as much as any Ford or Packard, requires refueling." He added: "No one would expect to drive along our highways with an empty gasoline tank."[47] But even as western conservationists courted business leaders and timber industry officials, they did not generally adhere to a strict utilitarian resource conservationist model of advocacy.[48]

The final task of writing out a guiding definition for the CLC in its first years fell to Carhart and Eastlick and, not surprisingly, led to heated exchanges.[49] New to the conservation game, Eastlick felt underqualified

Carhart and Eastlick confer as their library begins to take shape, ca. 1962. Denver Public Library, Western History Collection, Conservation Library Collection photos.

to construct the definition. Only a year before, his strongest connection with nature consisted, in the words of a friend, of having a glass of scotch in his backyard.[50] At the same time, he realized that plans needed to be set in motion as quickly as possible. And, as far as the DPL Commission was concerned, he was personally responsible for the CLC. Since materials continued to arrive at the DPL on a weekly basis, arrangements for cataloging and display and the need to define the purposes and boundaries of the collection became critical in the last months of 1961.

Carhart and Eastlick settled on an ambitious and open-ended definition that stated: "Conservation is thought and action directed by man to protect, maintain and fortify the environmental complex that supports and enriches life as it now exists on the planet earth."[51] This somewhat flabby definition was meant to get the debate over with and move forward with the business of building the Conservation Library. At the same time, they managed to include some sophisticated ideas. First of all, they recognized that perception was as important as action. To succeed, therefore, the CLC needed to concentrate on changing people's perceptions about the environment.

Three phrases that appear over and over in the language of the Conservation Library's founding documents strike the modern reader and, indeed, caused the greatest controversy at the time. The seemingly benign words "maintain" and "fortify" and the vague phrase "environmental complex" gave a few of the counselors pause. Overall, however, they provide key insights to Carhart and Eastlick's thinking.

The use of the term "maintain" reflects the attempt, on the part of the CLC founders, to move away from the ideal of perpetual progress and development that drove much of modern American history and formed the cornerstone of the remarkable post–World War II economic boom. This desire to freeze history, or even turn back the historical clock, reflects the declensionism inherent in the antimodernist alienation from the modern world. The use of the term "fortify" speaks to the same kind of thinking, but with a slight twist. When Carhart and the counselors spoke of "fortifying" nature, they meant the careful management of natural resources. The inclusion of "fortify" in their definition was aimed at calming the fears of CLC supporters in the timber industry and sportsmen's organizations, both of whom used the word to refer to active management of resources, emphasizing use.[52]

As soon as they drafted their definition, Carhart and Eastlick mailed it out to all the counselors, asking them to vote for or against it. Most of the conservation leaders surveyed approved this statement, but some terms made business leaders and industry spokesmen, such as Richard Smith of the U.S. Chamber of Commerce, nervous. He pointed out that the definition failed to include the key utilitarian conservationist phrase "wise use" and that the terms "maintain" and "environmental complex" sounded like the ramblings of an "impractical preservationist."[53]

An unrepentant utilitarian and an adherent to the modernist ideal of progress, Smith worried that omitting the phrase "wise use" from the definition might alienate conservative sportsmen's groups and timber industry people. For many conservationists of the Pinchot school, the inviolable mantra of "wise use" needed to be part of the CLC manifesto. The message of a definition that excluded "wise use" was clear to Smith: "This is a plea for the maintenance of the status quo," he wrote, "and you know that as long as man is around in ever increasing numbers you can't always maintain the status quo. I believe, therefore, that you should explain fortify by adding the words, at the end, 'and use it wisely.'"[54] Business leaders were not the only CLC counselors who maintained their allegiance to "wise use." Clarence Cottam, fearful that sportsmen would never support the CLC without it, also urged Carhart to include the phrase.[55]

On the other hand, Walter P. Taylor of the Oklahoma Cooperative Wildlife Research Center thought the definition too restrictive. He lamented the tendency of conservative conservationists to emphasize economic utility. "Esthetics, wilderness, and the true inward spirit of conservation," wrote Taylor, "and to Hell with the dollar values, should occupy a large and indeed climactic place in the Conservation Library Center."[56] When Carhart pushed Taylor to explain how to define the boundaries of the Conservation Library, Taylor responded, "Boundaries *should* be hazy. They do not exist in nature."[57]

Taylor's and Smith's very different points of view highlighted growing tensions within the conservation movement. On the surface, Smith's statements seem more overtly political and self-serving, with Taylor's position more ambiguous and complex. Yet Smith's statements actually reiterated the common logic of the conservation movement. His position was conservative but hardly regressive. Taylor's position, on the other hand, reflected the philosophical complexity involved in abandoning the old paradigm. Are there really no boundaries in nature? Does the exercise of defining boundaries somehow cede important intellectual territory to the utilitarian school of conservation, or even to anticonservationists? If environmentalism is everything, then what isn't environmentalism?

Taylor insisted that Carhart's questions about boundaries were better left unasked and unanswered. While Smith's position harkens back to the old school of conservation and Progressive politics, Taylor's serves as a harbinger of 1960s political activism and environmentalism. Smith chided Carhart and Eastlick for attempting to maintain the status quo. Obviously, in Smith's mind, the march of progress would continue on. Conservation could not, and should not, stop progress. Instead, conservationists should work to check waste. Taylor also chided Carhart about the status quo. He, too, thought that adherence to the status quo was dangerous and foolish. The change he advocated, however, differed radically from that proposed by Smith. Taylor argued for a break from the confines of the Progressive status quo that Smith, and others like him, had long maintained. Taylor recognized the politics of "wise use" and clearly understood that the future of environmentalism entailed more than a critique of grazing and timber harvests: it required a fundamental change in society. Taylor's friend Olaus Murie agreed with his position and backed up Taylor's assertions about the definition. The savvy Murie recognized the politics inherent in environmental language. "Conservation can mean so many things," he said. "Some people say it's 'wise use.' Who is to say what is wise?"[58]

Taylor's comments reflected growing concerns among many conservationists about the limitations of mainstream conservation. At the same time, his vague recommendation demonstrated the difficulty of defining an alternative without offering a systematic critique. Carhart was asking Taylor and others to define sharply their ideology at the exact moment when that ideology was the least organized and hardest to define. This meant that in the early 1960s, conservationists like Taylor confronted what amounted to an ideological crisis.

Although Taylor argued that boundaries "do not exist in nature," he affirmed a sharp dichotomy between wilderness (nature) and "the true inward spirit of conservation," on the one hand, and "dollar values" (humanity), on the other, thus implying a gap between nature and people. Humans, concerned primarily with economics and progress, became alienated from nature, creating an ethical dilemma: How to move beyond anthropocentrism (a human-centered view of the world) and toward biocentrism (a holistic, ecosystem-based worldview) without a shattering critique of the American market system?

For most of its history the conservation movement drew heavily on the ideal of the Progressive reformers.[59] Many of the older generation based their personal philosophies on the Progressive faith in careful management, multilevel governmental intervention, and linear progress toward balance between human needs and natural capacities. The dominant scientific and ecological paradigms of the period supported this thinking. The idea of a "climax community," Frederic Clements's brainchild, was in perfect harmony with the Progressive ideal. Over time, natural and human systems purportedly evolved until they reached a state of perfect balance.[60] If the nation could eliminate wanton waste and preserve priceless resources, conservationists believed, America could achieve ecological balance.

Clement's thinking served conservationists well in their attempts to manage lands and eliminate gratuitous waste in natural resource use. This ideal, however, failed to confront the fundamental problem facing the United States in the second half of the twentieth century: reconciling an economic system based on ceaseless growth with the dawning realization that scarcity was a real threat in the near future. The supplanting of Clements's climax theory with scientific holism in the 1950s cast further doubt among a growing number of conservation-minded individuals about the feasibility of reconciling the Progressive ideal with holistic ecology.[61] As the extent of the environmental crisis became clearer, many conservationists like Walter Taylor abandoned the Progressive faith and moved toward a more biocentric and socially conscious environmentalism. Taylor's desire to abandon borders reflected a new holistic environmental philosophy that gradually became entwined with a growing awareness of social and economic injustice in 1960s America. While Taylor and others sharply shifted the focus of the environmental debate, they still predicated their philosophy on the notion of scarcity. It would take an infusion of counterculture politics from a younger generation to push the environmental movement beyond scarcity and its concomitant antimodernism.

To a certain degree Carhart sympathized with Taylor's concerns, but in 1960 he was unable to see the complexities and subtleties of Taylor's point. Anthropocentrism continued to dominate Carhart's thinking about environmental issues. The tendency to fall back on an anthropocentric position surfaced most clearly in early discussions about nonrenewable resources such as oil and gas. The very fact that Carhart, Eastlick, and many of the counselors questioned whether writings and artifacts dealing with nonrenewable resources should be included in the collection demonstrated the naïveté in their early environmental philosophy. Taylor, for one, could not understand why they bothered to make the distinction at all. "Living matter," he argued "is simply one phase of the great stream of matter and energy which characterizes the world and probably the universe."[62] Taylor, who had made the leap of faith from atomistic anthropocentrism to holistic biocentrism, recognized the folly of trying to distinguish between "renewable" and "nonrenewable." When Carhart and Eastlick tried to explain how nonrenewables could be "conserved," all they could think of was "channeling it [a nonrenewable resource] to the best use, eradicating every possible type of waste in its use, and as great a degree of salvage and reuse."[63] The key word "use" continued to dominate in the early days. Carhart did not yet consider the consequences of the use, only the best way to maximize the longevity of the resource. The problem with oil and gas, in Carhart's early view, was not whether to use them but how best to use them. Carhart was, to paraphrase E. F. Schumacher, treating nonrenewable resources as income instead of capital.[64] Not surprisingly, the early policies of the CLC reflected the general emphasis among conservationists on planning for use instead of looking for alternatives to the status quo. The CLC's cautious approach to nonrenewable resources changed dramatically over time, particularly after a new group of younger staff took over the management of the library. After this critical generational change, the emphasis of the CLC shifted from collecting materials concerned with the problems of efficient use to acquiring materials concerned with the consequences of that use over time.

Unfortunately, from an administrative point of view, the thoughtful contemplation of the philosophical underpinnings of the library never led to a definitive statement of purpose that could be used to limit the scope of acquisitions to a manageable size. The counselors, Eastlick, and Carhart never stated definitively which would be accepted and which materials would not. Revealingly, for all his experience and genuine dedication to the cause, Carhart was never able to distinguish between quantity and quality in archival collecting. As boxes of manuscripts, artifacts, documents, and photographs began rolling into Denver, all thought of limits was lost in the excitement of discovery.

From the beginning, then, the directors and advisers of the Conservation Library cast their nets wide. As a result, they became very successful at acquiring a rich harvest of valuable materials. In many respects, from a researcher's point of view, this broad focus and general vagueness became an asset. For the administration of the library, however, the failure to resolve issues of scope had serious fiscal ramifications for the future of the Conservation Library. At the same time, the debate over how to define the project (and themselves) proved to be one of the most intriguing legacies of the CLC program. The collection they assembled remains today as a metaphor for the transformation of environmental thinking in the 1960s.

PEOPLE AND STUFF

Nineteen sixty-two was a crucial year for the Conservation Library. The national press took note of the grant from the American Conservation Association. The regional media also focused on the Conservation Library, which remained in the local spotlight throughout the following decade. Carhart, who understood the power of the press, made sure that every event connected with the collection received maximum coverage, issuing photos and press releases no matter how minor the occasion. The press picked up these stories more often than not.[65] National organizations began to seek information on the library, with some pledging moral and financial support. Following the lead of the Outdoor Writers Association of America and the U.S. Forest Service, the International Association of Game, Fish, and Conservation Commissioners (IAGFCC) made the Conservation Library its official depository. Commissioner Ira Gabrielson enthusiastically volunteered IAGFCC support and offered his own collections, telling Eastlick, "I've an attic full of stuff I'll send to you!"[66] The Conservation Education Association, the American Association for Conservation Information, and the Forest History Society followed suit. Excitement about the library reached a high point in March 1962, when 250 conservationists from around the country visited Denver as a part of the National Wildlife Federation annual meeting.

The Friends of the Denver Public Library organized a reception for the visiting conservationists. Refreshments and displays of recent acquisitions greeted the group, and guests were encouraged to browse among the shelves and burrow through boxes.[67] Eastlick and Carhart also used the occasion to explain the origins of the collection and encourage all National Wildlife Federation members to consider the Conservation Library as a home for their personal collections. The highlight of the evening was a presentation of a rare fishing book to Carl O. Gustafson, Conservation

Library counselor and representative of Lawrence Rockefeller.[68] The gift recognized Rockefeller's support of the library and his contributions to the conservation movement. One might ask, how do you thank a multi-millionaire for his support? In this case, by giving him an artifact whose perceived value transcends its market worth. The ritual giving of artifacts in recognition of achievement signifies the reverence these things inspire. Content becomes secondary. The real significance in such material things comes from their power as symbols. The fishing book symbolized the solidity and tradition of sportsmanship in America, a tradition worthy of substantial financial support from benefactors such as Rockefeller. The book also symbolized control. By accumulating and organizing the material relics of conservation, the founders of the CLC demonstrated the coherence of their belief system and their ability to control at least one aspect of an increasingly chaotic world. Nebulous and often conflicting ideas about conservation became comforting reality within the walls of the DPL; the solidity of the artifacts conveyed a sense of control over time. By sending their things and donating their money, conservationists might transcend their time, passing on their legacy of advocacy and tradition to future generations.

At the CLC, newly opened in spring 1961, the story of the preservation of wilderness untrammeled began, ironically, in a locked, temperature-controlled room full of decidedly human artifacts. Guests at the official grand opening, including conservation dignitaries and CLC supporters such as the Sierra Club's David Brower and the Wilderness Society's Howard Zahniser, were on hand to view the relics and peruse the manuscripts. Curious library patrons followed the crowds to the fourth floor, where they passed through two large frosted glass doors, emblazoned with the CLC's new icon. Tall oak cabinets and bookshelves with wire mesh doors contained conservation treasures from around the country. Every corner overflowed with archive boxes, trunks, and sacks of manuscripts. Wrought iron gates led into the rare book area. The prize possession, Howard Zahniser's personal book collection, carefully cataloged and lovingly displayed, occupied the center of the room.[69] Next to the Zahniser books, visitors could sort through a jumble of material artifacts. From the dusty shadows, a marble bust of William Gilpin, former Colorado governor and leading proponent of the "rain follows the plow" idea, locked startled visitors in his stony gaze, a particularly ironic icon for an environmental collection. Next to Gilpin sat John Muir's glasses, displayed alongside a small wooden box holding the presidential fountain pen used to sign a law protecting the American bison. A central case housed another of the library's prized possessions, Aldo Leopold's field notes and an early manuscript for *A Sand County Almanac*, decorated with marginal notes and pencil illustrations. In the corner of the room on that festive night, groups of conservationists gath-

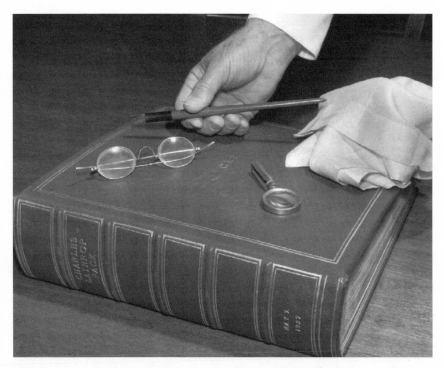

John Muir's eyeglasses, field magnifying glass, and silk scarf rest on a bound copy of Charles Lathrop Pack's journals. Carhart holds the fountain pen used by Theodore Roosevelt to sign the legislation protecting the American bison, 1960. Denver Public Library, Western History Collection, Conservation Library Collection photos.

ered around reel-to-reel tape players and listened to the recorded voices of elderly forest rangers recounting the glory days of the Forest Service.

Among the oddest artifacts in the vault of the Conservation Library was the great seal of the Ladies Auxiliary of the Colorado Ku Klux Klan. The presence of the KKK seal raises interesting questions about links between attempts to preserve race and sex purity and the drive to preserve the American wilderness.[70] Although Carhart and the founders of the CLC did not share the goals of the KKK, there are some intriguing parallels. Like the women of the KKK, very active in Colorado during the 1920s, Carhart and his peers feared changes in American culture and values during a period of prosperity and growth.[71] Both the conservation movement of the 1950s and the western women of the KKK in the 1920s responded initially to demographic changes that appeared to shift power toward groups they feared. And both groups "armed themselves with the rhetoric of moral righteousness and stood at Armageddon to battle for the return of power to the people."[72] By the late 1950s, Carhart and many of the older leaders of the conservation movement became increasingly concerned with the population explosion of the postwar years. Educating the public about the environmental consequences of overpopulation became one of the central goals of the library in the early 1960s.

Overpopulation has been a central concern of the American environmental movement.[73] In the early years, William Vogt, Conservation Library counselor and national executive secretary of Planned Parenthood, became the key figure in influencing the CLC's philosophy of population control. In the dawning days of the baby boom, Vogt wrote an influential and widely read book titled *Road to Survival*. More than most conservationists of his day, Vogt stood firm against the current of popular opinion. He had spent World War II working for the Pan American Union in Latin America, and the human conditions there appalled him.[74] Omnipresent poverty and ecological destitution in the region seemed, to Vogt, a direct result of overpopulation. Following the war, Vogt found himself increasingly alienated from the zeitgeist of American culture, with its focus on ceaseless growth. The growth that most disturbed Vogt was population. He viewed the baby boom as an aberration in human logic and wrote darkly of America's future. "Ancient civilizations fell," he lamented in *Road to Survival*, "and our own is tottering."[75]

Road to Survival was the best-selling conservation book before *Silent Spring*.[76] As executive secretary of Planned Parenthood, Vogt became one of the leading experts on population issues. In his capacity as CLC counselor, he exercised considerable influence in shaping the philosophy and growth of the Conservation Library.[77] One idea in particular struck a chord with many conservationists. Never one to mince words, Vogt stated emphatically, "We support as public charges . . . the senile, the incurables, the insane, the paupers, and those who might be called ecological incompetents, such as the subsidized stockmen and sheepherders. They exist to [destroy] the means of national survival . . . [and are] the source of environmental sickness."[78] The directors of the CLC expanded Vogt's categories to include the rapidly swelling urban youth population, along with other urban "victims" of unrestrained human nature as parts of a growing population of "ecological incompetents."

Notions of "human nature" influenced the early years of the CLC and reflected philosophies of the entire environmental movement.[79] Since many environmentalists of the early 1960s believed true communion with nature involved recreational experiences and wilderness, they tended to view uses of wilderness for recreation as healthy. On the other hand, those who used wilderness as a source of economic gain were lumped along with the "senile" and the "insane," individuals clearly not masters of their own nature. For a time, these notions about human na-

Cracking open a trunk of treasures from the American Bison Society in the heady early days of the library, 1961. Denver Public Library, Western History Collection, Conservation Library Collection photos.

ture and recreation posed no serious threat to the rapidly expanding library or to the environmental movement. As time passed, however, neo-Malthusian notions, coupled with ideas about human nature and the proper use of nature, came to haunt the CLC and the environmental movement. But in the heady days of 1962, everything seemed to be going as planned for the CLC and the conservation movement.

Fifth World Forestry Proceedings unveiled at a special ceremony, November 3, 1962. Left to right: Denver mayor Dick Bratterton, Douglas McHendrie, David S. Nordwall, Raymond Price, John Eastlick, Carhart, and Dr. Verne L. Harper. U.S. Forest Service. Denver Public Library, Western History Collection, Conservation Library Collection photos.

The grand opening of the Conservation Library was an unqualified success. Hundreds of active conservationists were exposed to the collection, with many sufficiently impressed to pledge their cash and collections. The event also ensured the Conservation Library's status as the nation's premier conservation archive. On November 3, 1962, Carhart, Eastlick, DPL Commission member Douglas McHendrie, and representatives from the U.S. Forest Service gathered in the office of Denver mayor, Richard Batterton, for the presentation of one of five copies of the proceedings of the Fifth World Forestry Congress. These rare documents came bound in three impressively large volumes especially embossed with a dedication to the CLC on the front cover. The actual significance of this collection of international writings on forestry was far less important than its publicity value. The presentation ceremony received wide press coverage all over the nation and in other countries. South African and Mexican papers even ran major stories on the event.[80] Once again, Carhart and Eastlick used the event to promote their vision of the Conservation Library as an antidote to the chaos of the cold war, which "clawed at rims of civilization that Saturday afternoon. Threats of armed strife boomed and bumbled in a tense world atmosphere. Missiles stood poised on Cuban soil."[81] Although the melodrama and fiery rhetoric proved overdrawn, both men recognized good publicity when they saw it, and contributions to the collection escalated dramatically after the publicity blitz of 1962.

In 1963, the Conservation Library received the second part of the American Conservation Association grant in the amount of $10,000. In addition to strong support from the national conservation community, the DPL Commission abandoned its cautious position and enthusiastically embraced the CLC. The wide press coverage, the ACA grant, and the quantity and quality of collections arriving almost daily more than convinced the administration of the DPL that the Conservation Library was a serious, worthwhile project. Consistently positive public reaction allayed fears of political controversy. The library increased the funding for the CLC to $7,500 to help cover personnel and administrative costs. With this support, the staff of the Conservation Library, previously limited to Carhart and his secretary, was expanded to include a librarian, Roberta Winn, and several part-time assistants. The CLC was given a spacious area on the fourth floor, just to the north of the prestigious Western History Collection. Boxes of manuscripts began to be organized and explored.

During 1963, two other important administrative groups joined the Conservation Library project. First, the Friends of the Denver Public Library came on board. This group of volunteers provided greatly needed financial support and volunteer labor to the CLC over the following years. The Friends had already demonstrated their willingness to help the library by hosting the reception for the National Wildlife Federation the previous year. Over the years the Friends remained one of the biggest supporters of the library, consistently making it one of their top priorities. The alliance with the Friends also proved politically beneficial. The Friends included among their members many men and women from prominent families with political connections. Their support helped ensure the backing of the DPL Commission and the city council.

The second group to emerge as a key supporter of the library was the Denver Public Library Foundation, a legal mechanism for channeling funds from sources outside the library directly into special collections

Conservation leaders tour the CLC, spring 1962. Left to right: Carhart, David Brower, Seth Meyers, E. Budd Marter, and Carl O. Gustafson. Denver Public Library, Western History Collection, Conservation Library Collection photos.

such as the conservation collections.[82] This foundation facilitated the grant-writing process by ensuring that funds granted by foundations or individuals would go directly into the Conservation Library budget, not into a general library fund. This financial arrangement eliminated one of the main stumbling blocks to securing outside funding and opened the door to more fund-raising. Even though the library had received the grant from the ACA and increased funding from the DPL, the Conservation Library's management required far more money than anyone had anticipated. As the quantity of materials coming into the library increased during 1963, the CLC required more staff simply to catch up with the volume of collections already received, let alone to train and support conservation activists.

CONCLUSION

The task of building the Conservation Library proved more complex than anyone could have foreseen. It entailed far more than simply rounding up collections of manuscripts and artifacts and finding space to house them. During the initial year of the project, Carhart and Eastlick worried about the reception the idea for the CLC might receive. The positive response enabled them to turn to the more difficult tasks that lay ahead. To succeed, the Conservation Library required money as well as space. In the years to come, finding and keeping the money became one of the most taxing and tedious chores for the managers of the CLC.

Administering an archival collection of the size and scope of the nascent CLC required far more organizational and political savvy than Eastlick, and certainly Carhart, could have imagined. For one thing, forging a coalition of supporters required skill and tenacity. Carhart contributed to the ceaseless work of developing the Conservation Library by serving as arbiter, moderator, and coalition builder. He enabled the CLC to assemble the impressive roster of counselors, who ensured that the library became a key part of the developing environmental movement. Bringing together various factions and new constituencies proved crucial to the early success of the project. Beyond these mundane concerns, the need to carefully define and delineate boundaries continued to plague all those involved in the CLC.

Boundaries are tricky things, since they often exclude as much as they include, and they often prove limiting and arbitrary over time. When Carhart started the Conservation Library, he thought he knew what conservation was. His years as an environmental advocate had taught him that there were "good" people and "bad" people, as well as people in between who could be won over to the cause if one knew how to talk their language. Although he was confident in his knowledge, he was not blind to the complexities of the situation. In fact, his vision of the conservation movement, and those who counted as allies, was in many respects more subtle and flexible than the views of many younger environmentalists who rose to prominence during the early 1960s.

Nonetheless, defining boundaries for the CLC taxed the imagination of all involved. The CLC was born with the modern environmental movement in an era of rapid and dramatic ideological change. The project of assembling discrete lumps of the physical world to represent ideas and movements forced many of those involved in the project to look closely at what they thought they were doing and why. Ideas about the proper relationship between people and nature, and among humans, bubbled to the surface. Unacknowledged assumptions about good and evil, human nature, and environmental purity drove the effort to define the collection. So, too, did the effort to reconcile divergent views on anthropocentrism and biocentrism, wise use, population, wilderness, and energy. For many people in America, the 1960s were a decade of introspection. Americans turned a microscope on themselves, and many did not like what they saw. When Carhart and Eastlick swung open the doors to their prized collection in 1962, they thought they were looking at the end of a life's work. In reality, the CLC and the environmental movement it represented stood on the edge of a new beginning.

CHAPTER FOUR

Wilderness, Birth Control, and Card Catalogs

There's a race of men that don't fit in,
A race that can't stay still;
So they break the hearts of kith and kin,
And they roam the world at will.
They range the field and they rove the flood,
And they climb the mountain's crest.
Their's is the curse of the gypsy blood,
And they don't know how to rest.
Robert Service, 1907

Anything that may have been a fallacy in Technocracy, . . . the worshiping of technological perfection and the beauties of pure science, is being burned out; a new, better, more balanced regime will come.
Arthur Carhart, Technocrash!

Around the turn of the century, the Scottish poet Robert Service wrote of those who chose a life outside the mainstream. Service dubbed his fellow travelers the "race of men that don't fit in," men who chose adventure in the wild places of the earth over comfort and security in the cities.[1] In many respects the poem rings even truer for that "race" of women, like Rachel Carson, Lois Crisler, and Kay Collins, who chose during the 1950s and 1960s to break the bonds of American gender norms and leave their homes and families to pursue a life of exploration, adventure, and political activism. As the Conservation Library established itself as the central repository for the American environmental movement in the 1970s, young women increasingly played important roles in the management and advocacy of the institution. As they contributed more to the management of the CLC, they brought a new perspective and a new political emphasis to the library. Across the country, a new generation of environmental advocates worked to forge diverse coalitions as definitions of conservation became increasingly contentious and environmental philosophies became more complex. By the mid-1960s, the conservation battle lines were less clear than they had been in the days when Carhart and DeVoto fought the "land grab." Environmental advocates in the

1960s were as likely to be supporters of Planned Parenthood as opponents of stock growers associations.

Questions about gender and generational tensions, as this chapter shows, are important facets of the history of the Conservation Library and the developing environmental movement. The coalition-building efforts in Colorado provide an example of the growing problems of gender and generational conflict within the environmental movement and raise important questions about the history of the Conservation Library project. For example, in what ways did the evolving policies and financial exploits of the CLC in the mid-1960s reflect larger changes in national environmental ideas and politics? How does the history of the CLC fit into the history of grassroots environmental advocacy in the battleground state of Colorado during the period between 1960 and the late 1970s? To what extent did the mundane concerns of funding and cataloging at the CLC reflect growing conflicts over definition, philosophy, and direction in the environmental movement? The underlying premise of this chapter is that environmental advocacy in the 1960s and early 1970s entailed significant social change, and the increasingly divisive debates about definition and leadership at the Conservation Library exemplify these changes.

Although historians frequently argue over the nature and extent of 1960s radicalism, few doubt that America in the 1960s witnessed a widespread revolution in thinking about the relationship between humans and the environment.[2] Most observers agree that, gradually, millions of Americans began to question long-standing assumptions about material progress and the desirability of development and growth. Even though initially not an explicit part of the counterculture, the environmental movement benefited greatly from the spirit of dissent radiating from a generation deeply disillusioned with postwar American culture.[3] One of the most jarring differences between the new generation of environmentalists and the old had to do with their contrasting views of technology. Counterculture-inspired environmentalists embraced alternative technologies as a solution to contemporary concerns over pollution and overpopulation because of a dawning realization, on the part of some, that America was entering a new phase in its development.

This new phase was envisioned as a "postscarcity" economy, where advanced industrial societies theoretically possessed the means to provide abundance and freedom and reconcile nature and technology if only they chose to do so.[4] Led by New Left social theorists such as Herbert Marcuse and Murray Bookchin, postscarcity adherents shared the belief that "the poison is . . . its own antidote."[5] In other words, technology used amorally and unecologically created the social and environmental problems of industrial capitalism; therefore, technology used morally and ecologically could create a revolution toward a utopian future. The New Left critics emphasized that social and environmental problems in America stemmed not from a lack of resources but from a misguided waste of the "technology of abundance."[6] If, these critics argued, the American people could be convinced to abandon their bourgeois quest for consumer goods, then valuable resources could be redirected toward establishing social equity and ecological harmony instead of consumerism and waste. In the late 1960s, postscarcity assumptions fueled a brief period of technology-based utopian optimism that profoundly influenced a generation of environmentalists.

New, more radical, environmental advocacy organizations grew out of this spirit in the 1960s. In addition, new modes of protest, political action, and grassroots organization helped established conservation organizations increase their support base and effectiveness as advocates for the environment. In the words of Kirkpatrick Sale, "The protest generation of the sixties was a distinct minority, but it could resonate with such power through the society because it was challenging assumptions, expressing disillusions, and asking questions that in some way reflected the hidden doubts and fears of the great majority."[7] This is not to say that in the 1960s everyone in the conservation community approved of the maelstrom of social change that engulfed them or approved of the younger generation's desire to play an active role in their organizations. On the contrary, many older conservatives inside the conservation community looked with horror on the counterculture and the rise of increasingly radical protest movements. Ultimately, however, this rising generation of socially aware Americans became the foundation for an unprecedented explosion of environmental advocacy in the 1970s.

WILDERNESS PROXIES

Between the turn of the century and the 1950s, preserving the American wilderness formed the basis for most environmental advocacy. Wilderness remained the central focus of the established conservation organizations into the early 1960s, culminating in a major national effort to enact a federal wilderness bill. At the same time, upstart organizations like the Rocky Mountain Center on Environment, the Defenders of Florisant, the National Congress on Population and Environment, and many local groups began to move environmental advocacy away from the traditional focus on wilderness.[8] Still, during the first half of the 1960s, wilderness preservation continued to dominate environmental politics and to preoccupy environmental advocates such as the directors of the Conservation Library.[9]

Since the days when Aldo Leopold and Arthur Carhart fought to establish a wilderness policy within the Forest Service, the effort to preserve America's wild lands was a reactive fight. Lilliputian
conservationists waged brushfire wars and holding actions against giant
developers and public land users who fought to open these lands to economic development. From John Muir's fight for Hetch-Hetchy forward,
national and grassroots organizations scraped together supporters and
funds to try to stop attempts to develop the public domain. Savvy developers with high-priced lawyers and publicists often easily outmatched
poorly funded conservationists. These battles culminated in the best-
known and most significant fight over the use of public wilderness: the
attempt to save Echo Park.[10]

The effort to save Echo Park ushered in a new stage of environmental advocacy. For the first time in American history, tens of thousands of
people, most of them far removed from the geographic location of the
fight, became personally interested in a wilderness controversy. The
Sierra Club and other national conservation groups mobilized a wide
support base and after a stunningly successful grassroots campaign
stopped the proposed dam.[11] After Echo Park, the movement to preserve
wilderness gained a significant amount of political clout and a substantial public following. Building on this momentum, advocates of wilderness preservation abandoned their defensive position and took the
offensive, pushing for permanent federal protection for Forest Service
wilderness areas.[12]

On the national level, Howard Zahniser, Conservation Library counselor, executive secretary of the Wilderness Society, and editor of *Living
Wilderness*, became the leading proponent of federal protection for
wilderness.[13] He spent more than a decade working to get a wilderness
bill passed to ensure federal legal protection for Forest Service Primitive
Areas. In appearance and demeanor, Zahniser was an unlikely
spokesman for wilderness. One colleague commented that in meetings of
the Wilderness Society, he "looked like a misplaced librarian, bald, be-
spectacled, and bookish."[14] Friends were more likely to find Zahniser
browsing in a used-book store than out on the trail. While this appearance made him something of a misfit among his rugged allies in the
wilderness movement, it also enabled him to move with ease in Washington political society. As a result, Zahniser became the most effective
voice for the wildlands in the nation's capital and the political point man
for the wilderness preservation movement. He roamed the halls of Congress, cornering senators and congressmen, tirelessly promoting his
brainchild, a federal wilderness bill.

Zahniser's love of books and wilderness made him a natural as a
counselor for the Conservation Library. Eventually his large personal li-

brary, ranging from ornithology to nature writing, became the nucleus of the CLC rare book holdings. During the 1950s, Zahniser and Carhart maintained a long correspondence and developed a strong working relationship and friendship.[15] Like Carhart, Eastlick, Murie, and other CLC counselors, Zahniser embraced an antimodernist fear of postwar technology and worried about military proliferation. "As we constantly become more and more nearly lords of creation," he said, "there is nothing so much to be feared as ourselves."[16] His concerns about the rise of technocratic thinking lent an urgency to his quest to protect America's remaining wildlands.

For Zahniser and the leaders of the wilderness preservation movement, Colorado became the key to their efforts to move the wilderness bill through Congress. In the late 1950s, Zahniser and others came to believe that grassroots support from Colorado was crucial to success.[17] Influential Colorado congressman Wayne Aspinall headed the House Public Lands Subcommittee; convincing him that the bill should be approved and released for a vote on the House floor became the crux of the fight.[18] Deeply suspicious of national conservation organizations, Aspinall looked to the people of his home state for answers to the wilderness conundrum.[19]

In Colorado, Edward Hobbs Hilliard, owner of the Redfield Gun Sight Company, was the driving force behind the organization of the Colorado wilderness coalition. One of his primary goals was to use the newly formed Conservation Library as the staging ground for his grassroots campaign. The organization of a diverse pro-wilderness coalition in Colorado formed a key factor in the ultimate passage of the federal wilderness bill in 1964. Conservationists, preservationists, rural sportsmen, urban nature clubs, women's clubs, labor unions, mountaineers, and business leaders came together in the early 1960s to form a unique environmental partnership. Hilliard had listened carefully to Carhart and Eastlick's plans to construct a national center for advocacy, and he took them at their word. To Hilliard, the time seemed right to make the CLC live up to the goal of creating a center for environmental advocacy. Yet, despite the oft-stated goal that the library become a focal point for political action, Carhart and Eastlick were wary of political conflict and tried to keep the CLC removed from the controversial wilderness issue.[20] Eastlick and Carhart worried that a messy political debate could jeopardize the CLC's status within the Denver Public Library system. As Carhart said, "I have to work with some folk who are quite opposed to this wilderness bill," and "I'll do my slugging as in this letter, entirely personally, on the side and stir no backlash in any quarter."[21] On a personal level, Carhart had too much at stake to risk everything so soon. After the turmoil of the first year, he had settled into a comfortable routine and had

Edward Hobbs Hilliard Jr., packing for a trip into the Colorado high country, 1960. Courtesy Joy Hilliard.

gotten used to the national attention and much-needed paycheck he received as official adviser to the CLC. By 1964, the "policy angle," in other words, trying to keep the DPL administration and city council happy, became more important than working in the trenches for actual environmental causes.[22]

Environmental politics in Colorado have always been complicated. Throughout the twentieth century, issues surrounding control of the public domain never failed to generate serious division within the state. In general, anticonservation forces maintained the upper hand in Colorado politics. An alliance between stock growers, extractive industries, and rural citizens provided a seemingly unbeatable challenge to conservation-minded citizens interested in protecting Colorado's vast wilderness resources.[23] Still, the state has a long tradition of local grassroots environmental advocacy, and over the years tenacious activists successfully fought conservation battles in the face of strong opposition. Economics played a key role in this transition.

Gold and silver first brought white settlers to Colorado in the 1850s. After the mineral rush faded, an ultimately more significant rush followed. Thousands of individuals relocated to Colorado to rejuvenate their physical and spiritual health in the crisp, thin air of the vast mountain regions of the state. Hardier souls came from around the world to climb Colorado's peaks, fish the state's wild rivers, and explore its dark canyons. The beautiful mountain landscapes became a resource worth more than gold or silver.[24] Many who came as sojourners in search of high adventure stayed and became advocates for preservation of the wilderness areas that had attracted them. The Colorado Mountain Club (CMC), founded in the early 1900s, quickly grew into one of America's premier outdoor clubs.[25] This active organization mobilized grassroots support for conservation measures as early as the 1920s. By the 1950s, the Conservation Committee of the CMC began to cultivate connections with national preservation groups such as the Sierra Club and the Wilderness Society.[26] It also corresponded with other Colorado groups that expressed interest in preserving the environment. When the Conservation Library was coming together in the first years of the 1960s, a highly motivated and idealistic group of local environmentalists began piecing together the framework for a statewide wilderness preservation and environmental coalition. Edward Hilliard quickly assumed a leadership role in this nascent coalition.

Edward Hobbs Hilliard, the son of a successful investment banker, was born in Louisville, Kentucky, on October 16, 1922. His interest in nature began in his youth, when he spent long summer days rambling through the woods around the family home, and later at prep school, where he developed a fondness for Robert Frost's nature poems. During the closing months of World War II, Hilliard left Louisville to serve as a second lieutenant in the U.S. Army Infantry stationed in Europe. Returning to America, he enrolled at Yale, where he received a bachelor's degree in applied economics in 1948.[27] In 1951, Hilliard married Joy Rushmore of Plainfield, New Jersey. In Joy, Ed Hilliard found a kindred spirit. The two shared a love of nature and wilderness and a growing concern with the direction of postwar society. Joy's interest in nature also started early. As a young girl she learned about wild animals and wild places through the pages of Ernest Thompson Seton's animal adventure stories.[28] Her concern about the wilderness grew as she and Ed began to explore and travel.

After a brief stint with his family's investment banking firm, J. J. B. Hilliard and Son in Louisville, Ed moved to Denver, where he took a job with the Westric Battery Company.[29] Joy joined him a few months later. The Hilliards were drawn to Colorado because of their love of mountains, camping, hunting, climbing, and skiing. In 1956, Ed was able to combine his interest in outdoor sports with his business career when he became a managing partner in the Redfield Gun Sight Company of Denver.[30] Under Hilliard's dynamic guidance, the firm became a leading national manufacturer of rifle scopes and sighting equipment, eventually employing more than one hundred people. With his career in good shape, he and

Joy were able to spend more of their time exploring the Colorado mountains and pursuing their interest in environmental and population issues. Hilliard worked with various local groups on environmental and population control issues. He was, in his own words, "vitally concerned with the conservation of natural resources" and "keenly aware of the present and future tragic results of over-population."[31] In the 1960s, Hilliard found himself in an unusual position. He was a successful and prominent business leader, well respected in the conservative world of gun and hunting equipment manufacturing. Both a National Rifle Association national committee member and a trustee of the National Shooting Sports Foundation, Hilliard was gaining a reputation as a rising star in the weapons manufacture field.[32] Concurrently, he was becoming more and more involved in the world of conservation and environmental advocacy. Hilliard was not alone in his affiliation with gun manufacture and conservation, but in the 1960s individuals who were able to maintain such strong connections with both were exceptional.

Over the years, Hilliard became increasingly aware of the critical need to reconcile differences among sportsmen, business leaders and industry, and the federal government. He realized that the greatest threat to environmentalism rose out of philosophical divisions among wilderness enthusiasts. As a businessman, he personally knew prominent men who spent their spare time hunting, fishing, and camping, men who valued America's wildlands and yet often actively opposed conservationist plans that seemed to threaten business and industry. Hilliard thought that "businessmen should see the ultimate benefits of good stewardship of resources." Consequently, reconciling the business community and the environmental community became his passion.[33] He realized early on that the Conservation Library could play a key role in accomplishing this goal by providing a public forum for airing opposing viewpoints in an atmosphere of cooperation.

Convincing conservative business leaders that they shared a common interest with environmentalists was no easy task. Likewise, convincing environmentalists that it was worth their time to try to reach an understanding with business and industry, particularly the hunting industry, proved equally difficult. Nonetheless, Hilliard believed that cooperation and open lines of communication were crucial for future environmental advocacy; therefore, he worked to convey this message to friends on both sides of the fence. A conversation with Wilderness Society and CLC colleague Olaus Murie highlighted the difficulties on both sides. After listening to Hilliard's argument for a reconciliation between business and conservation, Murie commented, "I should like to think there are industrialists who see this far ahead." But, he continued, "it always seems we are in opposing camps—they have the money and the power and the influence and want no interference. We have only our belief and our stubbornness."[34] Hilliard had heard it all before, but he thought that regardless of the difficulty, reconciling all factions of the outdoor community was a prerequisite for the long-term success of environmentalism.

Hilliard brought to the conservation movement a levelheadedness that gained him a reputation as a consummate negotiator. He was able to bring various factions together, build bridges in understanding, and overcome the often paralyzing polarization between industry, conservation groups, and government agencies.[35] With one foot in the conservation camp and one in the gun industry, Hilliard was in a unique position to act as a mediator and leader of the environmental movement in Colorado as the nation mobilized to fight for the wilderness bill. In the words of Roger Hanson, Hilliard's friend and colleague in conservation, Hilliard "knew how to idealize, organize, synthesize."[36] To achieve a synthesis of environmental supporters that transcended traditional political entrenchments, a new organizational mechanism was required, an environmental "United Nations" that could provide the neutral ground for negotiation and reconciliation. In his capacity as adviser to the CLC, Hilliard worked to mold the library into just such a place.

During the 1960s, Hilliard expanded his involvement in the national environmental movement, quickly rising through the ranks at the Wilderness Society. Initially serving as a member of the governing council, he eventually rose to the rank of vice president.[37] Still, while his reputation as a national environmental leader grew, he continued to focus most of his energy and personal financial resources on the effort to construct a framework for grassroots environmentalism in Colorado. Between 1958 and 1964, Hilliard concentrated on uniting various groups behind the effort to preserve wilderness. He gathered supporters from Colorado outdoor groups and the business and hunting communities and assembled two wilderness lobbying organizations, the Wilderness Committee of Colorado and the Conservation Council of Colorado.[38] These organizations coordinated the lobbying effort in Colorado for the wilderness bill, bringing sportsmen, conservationists, preservationists, population control advocates, and urban outdoor clubs together for the first time in a united effort to influence federal public land policy. Joy Hilliard worked with Ed to made sure that Planned Parenthood was included in the coalition, and that supporters of population control became a part of the effort to save wilderness.

The inclusion of population control advocates within the wilderness coalition highlights a complex ideological dynamic that evolved during the mid-1950s. Population control can serve as a means of repression and social control or as a means of personal and social empowerment. During the 1960s, men and women, conservatives and liberals, environmentalists and antienvironmentalists all used the rhetoric of population control to make various points about the proper relationship between humans and the environment. The liberal position most often voiced by environmentalists argued that overpopulation places an undue strain on ecosystems, ultimately leading to environmental crisis. Therefore, population control must be a cornerstone of environmental advocacy.[39] Outside certain religious denominations, few disagreed that rampant human population growth endangers ecosystems and the environmental health of the planet. Yet population alone cannot explain the environmental crisis of the late twentieth century. Serious overpopulation tends to be a third world phenomenon. On the other hand, the "first world," where overpopulation is less of a problem, is most responsible for resource depletion, pollution, overdevelopment, and overconsumption. The population control debate, therefore, has often centered on the politics between developed and undeveloped nations.[40]

Equally complicated are the gender aspects of the population control issue. Feminists point out that oftentimes "population control is a euphemism for the control of women."[41] As a result, centralized population control efforts, usually directed by men in leadership positions, often tend to bolster established unequal gender relationships and limit women's right to reproductive control, while implicitly blaming the environmental crisis on women.[42] Yet, at the same time, population control efforts spearheaded by women increasingly became avenues to greater individual control and empowerment.[43]

Through their work in organizations such as Planned Parenthood, Joy Hilliard and others, consciously or not, helped to integrate reproductive rights into the framework of environmental advocacy from a women's perspective. Joy and Ed Hilliard realized that one of the tasks of a successful environmental coalition was to reconcile population concerns with more traditional issues like wilderness. Joy Hilliard's participation in the Colorado wilderness coalition ensured that the Colorado environmental coalition included the perspective of women working on population issues.[44]

The Hilliards' successful effort to build a diverse environmental coalition in Colorado became a model for national environmental advocacy in the decades to come.[45] Ed Hilliard used his work with the grassroots wilderness movement in Colorado as a springboard for other related projects, such as "Operation Respect," a nationally recognized effort to improve relations between landowners and sportsmen. The very name of this project perfectly captures Hilliard's advocacy philosophy. In 1963, his efforts were recognized nationally when he received the coveted American Motors Conservation Award. For Hilliard the award came as a surprise. Writing to his sister, he called it "quite an honor." But, he went on, "I think it's premature as hell because I haven't had time to do 1/10 of what I hope to do before I hit the sod."[46] Ironically, the recognition was more timely than Hilliard thought. With only six years to live, in 1964 he was at the height of his career.

The same year Hilliard won the AMCA, the battle over the wilderness bill reached a dramatic conclusion. A series of public hearings held in Colorado turned the tide of public support for the bill, with Colorado's two main wilderness lobbying groups, under the direction of Ed Hilliard, playing a key role in this victory.[47] The two groups comprised Colorado's various wilderness supporters. For instance, the Conservation Council was a federation of sportsmen's clubs and business leaders, whereas the Wilderness Committee of Colorado united preservationists, conservationists, mountain clubs, hiking clubs, garden clubs, women's clubs, and the local chapters of national conservation groups under one umbrella organization. The development of these two successful groups represented the culmination of Hilliard's reconciliation efforts. Working together, the two organizations put intense pressure on Wayne Aspinall, Colorado congressman and chair of the House Public Lands Subcommittee, at national and local congressional hearings on the wilderness bill.[48] The campaign helped turn the tide of popular opinion in Colorado, forcing Aspinall to release the bill, which was promptly passed and signed into law by President Lyndon Johnson in 1964.

The passage of the Wilderness Act was a sweet victory for Colorado conservation leaders and Ed Hilliard in particular. By presenting a united front in the face of strong opposition, they played a vital role in the wilderness bill's ultimate success. In the process, they substantially altered the ideological orientation of the state, blurring the distinction between conservation and preservation and fostering a climate of grassroots cooperation crucial to the development of modern environmentalism. All this was good news for the Conservation Library, which, despite a conspicuous silence on the wilderness issue, gladly reaped the benefits of a greatly expanded environmental awareness in Colorado and the nation.

By the end of 1964, the Conservation Library was well established on its fourth-floor home, receiving a steady stream of visitors. Later that year, the CLC received a ringing endorsement from the Forest History Society and a $1,000 grant from the Wildlife Management Institute.[49] The holdings of the CLC at this time amounted to approximately five hundred linear feet of manuscripts, five thousand books, and fifteen thousand pamphlets and clippings. The Conservation Library did not receive the same level of use as its more prestigious neighbor, the Western History Collection. Nonetheless, its fifteen to twenty visitors a day provided strong evidence of the popularity of environmental issues and the growing notoriety of the Conservation Library.

Elwood Maunder, executive director of the Forest History Society, helps Carhart and Eastlick hang plaque in CLC recognizing the status of the library as official repository for the society, May 1964. Denver Public Library, Western History Collection, Conservation Library Collection photos.

CONTINENTAL DREAMS

In the mid-1960s, American popular opinion shifted toward a greater acceptance of environmentalism. Information about the environment, wilderness preservation, the population explosion, and pollution became common fodder for the popular media.[50] This dramatic expansion of public awareness meant that conservationists and environmental organizations no longer had to operate on the fringes of society, fighting for every dollar. Supporting environmental causes became popular and politically acceptable.

The Conservation Library benefited greatly from this changing climate of opinion. Grants, previously so hard to come by, began to materialize. In addition to the $12,500 from the American Conservation Association in 1964, the library received a $5,000 grant from the Max C. Fleischmann Foundation of Nevada and $1,000 from the Wildlife Management Institute, bringing the 1964 total funding, including DPL support, to just over $22,000.[51] Still, the budget was barely large enough to cover the expenses. For the CLC, growth was impossible without a large increase in funding and a permanent endowment.

With this long-term funding requirement in mind, the counselors and Eastlick agreed that Carhart should spend his time, and a large chunk of the CLC budget, traveling to the East Coast to try to secure long-term financial agreements for the library. Between 1962 and 1964, Carhart traveled extensively, promoting the library to foundations and at conservation conventions around the country. Back in Denver, staff members simply gave up on cataloging the ever-increasing collections and concentrated on producing glossy reports and plans to be presented to foundation heads over lunch at the Willard Hotel. Carhart visited Washington, D.C., regularly to meet with the officers of the ACA and to confer with the Conservation Library counselors, like Albright, Vogt, and Joe Fisher, who lived and worked in the area. These trips proved somewhat successful in bringing in money and more so in securing additional collections. Likewise, the appearances in Washington enabled Carhart to establish contacts with officials in the Forest Service and other agencies interested in the CLC. The ultimate dream of the counselors was to dip into the deep pockets of the federal land agencies. One day, they hoped, the CLC might be featured on a small line item buried deep within the impenetrable prose of an appropriations bill. Then the dream of building a truly national center might actually be realized.

In addition to maintaining good relations with the ACA, the CLC's only solid source of funding, the Washington trips eventually resulted in some fruitful agreements with federal agencies. The most significant of these was a cooperative arrangement between the Conservation Library and the Bureau of Sport Fisheries and Wildlife. In 1962, the International Association of Game, Fish, and Conservation Commissioners, an advisory group to the Bureau of Sport Fisheries, requested that the Conservation Library be designated as the national repository for the reports and information resulting from the Pittman-Robertson and Dingell-Johnson Acts.[52]

The Pittman-Robertson Federal Aid in Wildlife Restoration Act, passed in 1937, gave money from federal excise taxes paid by manufacturers of sporting arms and ammunition to states to fund game studies and programs. Most significantly, the money enabled states to conduct extensive research into regional game populations and ecosystems.[53] The IAGFCC was composed of directors of state fish and game departments in charge of implementing the Pittman-Robertson programs.

Carhart had close connections with Pittman-Robertson. In 1938, he was appointed to head the Colorado program, and he had firsthand experience dealing with the reports and bulletins it generated. On his frequent Washington trips, he often stopped into Bureau of Sport Fisheries. When the order came down to find a new home for the bureau's records, Carhart's Conservation Library came quickly to mind.

By the early 1960s, the members of the IAGFCC were growing concerned that the vast information resources resulting from the Pittman-

Robertson programs were not accessible to the general public, or even to trained professionals who might need to use the studies in their research.[54] A wealth of valuable wildlife data, paid for with millions of tax dollars, sat unused and unknown. The Bureau of Sport Fisheries and Wildlife chose the Conservation Library as the institution best able to store and catalog the study results and to create a Library Reference Service.[55] The plan for the reference service called for the use of the "latest in computer technology and information retrieval systems," making the tens of thousands of wildlife documents in the Pittman-Robertson archives available to researchers. The directors of the CLC and the IAGFCC hoped the project would become a model of modern cataloging and data management.[56] The plan called for the consolidation and storage of all Pittman-Robertson reports on IBM punch cards for rapid retrieval. Ultimately, an elated Carhart gushed, "the joint library service will provide the greatest source of information on wildlife needs and problems in the world."[57] Best of all, funding for the project came directly from the U.S. Department of the Interior and the ongoing Pittman-Robertson program, providing a much-needed injection of federal funds into the CLC.[58]

The original IAGFCC contract provided $57,000 annually to cover the costs of hiring three librarians to develop and manage the information systems relating to the Reference Service.[59] According to the press releases announcing the agreement, this was the first informational service contract between the federal government and a municipal library.[60] As usual, the CLC made sure that the announcement was widely disseminated to the press.[61] During the next five years the program expanded greatly, with budgets reaching as high as $130,000 per year. For the Conservation Library the program meant stronger ties with federal conservation programs and officials.

But the money came with strings attached. The Pittman-Robertson work required the already overwhelmed staff of the library to cope with an ever-increasing workload, fielding questions from across the country and creating a backlog of cataloging work. Despite significant problems, notably an almost complete lack of archival management, nationally celebrated programs like the Library Reference Service led Carhart, Eastlick, the CLC counselors, and the members of the DPL Foundation to consider expanding the library.

By spring 1965, the directors and counselors of the CLC could not help feeling a little smug. Their brainchild had achieved a level of acclaim unimaginable only four years earlier. The Conservation Library was the toast of the American conservation movement, and it seemed there was no limit to the potential for future growth. The counselors decided that the future of the collection needed to be carefully plotted in light of the tremendous success of the previous four years. The publicity, acquisitions, and support for the library far surpassed even the most optimistic early visions. Despite continued funding questions and serious archival management problems, all thoughts of limiting the CLC were washed away in a sea of favorable press and popular approval.

By 1964, the Conservation Library staff, counselors, and directors seemed far removed from the thoughtful discussions of limitations and boundaries of the previous years. Convinced of the bright future of the CLC, they abandoned their cautious plans and drew up a blueprint for expansion—major expansion. John Eastlick summed up the mood when he commented, "We have in the CLC beginnings of a vital, desperately needed continental institution." He added, "There can be no small plans that will fit the destiny of the Conservation Library Center."[62] Indeed, small plans were not a consideration in 1964, even while the day-to-day management of the collection was left in the hands of DPL staff librarians who muddled along as best they could, scratching their heads at all the grand talk. Later that year, the counselors drafted a proposal to the ACA, asking it to fund a special conference to chart the future of the Conservation Library. In September the ACA granted the request and appropriated $5,000 to hold the event in Denver, to fly in counselors, and to produce a formal report of recommendations.[63]

On November 11, 1965, CLC counselors, members of the DPL Foundation, local environmentalists, and local sportsmen gathered in Denver to brainstorm for the library. Conference participants included Dr. Lemoyne Anderson, Colorado State University; Arthur Carhart; G. Christian Crosby, Colorado outdoorsman; John Eastlick; Edward Hilliard Jr., Redfield Gun Sight Company; Dr. Sydney Howe, Conservation Foundation; E. R. Kalmbach, biologist; David G. Leo, consultant, DPL Foundation; E. Budd Marter, executive director, OWAA; Bernard L. Orell, president of the Forest History Society; Gerald P. Peters, president, DPL Foundation; Dr. Horace Quick, University of Colorado; Dr. Bettie Scott-Williams, Thorne Ecological Research Station; Dr. Paul B. Sears, former director, Yale Conservation Program; Dr. Robert L. Stearns, University of Colorado; Harry R. Woodward, Colorado Game, Fish and Parks Department; and Roberta Winn, DPL librarian, secretary for the CLC. The purpose of the conference was to determine how the CLC could be expanded, who it would serve, and how much the project would cost.[64]

Significantly, no representative from the consistently pragmatic Denver Public Library Board attended the event other than Eastlick, and his involvement certainly did not guarantee the board's support. In fact, the makeup of the conference virtually guaranteed a positive response to the expansion idea.

For the most part, participants in the CLC planning conference came from the old school of conservation. Issues such as wilderness, forest resources, and population control dominated the discussion of acquisitions and collection management.[65] Yet, for the first time, there was a dawning realization that the movement to preserve the nonhuman environment was about to head in very different directions. Paul Sears, former head of the Yale Conservation Program, argued that "we must meet the shifting emphasis and new demands of conservation."[66] Sears wanted to see the CLC become a primary repository for ecological research and move away from traditional conservation topics such as forestry. On the other hand, Bernard Orell, a vice president of Weyerhaeuser, strongly cautioned that the CLC should maintain ties with the forest products industry and use the library as a center for arbitration between industry and conservationists. "The Conservation Library Center," he said, "has the responsibility for . . . providing an impartial ground for discussion of these [controversial] problems."[67]

For Carhart, the relationship between the CLC and the timber industry was a particularly touchy subject. Throughout his career, he had worked to maintain a reputation as a moderate who had friends on both sides of most conservation issues. One of the connections he had carefully maintained through the years was with the American Forest Products Industries Association (AFPI). In the 1950s, he worked with the AFPI to produce booklets aimed at convincing sportsmen and conservationists that the timber industry had their best interests at heart. "People interested in timber," he argued in one such publication, "and those interested in wildlife can assist each other."[68] Carhart's steadfast belief in the value of cooperation between the forest industry and conservationists earned him the AFPI Distinguished Service Award in 1965.[69]

Despite Carhart's strong personal feelings about cooperation, other participants in the conference were less sure about the politics of close ties between industry and the CLC. Ed Hilliard, for one, was happy to help foster cooperation between the outdoor sports world and the CLC, a collaboration between two groups he believed shared many interests. Still, he and others were less sure about the timber connection. In the end, despite these differences, everyone involved agreed that the scope of the CLC needed to be dramatically expanded. They decided that the library should move away from its role as museum for past glories and work toward a more active role as a center for education and advocacy. All agreed that environmental advocacy was progressing in new directions and that the CLC should be in the vanguard of the new movement.

On the final day of the meeting, the participants mapped out a future for the Conservation Library that would have seemed fantastic only three years before. Their plan was bold and, in hindsight, completely unrealistic. In 1965, the Conservation Library reached its zenith of popularity and influence; significant manuscript collections, money, and moral support poured daily into the DPL. At this point two roads lay open to the directors of the library. First, they could step back and take stock of the vast array of materials they possessed and begin a serious effort to organize and catalog. This was the most reasonable option, but in the pervasive atmosphere of excitement and enthusiasm among those connected with the project, such a conservative plan was unthinkable. They instead chose the second road: massive expansion in scope, structure, and mission. The humble Conservation Library became, at least on paper, the Conservation Library Center of North America.[71]

The participants at the planning conference took their roles very seriously. During the course of a long day, they bolstered each other's confidence and fostered a sense of unlimited possibilities. In the heady days after the publication of Rachel Carson's *Silent Spring* and the passage of the Wilderness Act, it seemed that anything was possible. And the CLC supporters at the conference assumed that concerned citizens everywhere were behind them in their noble efforts to build an environmental library worthy of international recognition. As pots of steaming coffee disappeared, a plan began to take shape. Not only the scope and mission of the library but also its location was going to change.

The cornerstone of the expansion plan was a proposal for a fifty-five thousand-square-foot addition to the DPL's main building, designed to house researchers and educators. The plan called for a staff of up to thirteen librarians, consultants, and professors to run the new center and proposed an annual budget of over $190,000.[71] The idea for the Conservation Library Center of North America received ringing endorsements from Denver mayor Thomas Currigan and Colorado governor John Love. In a letter supporting the project, Currigan stated, "Realizing the importance of conservation . . . we will do all we can to assist you in the furtherance of your splendid goal so that all mankind may profit."[72] The expansion was to be funded through the city and county of Denver and by a fundraising campaign through the DPL Foundation. Additionally, it was assumed that the federal government, via "several government agencies," would provide substantial future funding.[73] The ultimate goal of the fundraising drive was $5.7 million. Of this proposed budget, almost $1 million was to cover the expense of constructing the new building. Before 1965, the Conservation Library's annual budget had not exceeded $19,000 per year, or $90,000 total over the life of the project; the staff consisted of only six persons, including Carhart. Again, in hindsight, it seems that the directors of the CLC, the counselors, and the members of the DPL Foundation were not thinking rationally when constructing these plans. Despite the CLC's remarkable success in accumulating an unprecedented body of conservation manuscripts and artifacts, the possibilities of raising the large amounts of money required for the expansion program were remote.

Part of the problem with this bold plan was that it focused on the future at the expense of programs desperately needed at the moment. The plan met with skepticism from the DPL Board and from some of the Conservation Library's major supporters. For the previous two years, CLC supporters had tried to secure funding from the Old Dominion Foundation, a philanthropic organization that had supported conservation programs in the past and one with which Carhart had some personal connections. In the fall of 1965, Carhart traveled to Washington to meet with representatives of Old Dominion, especially with Monroe Bush, its director and a longtime supporter of the Conservation Library. Bush listened to the plan for the Conservation Library Center of North America, but he was not as enthusiastic as Carhart had hoped. He was concerned that the DPL Foundation was using the CLC as an excuse to expand the main library with foundation funds that would end up supporting general Denver library services. Very sensibly, Bush thought that the relationship with the DPL was problematic, to say the least. What, he prophetically wondered, would happen "if there might be a Mayor or Librarian in some days ahead who would decide to wipe out the character and objectives of the CLC and simply throw the whole collection into the general library?"[74] With the stakes so high, Bush speculated that it would behoove the CLC to get a few of the counselors onto the DPL Board. Taken aback by this line of questioning, Carhart became defensive when Bush asked if the counselors were "names only for prestige."[75] The meeting ended with a disappointed Carhart leaving Washington with the impression that any funding would be hard to come by, let alone on the scale proposed by the expansion plan. Like a sleepwalker suddenly shaken awake in midstride, Carhart found himself wondering about plans for the Conservation Library Center of North America. He found himself deeply troubled at the prospect that the CLC faced an uncertain future.[76]

During this period of bold planning and big dreams, only one voice, that of DPL librarian Roberta Winn, remained consistently pragmatic. Following the conference, she warned that the plans for the Conservation Library Center of North America were a fantasy endangering the long-term health of the project. Having joined the CLC project shortly after the first boxes arrived at the DPL, she was the heart of the daily operation from the beginning and maintained this position throughout the 1960s. More than anyone involved over the years, Winn was able to step back and realistically evaluate the possibilities and limitations of the CLC. After the CLC planning conference, she was concerned that things were moving in the wrong direction. "Above all," she wrote, "I feel that we should continue to emphasize quality librarianship and not try to perform more than we can do well."[77] Although Winn urged caution, she was not recommending a retreat from the advocacy and education program. On the contrary, unlike Carhart, Eastlick, and many of the older counselors, Winn understood that for the CLC to make an impact on the environmental movement, pie-in-the-sky plans like a $5.7 million pipe-dream expansion had to be abandoned. The CLC could better serve the project of environmentalism, she argued, through direct work with local and regional environmental groups. She worried that money that could go directly into environmental action would be spent on grandiose building schemes and monuments for conservationists no longer actively contributing to the movement.[78]

Winn remained unconvinced that the CLC could become a "continental institution." Unfortunately, the counselors paid little attention to her during the meeting or in the months following. Past presidents of national organizations, distinguished professors, and successful local business leaders apparently were unwilling to seriously consider the opinions of a lowly female librarian. The frustration Winn felt at this treatment surfaced after the meeting. She wrote: "I alluded to the problem of whether or not we *can* be a national conservation library. . . . whether or not we can find a place to serve as a national conservation library is debatable."[79] More than anyone connected to the project, Winn understood that, lofty ideas aside, the CLC was an archive in desperate need of careful management. She also knew that, for the artifacts and manuscripts that formed the heart of the collections to have any value for the environmental movement, librarianship had to be taken seriously. Over the next years, Winn consistently worked behind the scenes to reconcile environmental advocacy with library science in the face of strenuous institutional resistance.

In the meantime, undaunted by questions about the feasibility of the expansion project, the CLC counselors used the money remaining from the planning conference to hire a consultant to prepare an expanded definition of conservation and to outline the goals for the future Conservation Library Center of North America. They chose David Fischer, a doctoral candidate in resource economics at Colorado State University, to work on the project.[80] Fischer was the ideal person for the job. His expansive personal environmental philosophy meshed perfectly with the dreams of the counselors. In a lengthy report, Fischer outlined the "broadened concept of conservation by the CLC."[81] This concept abandoned previous attempts to limit the boundaries of the library and explicitly embraced modern environmentalism. Fischer argued that the library should have few boundaries. It should actively assemble materials dealing with all phases of the environmental crisis and should also take an active role in environmental politics. In his view, only after the CLC abandoned all limits could it move forward and become "the *dominant* research base for the conservation movement."[82] Further, the new building should be a national meeting place where disputes between environmentalists and industry leaders or policy makers could be debated in public forums.[83]

Fischer's hyperbole played well to the directors of the CLC, who were looking for confirmation that their monumental plans were viable and realistic. The directors, quickly forgetting the pragmatic and sensible arguments of Roberta Winn and Monroe Bush, reveled in Fischer's Olympian vision. At the end of his report he triumphantly proclaimed, "It is here [CLC] that the ultimate answers may be found."[84] Blinded by favorable press and ego-boosting letters from regional dignitaries, Carhart and Eastlick abandoned all reason and plunged headfirst into the project without checking the depth of the pool.

One of the cornerstones of the new plan was education and training for young conservationists. The Conservation Library Center of North America was to become a focal point for national environmental education and a boot camp for grassroots activists. Yet Fischer never explained how the library should implement this expanded activist role or how this plan could be possible within the confines of the DPL system. The directors of the CLC and the counselors seemingly ignored the gaping holes in the plan, somehow convinced that the details would work themselves out. Illustrating their enthusiastic convictions, the bold statement on the front of the expansion proposal read, "We will apply Research, Education and our Knowledge for Man's Survival."[85] With the survival of the human race on the line, who had time for administrative details?

Convinced that the CLC's future as an archive was a foregone conclusion, Carhart and Eastlick began to focus on developing an education and public outreach program. As a first step, a search began for a "conservationist and educator" to direct a conservation education program. The ultimate goal was to build a graduate program in "conservation" to train future leaders of conservationist organizations. With this in mind, Eastlick contacted the University of Denver (DU) Graduate School of Librarianship about the possibility of setting up a graduate program to train "conservation librarians."[86] Eastlick had taught classes at DU and had contacts within the school administration. At the same time, Carhart approached the Resources for the Future Foundation (RFF) to see if it would be interested in funding such a program. Resources for the Future was a well-endowed organization, funded mostly by the Ford Foundation, that had been started in the 1950s by CLC counselor Horace Albright and others.[87] Because of the Albright connection, the directors of RFF were predisposed to approve of the CLC and its desire to expand. Both DU and RFF responded quickly and enthusiastically.[88] The directors of RFF offered to fund a full scholarship program at DU to inaugurate the program. And it was agreed that as soon as a suitable candidate was lo-

Students of the University of Denver graduate school of librarianship study surrounded by the tools of their trade. DU brochure, 1962.

cated, the "conservation librarianship" program would be implemented with full funding from the foundation.

Carhart did not have to think long about his personal choice for a candidate. He quickly recommended Kay Collins, a young historian from the University of New Mexico. She was the daughter of well-known naturalist and forester C. K. Collins and a longtime family friend of the Carharts. She had used the Conservation Library two years earlier to complete the research for her master's thesis on transmountain diversion of water from the Colorado River.[89] During the time she spent at the DPL doing research, she impressed Carhart and all she met with her knowledge of environmental issues and her interest in environmental advocacy. Other candidates were proposed, but it was assumed by all that Collins would win the scholarship.

Collins was honored to be the recipient of the RFF fellowship and began an accelerated program in conservation librarianship in the fall of 1967.[90] The scholarship started a long, fruitful relationship between the CLC and Collins, who played a central role in the library's development for the next thirteen years. Under Collins's leadership the CLC entered the second phase of its history, moving in directions quite different from those imagined by Carhart and his generation of conservationists. Along with Ed Hilliard, Collins was responsible for establishing a stronger relationship between the CLC and the grassroots environmental community in Colorado. An activist herself, she consistently worked to make the library

Kay Collins as a young library student, ca. 1967. Denver Public Library, Western History Collection, Conservation Library Collection photos.

a vital part of the modern environmental movement. Unlike Carhart, Collins was not afraid to bring the CLC directly into debates on controversial environmental issues. She participated in the meetings and gatherings of local environmental groups and spoke in favor of their policies. Even though this practice led to some reprimands from the DPL administration, Collins was unwavering in her devotion to the local environmental community. But all this was in the future. First she had to jump through the hoops of graduate school, and she began her studies with relish. With the education program under way, the directors of the CLC turned to other issues.

Despite the inherent problems with the expansion plan, it did provide useful suggestions for future advocacy and education work at the CLC. One of the trends that began to emerge from the CLC planning conference and its aftermath was a growing concern with generational tensions within the environmental movement. Most of the men who participated, with the exception of Hilliard, were older and retired. The one aspect of Fischer's report that seemed to raise some eyebrows among the older CLC supporters who read it was its constant snide references to "past achievements and disappointments" of the conservation movement.[91] Instead of focusing on past glories, Fischer argued, the CLC should aim its services at the younger generation and concentrate on education rather than veneration. To Carhart, this must have seemed something of an insult; for others like Hilliard, it was a call to action. Either way, those involved with the CLC project began to look for ways to bridge the gap between an aging generation of conservationists and a younger generation of environmentalists. The "conservation librarian" program was the first step in this direction.

CONCLUSION

In Colorado, Ed Hilliard was the driving force behind the effort to bring younger people into the environmental movement. In 1964, after the remarkably successful grassroots campaign for the wilderness bill, the informal Colorado wilderness coalition Hilliard helped build was reorganized as the Colorado Open Space Committee (COSC) after a conference in Breckenridge, Colorado.[92] This group grew quickly, by 1966 encompassing more than twenty-five state environmental organizations with a total membership of over fifty thousand. Hilliard personally funded the new organization and donated office space at the Redfield building.[93] As a result, a younger generation of environmental advocates, without money or connections, could pursue environmental advocacy full-time. Hilliard's patronage likewise enabled them to build a strong network of support without having to worry about paying the bills. In the cramped office space above the Redfield sight-manufacturing works, young environmental activists such as Roger Fuehrer, Hugh Kingery, and future Colorado governor Richard Lamm sat around reading *Silent Spring*, *A Sand County Almanac*, and Stewart Udall's *Quiet Crisis* as they planned the future of environmental advocacy in Colorado.[94]

From the beginning, Hilliard and the others who organized the COSC wanted to attract younger members and generate interest in environmental advocacy in a new generation of Coloradans. Looking back on this time, Richard Lamm commented that "without Ed Hilliard's moral and financial support none of this would have been possible."[95] More than anything else, Hilliard thought that young people had to be educated about the environmental crisis and the value and power of grassroots environmental organization. At a time when generational tensions ran high, Hilliard developed a "growing understanding of the environmental action of the *next* generation."[96] As Hilliard's friend and colleague Roger Hanson stated, Hilliard could "identify and communicate with . . . that uncertain restless generation most of us cannot now reach."[97]

With the formation of COSC, environmental advocacy in Colorado started to move away from the radical amateur tradition dominated by older established social elites. The next generation of environmental leaders in Colorado started at a young age, with many making a career of advocacy. In fact, the Colorado method of coalition building and professionalization became the model for national environmental advocacy in the wake of the Wilderness Act. In addition to his work bringing young people into the Colorado environmental coalition, Hilliard also tried to think of ways to involve them in the CLC and to bring the CLC into the new environmental coalition.

The strange reticence of Arthur Carhart and the Conservation Library during the wilderness fight disturbed Hilliard and others connected with the CLC project, for they took seriously Fischer's call to action. What better time, he thought, to jump into the fray than during the culmination of the seventy-year battle to preserve the wilderness? Likewise, many wondered, if the leaders of the CLC were unwilling to stand up for wilderness, then what possible role could the library play in future, more controversial, fights? By 1966, it was becoming increasingly clear that for the CLC to become a center of advocacy, new leadership was required. Although Carhart, Eastlick, and the older members of the CLC counselors were willing to listen to and even endorse plans for more radical political action, when the time came to make a public commitment, they balked. It seemed as if the CLC was mired in a cautious, dated style of conservation advocacy. As a result, the library appeared to be teetering on the brink of obsolescence at the moment when its popularity reached new heights. All these concerns about the future of the library came to a head when Arthur Carhart suffered a crippling stroke in May 1966.

At seventy-four, Carhart had been in poor health for some time. The stress of constant travel and voluminous correspondence for the Conservation Library was intense and relentless. During this same period, Carhart's wife, Vera, became seriously ill. When he was not working for the library, he was caring for her and maintaining their household. During a cold spell in 1965, Vera died, leaving Carhart alone with only the staff of the CLC and local friends for comfort. The shock of his wife's death pushed Carhart's already precarious health to the limit, eventually leading to his collapse. The stroke left him paralyzed on one side and unable to speak. It was not clear for a number of weeks whether he would ever regain his ability to communicate.[98]

The news of Carhart's illness sent shock waves through the conservation community. There were fears that with Carhart incapacitated the CLC would cease to exist. From the very beginning of the project, Carhart had been so closely associated with the library that many of the advisers could not conceive of it continuing without him. After the stroke, letters and calls poured into Eastlick's office. Some donors wondered if their materials were safe or if the library would be disbanded. Eastlick quickly responded by preparing a long memorandum to all the conservation counselors, explaining that Carhart was expected to recover and that, regardless of his health, the CLC would continue in its present form. He reassured them, "It must be remembered the Conservation Library Center, as part of an important institution known as the Denver Public Library, has long-range and important goals, and that as an institution neither individuals nor the vicissitudes of daily living can terminate them."[99] Although this announcement placated those who were worried about an imminent collapse, it did not completely erase the sense that without Carhart the Conservation Library's future seemed less sure.

The successful discovery of a promising young candidate for the conservation librarian program, along with an extension of funding from the ACA, partially alleviated the sense that the CLC was in trouble. Although everyone connected with the project was deeply concerned about Carhart's health and welfare, there was also a sense among some of the counselors that Carhart's departure could be turned to their advantage. For Hilliard and others interested in positioning the CLC within the growing Colorado environmental coalition, Carhart's unfortunate illness meant that the library could start to move in new directions. During the four years between Carhart's stroke and his death in 1970, Ed Hilliard worked with the new generation of CLC leaders to make sure that the library lived up to its promise as a center for environmental advocacy. The key to that promise was Kay Collins. As she advanced through her studies in the unique DU program in librarianship and then moved into a leadership position at the CLC, it seemed for a time that the bold proclamations of the planning conference might actually come true. With Carhart out and Collins in, a new phase in the history of the CLC began.

CHAPTER FIVE

A Library of Her Own

My library was dukedom large enough.
Prospero, The Tempest

It is paradoxical that a movement that has been fueled by women's concerns and largely sustained by women's labor, one that offers the potential to provide a more hospitable working environment for women than most, should be so mired in conventional male power structures.
Joni Seager, Earth Follies

If the first decade of the Conservation Library's history was characterized by a veneration of the past and a reverence for the grand old men of conservation, the next decade was quite different, indeed. Carhart's stroke sparked an identity crisis for the CLC. During a prolonged leave of absence, he slowly regained his ability to speak but gradually realized that he could never again work on the project full-time. Many genuinely wondered if the Conservation Library could go on without him.[1] The process of reorganizing the administrative structure of the CLC revealed generational and gender issues that were, by the end of the 1960s, shaping both the CLC and the environmental movement. As in the civil rights movement, many women and younger people who constituted the front lines of grassroots environmental battles began to question the leadership of an older generation that did not seem willing to relinquish authority.

When the new generation of CLC leaders eventually found themselves in control of the library, they faced a complex set of sometimes conflicting national and local environmental imperatives, with little in the way of a plan from their former superiors. Carhart and his cohort had set a bold and sweeping agenda. Unable to clearly define their own position, including pretty much everything as an environmental issue, they left it to their heirs to deal with the increasing subtlety of environmental questions grounded in real conflict: economic, philosophical, and social.

Interpretations of environmental politics in the 1960s and 1970s often focus on changes in philosophy and direction as Progressive conservation evolved into environmentalism. New environmentalists, in the standard interpretation, inspired by the work of Rachel Carson and others, embraced environmental holism and rejected the utilitarianism and "technological optimism of Progressive conservation."[2] Renewed scarcity fears coupled with this new sense of environmental holism inspired the wilderness preservation movement and led to the passage of the Wilderness Act in 1964. Following the victory of the Wilderness Act, a significant split developed between local, grassroots activists and national, beltway-based organizations that practiced the cautious politics of bureaucratic maneuvering.[3] This split led to a fragmentation of the new environmental alliance and a period of confusing stagnation that has lasted until the present day. To a certain extent the CLC story supports this well-articulated view of American environmental politics. As the 1960s progressed, a significant change in the composition and methodology of the environmental movement occurred as environmental organizations moved away from their grass roots. As conservation became environmentalism, new factions formed as old coalitions realigned or dissolved. The shift from Arthur Carhart's grassroots library toward a federally funded technological information clearinghouse under the direction of Kay Collins reflects this transition.

There are, however, several problems with standard explanations of changes in environmental advocacy in the twentieth century. First, how can one explain the significant numbers of conservationists who, throughout the twentieth century, used Progressive modernist means to act on decidedly antimodernist fears of technological progress? What do you do, for instance, with someone like Arthur Carhart, whose career touches on almost all aspects of conservation, preservation, and environmentalism and does not support the shift from utility to holism? Second, how can this model of change account for the strange convergence, in the 1960s, of back-to-nature primitivism and renewed technological enthusiasm? Both of these positions were expressed, sometimes simultaneously, by a younger generation of environmental advocates. What place is there in existing historical models for individuals and organizations that defy easy categorization, for example, Stewart Brand and his *Whole Earth Catalog* or Kay Collins and her Conservation Library? Finally, what role do social politics play in the changing landscape of environmentalism in the 1960s and 1970s?

The example of the Conservation Library obviously cannot fully explain the myriad contradictions of environmental advocacy in America. Still, a close look at the evidence from the Conservation Library raises intriguing questions and provides some insights toward a more complex explanation of what happened to environmentalism, as a social and political force in the late 1960s and 1970s.

At the Conservation Library, environmental advocates and environmental organizations began to cope with political and social contingency and complexity in a typically modern American way. They turned to specialization and professionalization in newly invented methods of data gathering and generation, and to new environmental sciences and policy studies, while continuing to generate local projects. In ways that apparently contradict traditional historical explanations of change, the new generation of participants in the CLC project embraced wilderness preservation, holism, wise use, and back-to-the-land ethics; most important, inspired by New Left politics, they advocated a renewed technological enthusiasm predicated on counterculture notions of postscarcity economics. The transformation of the CLC under the leadership of Kay Collins exemplifies these trends.

When Arthur Carhart started the Conservation Library, there was no such thing as "environmentalism." The conservation movement was a much narrower, more elite, more compartmentalized political entity than its successor. The debates about the nature of conservation in the first years of the CLC indicate that there was little agreement even among conservationists about how to define their shared project. The problem of defining "conservation" was, in some ways, a harbinger of a future in which environmental issues would affect so many people, in so many ways, that virtually everyone could make some claim to know and care for "nature"—from the Mothers of East Los Angeles to Department of Energy (DOE) field office heads and chamber of commerce boosters in proposed nuclear waste disposal sites. There was, in other words, a spectrum of putatively environmentalist positions on most issues in the 1970s. The transformation of the CLC in this decade reflected this spectrum, with all its social complexities and political gray areas.

Part of the changing politics that affected environmentalism and the Conservation Library stemmed from subtle gender and generational conflicts, which were magnified in the case of the CLC because of parallel trends in librarianship during the same period. At the same time that the environmental movement was experiencing challenges from within, with women seeking a more active role in leadership positions, American libraries faced a similar crisis as women, who constituted the bulk of library employees, began to question the hierarchy and compensation practices of public libraries. As a result, during the 1960s, public libraries became a focal point for the attempt to correct unequal status and pay in professions traditionally dominated by women workers and male managers. In this case, the story of the Conservation Library sheds light on the connections between trends in libraries and environmental advocacy, while similarly revealing crucial gender changes in environmental advocacy as the movement reached maturity in the 1970s.

LINES OF AUTHORITY

Arthur Carhart's departure from the CLC after his stroke forced John Eastlick to reevaluate the staffing and management of the library. Although on

Unidentified DPL librarian sits alone in the basement stacks, ca. 1958. Denver Public Library, Western History Collection, Conservation Library Collection photos.

paper Carhart had never been anything other than a "consultant," in reality he had acted as the director of the day-to-day operations of the CLC from its inception until his collapse in the spring of 1966. With Carhart out, Eastlick decided that the CLC needed a full-time administrator to oversee operations and to direct the staff members working directly and indirectly with the CLC. DPL librarian and longtime CLC staff member Roberta Winn was eminently qualified for the job. She had worked with Carhart from the beginning, and as a trained librarian she knew the collections better than anyone, including Carhart. Winn was poised and professional, but she had one major disadvantage: she was a woman. At the DPL, as at most American libraries well into the 1960s, higher-paid management positions were reserved for men, who often were trained not in librarianship but in business management or a related field.[4] On the surface Winn was

Kenneth Porter and John Eastlick confer as Roberta Winn looks on, summer 1969. Denver Public Library, Western History Collection, Conservation Library Collection photos.

passed up because, it was argued, she was already managing the Fish and Wildlife Library Reference Service Division of the CLC.[5] Although the job in the Fish and Wildlife operation was an important one, it was clearly a stinging slight to be passed up for the administrative position after nine years of dedication to the CLC project.

The man Eastlick picked for the job of Conservation Library "administrator" was Kenneth A. Porter, twenty years younger than Winn and with no library experience. Porter was educated at Iowa State University, where he received a B.S. in animal science, and at Colorado State University, where he got his M.S. in wildlife management. Before coming to the DPL, he worked for the Colorado Department of Game, Fish, and Parks and with the U.S. Forest Service.[6] Despite his lack of experience in library management, Porter became an energetic and enthusiastic administrator with strong ties to the local environmental movement. A member of the Colorado Mountain Club and trustee of COSC, he spent much of his brief time at the CLC trying to build links between the library and Colorado's environmental organizations.[7]

As administrator, Porter was supposed to ensure that the CLC would be organized and cataloged, a Herculean task considering the eight-year backlog. How Porter was supposed to know how to manage this huge job was a question no one seems to have asked. Although he did make an effort to direct staff members toward cataloging and organizing the library, from the beginning Porter clearly was more concerned with advocacy than with the tedious minutiae of librarianship.[8] One of his first memorandums informed the CLC staff that establishing lines of communication with the grassroots community was now the library's primary goal. "Very soon," he wrote, "we should begin attending meeting[s] of these various groups."[9] This focus on activism was all well and good, but what the CLC needed was someone who could foster connections with the environmental community *and* manage the details of the library. Luckily, Kay Collins was on hand, eagerly waiting to step into Porter's place.

Collins began to work more directly with the CLC in 1966 as a part of her training in the DU library program. Her course of studies called for her to finish her formal training at the Conservation Library.[10] Graduate training at the DU library school was rigorous and demanding. The University of Denver—the first American school to offer graduate degrees in librarianship—prided itself on turning out some of the best-prepared students and providing a "course of instruction designed to . . . develop librarians who are capable of being leaders in their profession and participants and leaders in all community efforts to create and sustain an enlightened citizenry."[11] Collins's background in environmental history, her experience as an environmentalist, and her training in librarianship made her the logical choice as the future director of the CLC.

When Porter took over, however, Collins was still fresh out of the DU program and had not been seriously considered for the job of CLC administrator because of her youth (she was only twenty-six years old) and, as was the case with Winn, because of her sex. In 1966, there were no women in the DPL management structure. Although she was certainly the best trained, Collins would have to wait for her chance to take over the CLC.

In the meantime, Eastlick was relieved that Porter was proving an energetic promoter of the CLC and seemed to be running a tight ship. If successful management can be measured by the number of reports generated, Porter was a major success. With comforting regularity, bold-faced reports appeared on Eastlick's desk, temporarily allaying fears that nothing was really happening. Also pleasing to Eastlick was the return of Arthur Carhart to the library. After only three months of convalescence, Carhart was back at work part-time, but he was, in many respects, a broken man. He had aged remarkably during his illness and was hardly a shadow of his former vibrant self; he was barely able to speak and remained very weak. Everyone realized he would never be able to maintain the pace of work that he had managed prior to his stroke. Although everyone was glad to have him back, his presence in active work areas was less appreciated by the busy staff of the CLC.

From 1966 until 1969, Carhart played a minimal role in directing the CLC. Still, every day he dressed in his dark suit and spent at least a few hours at the library, carefully writing letters to the CLC counselors and preparing meticulous lists of documents and artifacts. Working quietly with the CLC staff, he spent much of his time telling the stories of the pioneer conservation movement so the younger generation might come to know the key players and events.[12] During this time, Carhart's personal life deteriorated along with his health. He was unable to write or fulfill consulting contracts, and thus his finances suffered.

After his stroke, Carhart began contemplating a move away from Denver. The big house on Eudora Street, where he had lived with his wife for forty years, was now too much for him to handle alone. Additionally, his deteriorating financial situation made it impossible for him to keep the maid who had helped cook and clean during Vera's illness and after her death. Maintaining the pristine yard, once his pride and joy, became a chore delegated to neighbor boys.[13] Carhart reasonably decided it was time for a change, and in the spring of 1969 he sold his Denver home. The move meant that a new wave of Carhart artifacts and manuscripts made their way to the Conservation Library. Sadly, however, Carhart, who was desperately in need of cash, sold his vast book collection to a local rare-book dealer. Many of his own rare 1930s novels and manuscripts were lost in the national maze of antiquarian book shops, some never to resurface again.[14] Inexplicably, especially to his friends at the CLC, Carhart chose as his new home a retirement community in southern California. Apparently he wanted to move to a warmer climate and had seen an advertisement for a community in Lemon Grove, California. He had no friends in southern California, and the move left him completely isolated from the CLC and his Denver friends. With hindsight, the decision to relocate to California proved disastrous. The story of the final years of Carhart's life is one of loneliness and isolation. The hale and hearty outdoorsman who prided himself on his physical strength and national reputation as a man's man spent his last years surrounded by "bridge playing old ladies." He was one of only a handful of men in the whole place.[15] During his remaining years, Carhart maintained his relationship with the Conservation Library through letters and tape-recorded messages. Kay Collins, coming to the CLC via her connection with Carhart, carefully kept him abreast of developments. Despite this regular correspondence, after 1968 Carhart no longer played a significant role in the Conservation Library.

Only a few months after Carhart departed for California, the CLC's other founder and benefactor, John Eastlick, announced his retirement as the head of the Denver Public Library to begin a new career at the University of Denver Graduate School of Librarianship. Eastlick spent the next two decades making a name for himself as a professor at DU and the author of several publications on the science of librarianship.[16] Eastlick left the DPL system with a new philosophy about public libraries. His experience with the CLC project had changed him. The once staid and conservative Eastlick became a champion of the public library as a center for social advocacy in a rapidly changing and chaotic modern world. "Libraries as traditional institutions," he wrote, "have found it difficult to cast off their bureaucratic structure and develop new avenues of effectiveness to meet the problems of racial and minority unrest, student demonstrations, [and] the generation gap."[17] The decade of work building the Conservation Library left a lasting impression on Eastlick. He was convinced that the only way libraries could remain relevant and combat the problems of the 1970s and beyond was to face head-on the controversial social issues of the day and to foster those who might use the library as an instrument of social change. Later, at the DU Graduate School of Librarianship, he preached this message to his students and acted as mentor to a new generation of activist librarians.

The departure of the Conservation Library's two founders and strongest promoters in the same year represented a clean break with the past and paved the way for a younger generation to take the CLC in new directions. Eastlick was replaced by Henry G. Shearouse Jr., a pragmatic and efficient manager who was seemingly immune to the spirit of activism. Unlike Eastlick, Shearouse was not an environmentalist and not particularly interested in environmental issues. Even though he entered the job as city librarian with a fairly open mind, he never made the kind of personal commitment to the Conservation Library that Eastlick did. Consequently, his relationship with CLC staff was often strained at best and openly hostile at worst. Shearouse considered the CLC just a small and unimportant piece of a large, complicated library system. He quantified library achievements in thousands of units circulated and safely returned. By this measure, the CLC appeared decidedly underused and therefore insignificant. Still, Shearouse was willing to support the CLC as long as it pulled its own weight and did not place a burden on the DPL system. Although he appreciated the archival role of the CLC within the structure of the system, he had little tolerance for any on-the-job environmental advocacy. He viewed the CLC simply as a manuscript collection open to researchers with an interest in conservation, not as a center for grassroots environmental advocates, and certainly not as a platform for DPL employees to parade their liberal environmental politics. This conservative view led to serious conflict with younger CLC staff, many of whom came to the library in the early 1970s energized by environmentalism and personally committed to a political agenda that seemed extreme and dangerous to Shearouse.[18] His relationship with Kay Collins in particular deteriorated as the two came to disagree over the best course for the CLC and the appropriateness of environmental politics in the public library. Moreover, the idea that a young woman, whose dress and actions were decidedly unmatronly, was controlling the daily activities of a significant section of the city's central library seems to have rankled the conservative Shearouse.

THE GENTLE SCIENTISTS

Between 1966, when she received her degree in conservation librarianship, and 1969, Kay Collins worked as the CLC librarian.[19] Collins was the first DPL librarian whose sole responsibility was to work with the collections of the CLC. Roberta Winn had spent almost ten years serving as the CLC's primary librarian, but the CLC was never her sole responsibility, and she had never been officially recognized as *the* CLC librarian. By the late 1960s, she was entrenched as the head of the Fish and Wildlife Reference Service, where she directed three librarians and a small administrative staff. Collins, therefore, was hired as librarian for the CLC over the more experienced Winn. In this capacity, Collins moved to increase her work with the local environmental community and to travel to conferences around the state promoting the CLC to environmental groups and organizations.

As the first professionally trained conservation librarian, Collins had a vested interest in promoting environmentally oriented collections in libraries. At a meeting of the Special Libraries Association in Los Angles in 1968, Collins helped form a Natural Resources Division of the association to help promote both her new field and environmental politics in public libraries.[20] In the following years she became a leader in the movement to bring environmentalism into the discourse of library science and edited a national newsletter on the subject.[21]

Kay Collins was certainly not the first woman to use a position at a public library to pursue an activist agenda and establish a power base within a larger community.[22] Particularly in the American West, libraries have always been centers of social and political activity for women. Between 1880 and 1930, Progressive women turned public and university libraries into centers of the female community and used the library as a platform for social activism. Historian Joanne Passet refers to these library activists as "cultural crusaders," women who worked with a missionary zeal and thought library work was more than just a profession; it was a means of bettering society and improving communities.[23] The spirit of activism in libraries was so strong during the Progressive Era that the years between 1870 and 1917 have been called a golden age for women in librarianship.[24]

As early as the 1850s, women began staffing public libraries, and by the 1880s women constituted almost 80 percent of all library workers.[25] By the 1920s, that figure had risen to over 90 percent, with libraries employing a larger percentage of women workers than either social work or teaching.[26] Figures for women in librarianship dipped during World War II but rose again once the soldiers returned. By the 1960s, the percentages were near the 1920s high.

Like other professions in which women dominated, American librarianship "both embodied and challenged contemporary gender ideology."[27] When women began moving into the profession in large numbers during the Progressive Era, they helped support the notion of women as guardians of culture and morality. At the same time, they used their jobs in libraries as avenues toward personal empowerment and more active roles in the public sphere. The acceptance of women in librarianship was due, in part, to the prevailing perception that libraries were appropriate places for women. The work required meshed perfectly with dominant notions about women's "natures" and capabilities. Librarianship quickly came to be viewed as a "feminized profession," with the work particularly suited to stereotypical female characteristics such as "passivity, emotionalism, and intuitiveness," thought to be important factors in the ability to do tedious hand cataloging.[28]

The large percentage of women in librarianship in the early twentieth century contributed to the debate over the professionalization of libraries. Librarians, like their middle-class counterparts in other relatively new professions, were "still in the process of negotiating their claim to professional status" during the first half of the century.[29] For the men who controlled library administration and the management structure of America's libraries, the issue of professionalization was an important one. Because of the perception that library work was women's work, the men in charge needed to differentiate themselves from the women who worked with them. They did this by creating a rigid structure of authority within libraries that generally excluded women from the top positions. Young men straight out of college were often hired to manage large staffs of highly experienced older women librarians. Historian Abigail Van Slyck has argued that this tension between professionally focused male management and subordinate female labor even influenced twentieth-century library design. The spatial arrangement of libraries came to reflect perceptions of the proper role of women in a public profession and the sharp distinction between professional male managers and subordinate female library staff.[30] For example, well-paid male managers occupied enclosed offices suitably removed from the general public that helped maintain their status as executives in control of the business of the library. Female staff, on the other hand, usually had no private offices and worked in the open with the patrons or behind the scenes, where the thankless work of cataloging took place. Thus, although libraries developed over the twentieth century as refuges for educated women in search of a career, they remained highly segregated by gender and entrenched in traditional power hierarchies.

The reality of library work differed significantly from the ideal of the Progressive library schools that were training thousands of young women as professional librarians. At the University of Illinois and other schools, pioneer library educators such as Katharine Sharp emphasized the social reform role of the library and the librarian.[31] Between the years 1900 and 1917, the women trained at the library school often found that they were able to use their careers to further the Progressive agenda of social reform. By the end of World War I, however, the missionary era of library development in America was coming to a close. Most institutional libraries grew into large bureaucracies run by male managers. Library work became more routine, and librarianship no longer seemed like a viable avenue for social advocacy. Still, young women librarians after 1917 left American universities anticipating an exciting career of social activism. When they took jobs as librarians, they expected to be treated like professionals. Instead, they usually found that the male library managers who hired them expected them to be secretaries. After long hours of tedious clerical tasks, little time remained for work on community issues such as public health, child welfare, or temperance. The reality of institutional library work, with its rigid hierarchies and long hours, fell far short of the spirit of activism that had characterized library schools in the previous decades.

For many female librarians, the managerial revolution of the Progressive Era seemed to have killed the social movement in the library. This was true to some extent; libraries and librarianship entered a protracted phase of quiescence. But the social aspect of library work was not dead; it was in stasis, caught in a holding pattern until a new generation of women activists resumed the tradition.

The social movement in America's libraries came alive again in the 1960s.[32] In the 1960s, the normally quiet and conservative annual meetings of the American Library Association (ALA) took on the atmosphere of a raucous political carnival. Open debates on highly charged political subjects, such as segregation, urban poverty, and women's rights, became commonplace.[33] The ALA meeting saw protests from groups of young Chicano activists and African-American civil rights advocates who called for America's public librarians to abandon their antiquated traditions of political neutrality and take a stand on the issues of the day. A new generation of women librarians began to demand equal treatment and equal pay. And environmentalists, like Kay Collins, began to demand that librarians deal frankly and openly with the environmental crisis and to use the public library as a means of generating grassroots support for environmental reform.

This new activist trend reached a climax at the 1970 annual meeting of the American Library Association. By this time, women librarians were ready for a revolution. Libraries had played a significant role in the civil rights movement during the 1960s, exposing thousands of women librarians to the power of grassroots advocacy.[34] Upon arriving at the convention in 1970, women librarians organized the SRRT Task Force on the Status of Women in Librarianship, which began challenging sexist rhetoric in ALA publications and guidelines and even went so far as to deface displays that it found biased and offensive.[35] The dam that held back feminism burst in the 1960s, hitting America's libraries like a tidal surge. As one historian stated, "The women's movement had a dramatic impact on libraries. Women actively worked to reclaim leadership . . . and expose unequal power structures [and] gender bias in material and even space."[36] By the early 1970s, women library workers were actively challenging the status quo within individual libraries and in the profession as a whole.

After the 1960s, librarianship would never be the same. As one historian of the period writes, "Certainly the efforts of activists contributed to the end of the field's self-imposed naiveté and stimulated an engagement with social issues and groups beyond previously accepted boundaries."[37] Prior to the 1970s, the terms "conservation" and "preservation" uttered at an ALA meeting conjured images of water-stained books, threadbare jackets, torn pages, and crayon marks. Collins hoped to change this. She wanted to make environmentalism a part of the social agenda of American librarians, and she made a significant leap in this direction with the formation of an ALA committee for natural resources librarians. The degree to which this group was influential in changing librarians' perceptions of conservation issues and in helping to bring environmental advocacy into the mainstream of American librarianship is difficult to determine. Still, pioneering efforts like this opened new avenues within the profession and represented a meaningful effort to expand the boundaries of library activism.

Back in Denver, Collins used her new leadership position to turn the CLC from a passive repository into an active center of social advocacy. In July 1969, Kenneth Porter left the CLC to take a job teaching at a local private academy.[38] With Porter gone, there was once again an opening at the top of the CLC hierarchy. In the months that followed, Collins acted as the de facto head of the CLC while Shearouse decided what to do. Shearouse

Kay Collins poses with some prized collections and recent brochures, April 1970. Denver Public Library, Western History Collection, Conservation Library Collection photos.

took his time making the decision, but early in 1970 he announced that Kay Collins would become the director of the Conservation Library. Shearouse remained skeptical about Collins's activism, and the two never had a good working relationship, but in 1970 they resolved to give it a try. Both began with high hopes for the continued success of the Conservation Library as it moved into its second decade.

The year 1970 proved a bellwether for American environmentalism and the CLC. In April, Americans participated in environmental advocacy in record numbers when they celebrated the first Earth Day. The Conservation Library benefited greatly from the publicity surrounding Earth Day and enjoyed an unprecedented influx of young patrons energized by the new spirit of environmental awareness.[39] Earth Day came to symbolize a shift in the American environmental movement from the older generation to the younger.[40] This transfer of power was highlighted by the announcement that Kay Collins was awarded the American Motors Conservation Award in the spring of 1970.

Collins was one of twenty AMCA winners, eight of whom were women.[41] The large number of awards to women marked a major change in the American Motors program and indicated a significant shift in the leadership of the American environmental movement. American Motors was well aware of the significance of the change and proudly proclaimed that "U.S. women, who have taken up the conservation cause in ever increasing numbers, have claimed a record" number of awards.[42] Collins's award praised her work at the CLC, her status as the first professionally trained "conservation librarian," and her efforts for regional environmental causes.[43] The recognition from the AMCA could not have come at a better time for Collins. The prestigious national award seemed to confirm Shearouse's decision to elevate her to the head of the CLC and helped solidify her power within the library. In addition, it gave her the authority to speak as one of Denver's leading environmentalists. After 1970, she was often sought out for speaking engagements and by the local press for information on environmental topics.

Of course, prior to 1970, women had also played significant roles in the Conservation Library and the American environmental movement in general. In fact, women traditionally formed the front lines of grassroots environmental advocacy and played key roles in national environmental organizations. In the fight for the wilderness bill of 1964, for example, women mobilized community support and organized huge letter-writing campaigns that ultimately turned the tide of opinion. Still, the leadership of the conservation movement remained heavily male. Even major environmental figures such as Rachel Carson and Rosalie Edge remained, for the most part, on the outside of the movement hierarchy; and most major conservation organizations had few or no female board members, managers, or executives well into the 1960s.[44] Prior to 1970, only 21 out of the previous 264 winners of the AMCA were women.[45] Therefore, the awarding of 8 out of 10 awards to women in 1970 signaled a significant change in the role of women in the conservation hierarchy. As with many of the social movements of the 1960s, the environmental movement opened new avenues for activism and leadership roles for women within traditionally male domains. Many women who worked for better relations between humans and the nonhuman world also began to question traditional relationships between humans and other humans. Kay Collins's new leadership role at the Conservation Library exemplified an emerging feminism within American environmentalism.

The American Motors award recognized not only Collins's leadership role at the CLC but also her achievements as a grassroots environmental activist. By 1970, she was the chairperson of the Information and Education Workshop of the Colorado Open Space Council and one of the more popular public speakers in the Denver area.[46] She traveled throughout the Denver metropolitan area and the state, giving speeches and promoting environmental education at every opportunity. When presenting the AMCA, Roy D. Chapin Jr., chairman of the board of American Motors, identified Collins as one of "the most forceful speakers in the area on natural resource conservation."[47] In a letter of recommendation to the directors of the awards program on behalf of Collins's nomination, her mentor, Arthur Carhart, acknowledged the importance of shifting the leadership of the CLC to a younger generation more in tune with current trends in the modern environmental movement. He wrote, "Here we have young dedicated and informed leadership which God knows we need desperately."[48] Monroe Bush of the Old Dominion Foundation stated that "the conservation of tomorrow belongs to the young, [and] Miss Collins would be . . . a superb representative of this trend."[49]

At the age of twenty-nine, Kay Collins had achieved more than many activists manage in a lifetime. She was not, however, ready to sit back and enjoy her new status. As soon as she took charge of the CLC, she began to work to create an expanded role for the library in the environmental movement. The CLC under Kay Collins was quite different from what it had been under Eastlick and Carhart or Kenneth Porter. For one, Collins displayed little of the fear of controversy that her mentors had. In her first interview after receiving the AMCA, she made her politics clear by openly criticizing the American market economy and the ignorance of the American public. "Some parts of the economy can make the change," she said, "but I don't know if enough can. We're not playing around now—it's lives that are on the line."[50] Collins's uncompromising rhetoric endeared her to her fellow environmentalists but led to serious conflict with Shearouse and other library employees.

The most noticeable change in direction at the CLC under Collins's leadership was the new audience for the message. Carhart and Eastlick, like most conservationists of their generation, aimed their message at middle-class and prominent men, who were the ones with enough money and influence to get a project like the CLC moving. True, Collins worked the foundation circuit and catered to wealthy patrons but not to the extent that Carhart had. Such activities were never her first concern. She focused instead on speaking to ordinary people, especially young people and women. She realized that even though the Old Dominion Foundation or Resources for the Future might be valuable "sugar daddies," trying to change their fundamentally conservative views was a waste of time. She focused instead on groups of local women and young people who were eager for a more radical environmental message. "Groups of women tend to be more open and objective audiences than men," she said, "because men, especially business men, are faced with economic problems" and were, she felt, ultimately too materialistic and conservative to be converted.[51]

To some degree Collins, true to her times, failed to understand the implications of her politics. Reflecting on her leadership at the CLC, she viewed herself as a moderate. "I personally was a hybrid," she stated, "and always found myself between the two [generations] or bridging gaps."[52] The older generation of CLC supporters generally respected her and thought she represented the virtues of the new youthfulness in the environmental movement. She was clean-cut, well-spoken, and respectful. As one older foundation head said about Collins, "I would have been hard-pressed to decline such dedication, ability, and charm!"[53] Also, most of the older generation of conservationists would have readily agreed with her contention that she "always looked for those few people who were not so bound by 'the way it has always been done' and could work with more than one group and see more than one side."[54] Yet, whereas she charmed her elders in the conservation movement, the more politically conservative and uninvolved, like Shearouse, found Collins's bluntness and aggressive support of environmentalism shockingly different from the careful diplomacy and cautious language of Carhart and even Porter.[55]

However much her strong positions worried the bureaucrats at the DPL, they delighted her colleagues in the Colorado environmental movement and her audiences of young women and men interested in environmental issues. In addition to her disdain for status quo positions for the CLC's environmental program, Collins also chafed at the stifling conservatism and bureaucracy of the public library. Like other women librarians of the early 1970s, Collins wanted to see the old hierarchy replaced. When she attended ALA meetings, she was inspired by the work of civil rights activists and feminists who attempted to open librarianship. And through her work with the ALA section on environment, she hoped to make environmentalism a part of the social revolution in the American library.

In an attempt to accomplish this goal, she and Roberta Winn organized the seminar "Environmental Ecology and the Library" as part of the annual Colorado Library Association Conference in 1970.[56] The conference, conceived and run primarily by women, was aimed at librarians, both male and female, with an interest in social advocacy in the public library. As one statement revealed, the purpose of the conference was to "assist librarians to become better acquainted with materials on environmental problems and possible solutions."[57] Further, the hope was that the conference would inspire librarians to work outside the library and become "more effective in their communities."[58] To achieve this purpose, Collins led an hour-long session on community relations that stressed the ways in which librarians could use their public positions to further social causes such as environmentalism. Winn likewise gave a talk on reference and the environmental movement, with an emphasis on helping environmental advocates and grassroots organizations make the most out of the free resources of the public library.[59] The message of the conference was clear: libraries were centers of social action, and librarians should do everything in their power to facilitate the use of the library to further the social revolution of the 1960s.

Clearly, the focus of the Conservation Library changed dramatically under Collins's leadership. She brought to the library the idealism, energy, and naïveté of youth. In addition, as a woman who came of age in the 1960s, she brought a nascent feminist perspective, radically different from those of her predecessors. Still, it would be a mistake to assume that this new focus completely changed the way the CLC operated on a day-to-day basis. When Kay Collins inherited the CLC, she gained more than a stage for political protest and environmental advocacy. She also inherited the administrative problems of how to define, organize, and fund the financially troubled project. In many ways, her vigorous political advocacy and dedication to community action and community support made the task of managing the CLC more difficult.

THE FIVE-YEAR PLAN

At the Conservation Library, the years immediately preceding Collins's arrival were dominated by schemes for building the CLC of North America. This plan, which called for a major expansion in scope and size and the construction of a multi-million-dollar environmental complex next to the existing DPL main library, completely occupied Collins's predecessors. Carhart spent his last productive months at the CLC concocting more and more grandiose plans for the expanded library. Still, by 1967, it was clear that the idea was not going to become a reality. There were no serious attempts to raise the endowment money necessary to begin the project, and the CLC continued to suffer from a lack of qualified staff. The Department of the Interior provided significant funding for the Library Reference Service, but this money went entirely into that particular, understaffed program. Complicating matters further, the Reference Service was moved out of the main library building in 1966 because of overcrowding.[60] As a result, its staff was separated from the CLC, making cooperative staffing arrangements untenable. Prior to this move, the Reference Service staff was able to help with the administration of the CLC and provide some cataloging assistance. With this shift and Carhart's change to part-time status after his stroke, the CLC was left with a serious cataloging backlog that seemed insurmountable. At the beginning of 1967, however, the library received a major boost in funding that seemed to be a positive indication that the staff problems, at least, would soon be resolved.

After years of lobbying by Carhart and Eastlick, the funding came in the form of a $25,000 grant from the Mellon family's Old Dominion Foundation. Established in 1941 by Paul Mellon, the foundation listed conservation as one of its primary missions and granted more than $5 million annually.[61] Carhart's friend Monroe Bush proved instrumental in arranging the deal. The conditions of the grant stipulated that the DPL Foundation had to raise matching funds during the following calendar year. If the CLC was able to raise the match, then an additional $25,000 was promised.[62] Considering the drought of funding from the Denver area over the past years, the likelihood of coming up with the matching funds seemed low.

As enthusiasm over the expansion project faded, it became increasingly clear to all involved that the DPL Foundation was only willing to raise money for the CLC on its own terms. Eastlick wondered if it would support the matching grant proposal.[63] These fears, however, proved premature. Although the DPL Foundation had moved away from supporting a major expansion of the physical plant, it was enthusiastic about raising money to continue to gradually expand the Conservation Library and to work slowly toward organizing and cataloging existing manuscripts and materials.

In fact, the following year saw an unprecedented level of successful local fund-raising. The DPL Foundation was able to secure a $15,000 grant from the Denver-based Boettcher Foundation and scrape together the remaining $10,000 from smaller donations and grants. This local money ensured that the CLC received the additional funding from Old Dominion. Money worries continued to plague the CLC, although the quality and quantity of donated material and manuscripts was actually on the upswing.

In 1968, the Wilderness Society agreed to make the Conservation Library the official repository for its vast records. This agreement was a major coup for the CLC, culminating years of negotiations. Theodore Swem, the president of the Wilderness Society and former assistant director of the National Park Service, engineered the agreement. An acquaintance of Arthur Carhart, Swem was an early convert to the CLC idea. His experiences with the National Park Service and the environmental movement had taught him the importance of maintaining a careful collection of records for legal research and future advocacy. Swem wanted to make sure that future environmentalists could learn from the victories and mistakes of the past.[64] Over the years, he personally shepherded several valuable manuscript collections to Denver, and he remained active in the CLC well into the 1990s.[65] Today the Wilderness Society collection is one of the largest and most valuable of the CLC resources.[66]

The money raised in 1968, along with the Old Dominion Foundation grants, provided the CLC with the luxury of additional staff members to help with a serious effort to organize the library, and Kay Collins was able to move into a full-time position at the DPL. The arrival of new materials had hardly slowed over the seven-year history of the library, and by 1967 only about one-tenth of the materials received had been cataloged. Staff members spent their time dealing with patrons, answering requests for information that arrived by mail or over the phone. In 1968, the CLC provided services to over fifteen hundred patrons.[67]

Making sure that all the significant collections were available to anyone interested remained a top priority, and the CLC staff received high marks from researchers who used the library for their work on theses, dissertations, books, and articles over the years.[68] A steady stream of historians, graduate students, environmentalists, industry researchers, wildlife specialists, and members of the general public called or visited the library. For example, the CLC was utilized by the first generation of environmental historians to research classic books of the field. Roderick Nash used the CLC in the mid-1960s to research *Wilderness and the American Mind,* and Donald Worster worked in the library in the early 1970s while completing early research on the American environmental movement.[69] Between 1967 and 1968, the CLC saw a large increase in the number of visitors. But the high volume of patron interaction, coupled with community outreach and fund-raising duties, left the overburdened staff of the CLC with even less time to process incoming collections.

One of the most consistent groups of CLC patrons was business and industry. Complicated issues surrounding water rights, natural resource use and conservation, timber management, wildlife regulations and control, and energy brought representatives from many regional businesses into the CLC.[70] By the late 1960s, the CLC was also developing a good reputation as a resource for the local business community. "As president of a small consulting company," one satisfied customer wrote, "I cannot hope to maintain the library and data banks . . . I need in my projects. For the last four years, I have come to rely upon the services and assistance of this library."[71] For many small businesses involved with the growing field of environmental management, environmental regulation, and environmental litigation, the CLC became a valuable tool for researching complex issues. The wealth of material collected in one central place was a boon to young companies trying to break into a new field.

The sight of researchers huddled over manuscripts hoping to solve some thorny contemporary environmental problem was gratifying to Kay Collins and the other CLC staff.[72] The atmosphere in the library in 1968 was charged with energy and excitement. There was a real sense that the promises of the early years were coming true: the Conservation Library had become a center of environmental research and problem solving.[73] Collins wanted to make sure that the CLC had anything and everything that these researchers might need. She realized that the environmental movement was changing and encompassing new subjects not necessarily covered by the existing CLC collections. Thus, she worked to ensure that materials on topics such as energy conservation, shale oil exploration, solar power, urban pollution, and nuclear waste could be found in the CLC holdings.

Although this buzz of activity was a welcome sight, the increased traffic brought up the perennial problem of how to define and limit the size and scope of the CLC manuscripts for management purposes. As described earlier, efforts to define conservation failed in part because the movement that the founders of the CLC were attempting to define and limit was constantly changing. Thus, from the beginning, the CLC was enmeshed in a web of structural change that undermined all efforts to limit and control growth. If the CLC were to succeed in meeting the needs of a rapidly expanding environmental ethos and capture the spirit of the movement, it would fail as a carefully organized archive. In fact, between 1960 and 1968, Carhart and Eastlick solicited any type of material related to conservation or the environment. These efforts paid off with significant rare books, documents, and manuscript collections. At the same time, literally tons of government documents and other bureaucratic debris found their way to the DPL, causing serious problems for the CLC staff and raising questions about the value of the collections for researchers.

When Carhart left the leadership of the CLC in the hands of first Porter and then Collins, there was a chance to step back and reevaluate the collection process, an opportunity to begin to weed out excess and nonessential materials and organize the collections according to sound principles of archival management. Had the leadership of the CLC gone into the expert hands of librarian Roberta Winn, this might have happened. For years, Winn argued that the ultimate success or failure of the CLC depended on sensible management. Once a management plan based on library science was in place, a process that might take years, the CLC could then provide future researchers with an environment much more conducive to careful research. Unfortunately, Porter was no better than Carhart at divorcing his environmental philosophy from the collection process. In fact, he was worse. The acquisition policy under Porter was more open and nebulous than ever before. He argued that "the term 'conservation' almost defies definition . . . hence none will be given for purposes of acquisition for the Conservation Library."[74]

What about Kay Collins? Her training seemed to make her the perfect person to resolve this ongoing conundrum. As an environmentalist and an environmental historian, she understood how the CLC might serve the environmental community. At the same time, her graduate training in librarianship gave her the expertise to organize and catalog the manuscript collections and to establish thoughtful guidelines for acquisitions. But Collins was no better than any of the other CLC managers at reconciling her environmental philosophy with the reality of librarian-ship. Caught up in the excitement of the time, she, too, and in many ways more so than any of her predecessors, focused on expansion and advocacy at the expense of organization and long-term planning. In retrospect, the task seems almost impossible and certainly beyond the means of any one individual. Still, this continuing failure to cope with the job of managing the library, a problem that seemed mundane, eventually came back to haunt the directors of the CLC and played a central role in the ultimate decline of the library as a viable institution.

By 1970, the CLC had not entirely succeeded in becoming the national center for grassroots advocacy that Carhart and Eastlick had envisioned. It was, however, a vital part of the grassroots environmental movement in Colorado, providing moral support and resources for research. Most important, the CLC contributed to the local grassroots environmental movement by providing a public center for the dissemination of environmental information and materials. Over the years, the CLC distributed tens of thousands of pamphlets about conservation and conservation education. These pamphlets were distributed to visitors to the CLC, general patrons of the DPL, local and national environmental groups, and the Denver community.

Public awareness of environmental issues formed a crucial aspect of the grassroots environmental movement. Often the greatest challenge activists faced was not corporate lawyers with deep pockets but apathetic citizens who were blissfully unaware of increasingly serious environmental problems. By acting as a clearinghouse for environmental information, the CLC made a significant contribution to the drive to change public opinion and combat anticonservation forces in Colorado and other parts of the American West.[75] Although the staff clearly leaned toward the side of environmentalism, they strove to maintain at least the appearance of objectivity. Sometimes this was more than simply an appearance. During this period there was little agreement, even among environmentalists, on controversial issues such as shale oil development and nuclear waste disposal. On many occasions, lawyers from both sides of a controversial environmental lawsuit used the resources of the library to research their cases.[76] In these situations, staff members were warned not to divulge what materials one side had used to researchers from the opposing side. Regardless of their personal feelings, the staff did not want to jeopardize the CLC by appearing to be openly biased.[77]

While staff members struggled with issues of fairness and political neutrality in the public library, Kay Collins began to face the ongoing problem of funding the CLC. When she took over Porter's post as head of the library, she found herself suddenly in charge of long-term funding. However much the large grants from Old Dominion and Boettcher helped, they still did not solve the problem of future funding, and there was not a large enough surplus to start an endowment. The constant pressure of fund-raising, Collins quickly learned, distracted her from the pressing need to catalog the collection and to work with the local environmental community. The DPL system provided fairly generous support for the CLC, but always with the understanding that the bulk of the funding would come from outside sources. Collins lobbied hard in her first year as head of the CLC to get the DPL to expand this funding. In light of the success of the first decade, she hoped that the DPL might agree to make the funding of the CLC a part of the permanent library budget, similar to the arrangement the Western History Collection enjoyed. The support of Denver's mayor, William H. McNichols Jr., was crucial to getting the funding plan past the city council. The Development Program, as the plan to secure city funds was called, had the full support of Henry Shearouse and the DPL Commission. For Shearouse, the plan seemed like an ideal way to either make or break the CLC. No matter what happened, he would have less to deal with: either a fully funded archive that contributed to the prestige of the DPL or no CLC, which meant the removal of the troublesome environmentalists running around on the fourth floor.

In 1971, the lobbying effort paid off. The city and county of Denver, with McNichols's strong endorsement, agreed to provide all basic operating expenses for the Conservation Library for a five-year period. The total amount appropriated was $264,355, to be used to offset all of the CLC's expenses while a major fund-raising effort was launched to secure a permanent endowment from private sources.[78] This agreement provided the first real opportunity for the directors of the CLC to concentrate on the long-term financial situation without having to worry about the immediate future. To kick off the five-year plan, the CLC and the DPL Foundation held a fund-raising dinner.[79]

With their funding secure for at least the next five years, Kay Collins and the staff of the Conservation Library settled into a comfortable routine. New assistant librarians were hired, and serious organization and processing of the manuscripts began in earnest for the first time in the CLC's history. Along with the cataloging, the staff dealt with thousands of annual requests for environmental information. The number of local visitors to the library actually declined during these years, but requests for information via phone or correspondence from other parts of the nation rose.[80] The CLC moved down to the second floor to less assuming, but more public, quarters.

The move to the public space of the second floor and away from the rarefied atmosphere of the restricted research area on the fourth floor symbolized the CLC's shift in focus under Kay Collins. Although Collins

Working in the CLC in its new second-floor home, February 7, 1971. Denver Public Library, Western History Collection, Conservation Library Collection photos.

corresponded with Arthur Carhart and consulted regularly with the CLC counselors, the focus of the CLC was no longer on the preservation of the past achievements of the conservation movement. Collins and the young staff she hired were much more concerned with current events and public access.

When Carhart and Eastlick ran the CLC, the exclusiveness of the fourth floor appropriately reflected their desire to maintain the collections in pristine condition for researchers and visiting dignitaries. Carhart delighted in taking his friends through the quiet rare book areas where the general public was not allowed. For him, appearances were important if the CLC wanted to impress the representatives of the Rockefeller or Mellon families. Photos of the books and artifacts were carefully staged, and a strict dress code was maintained. Captions to photos published during the early history of the CLC always emphasized the care taken to keep donated items out of the reach of marauding children and other undesirables. In these years, the fourth floor had a decidedly paternalistic feel, and even though anyone could get in if he or she made the effort, the atmosphere surely drove many away. But if some potential researchers may have been frightened off, the artifacts and manuscripts of the CLC were kept carefully intact; they were safe from theft, from careless patrons, and, more important in the long run, from disbursement into other sections of the DPL. On the fourth floor, the CLC was a clearly autonomous place with a separate identity within the library system. On the second floor, the distinction was less clear.

Along with the open new home on the second floor came a new emphasis on outreach to regular library patrons. Collins and her staff did not simply sit quietly and wait for researchers to come calling. They built elaborate displays and exhibits to draw in the general public and held open forums to discuss environmental politics and topics. Clearly, the mood at the CLC in the 1970s differed dramatically from that of ten years earlier. Staff members dressed more casually, though often in the unfortunate style of the 1970s, and some male employees sported shoulder-length hair, absolutely unheard of in the crew-cut days of Carhart and Eastlick. The rules of decorum were more lax under Collins's leadership as well, and visitors were occasionally treated to loud arguments and open political debate.[81] The atmosphere in the CLC left some critical, or perhaps envious, DPL staff wondering if anyone *was* in charge. Not only were library workers near the CLC area concerned, but Shearouse was beginning to hear stories from some offended CLC staff about a lack of leadership at the CLC.[82] The already strained relationship between Collins and Shearouse deteriorated precipitously during this period and never really recovered. The enmity between the two did not bode well for the future of the Conservation Library.

One of the dilemmas Collins faced during her tenure as head of the CLC was reconciling her commitment to grassroots environmentalism with the need to closely supervise the daily operations and staff. Since Collins was a popular speaker, she spent a great deal of her time traveling to give talks promoting the CLC and environmentalism in general at club meetings, branch libraries, schools, and environmental groups.[83] These engagements meant that she was often away from the library and unable to keep a close watch on the activities of her staff.

When Collins was at the library, she spent her time responding to the huge volume of correspondence the CLC received or personally helping patrons. As soon as she took over, the volume of information requests rose dramatically. "Since Earth Day," Collins told a reporter, "interest has been high." In a letter to Carhart, she added, "The statistics at the Conservation Library have doubled in the last two years. Our staff has not. And as usual, the material keeps coming in at a tremendous rate."[84]

Another factor that contributed to the huge increase in requests for information was the passage of the National Environmental Policy Act (NEPA) of 1969, which stipulated that virtually all major construction projects required an environmental impact statement (EIS) before any work could begin.[85] Suddenly there was a national rush for environmental information. Developers, municipal contractors, and city and state government officials needed help in completing EIS work, and many turned to the Conservation Library.[86] The interest in environmental information at this time was widespread enough to inspire the creation of

Library assistants Bob Junk, left, and Mark Zarn examine CLC's Collection of Forest Service Policy Manuals, February 1973. Denver Public Library, Western History Collection, Conservation Library Collection photos.

Opening day at ECOL: librarian Julia Copland, Sigurd Olson, and library assistant Wendy Adamson, April 16, 1972. Courtesy of Minneapolis Public Library, ECOL papers.

another environmental library in the United States, the Environmental Conservation Library (ECOL) at the Minneapolis Public Library. Founded in 1972 by a group of students, conservationists, librarians, and University of Minnesota faculty, the newer library was remarkably similar to the CLC.[87]

The similarities are not surprising considering that one of the founders of ECOL was Sigurd F. Olson, a Carhart colleague and CLC counselor.[88] Olson was a strong supporter of the CLC and sent a significant percentage of his own papers to Denver. He was, however, never sold on the idea that there should be only one central environmental library. Carhart did such a good job of convincing Olson of the importance of environmental information as the key to successful environmental advocacy that Olson wanted a library in his own backyard. At the opening of ECOL, on April 16, 1972, Olson gave a keynote address to an audience of over five hundred Minnesota environmentalists and supporters. "Wisdom," Olson told the crowd, "is what this environmental library is all about . . . the dissemination of wisdom so that we can meet these battles intelligently, and with a possible chance of winning."[89] Carhart corresponded with Olson about the Minnesota library and urged him to limit his support to the CLC, but Olson saw no problem in supporting both, so convinced was he of the importance of getting information into the hands of those who needed it.[90]

From the very start, because of the timing of its founding, ECOL was a center for Minnesota EIS research and the primary repository for impact statements from the state.[91] ECOL got substantial funding from the state of Minnesota as well as some federal government funding in the form of a $5,000 grant from the U.S. Office of Environmental Education. In addition to amassing a large collection of environmental books and magazines, several thousand by the early 1990s, ECOL also became a repository for the Nuclear Regulatory Commission's public documents.[92] Although mainly a volunteer-run operation, ECOL did have one full-time librarian paid for by the Minneapolis Public Library. Because they were mainly volunteers, the ECOL staff seem to have had an easier time than Collins and her paid staff in integrating activism with library work. The ECOL volunteers were not bound by the politics of the library bureaucracy and were very open about their politics and affiliations with local environmental groups. Like the directors of the CLC, ECOL volunteers worked to present an image of objectivity when dealing with controversial environmental subjects. They were less cautious, however, in making their true loyalties known. Joann Dennis, coordinator of ECOL volunteers in the mid-1970s, took care, one supporter wrote, "not to present moralistic, preachy material, but includes all (?) sides of the issue."[93] The question mark, one assumes, was meant to suggest that obviously there was only one supportable side to environmental issues. By remaining relatively small, with a primarily volunteer staff focused on regional issues, ECOL was apparently able to avoid many of the conflicts that often overwhelmed the CLC. Despite its lower profile and less tumultuous history, ECOL ultimately shared the CLC's fate, as changing politics conspired to undermine this sister project despite the best efforts of local supporters.[94]

Back in Denver, the passage of the NEPA and the new emphasis on EIS research at the Conservation Library marked a significant change in the client base. Prior to 1970, most of the patrons had been academic researchers, amateur environmentalists, and local government and business people. After the passage of the NEPA, the CLC moved to serve individuals and organizations dealing with new federal legislation and federal environmental programs. The shift was subtle at first but gained momentum through the early 1970s. Eventually, the CLC focused on the increasingly complex web of federal environmental legislation and bureaucracy. As a result, it moved farther from the local environmental community that had formed the foundation of its support.

With all these new developments, little time remained for Kay Collins and the CLC staff to think about fund-raising. As the deadline on the five-year development plan came closer, almost nothing had been done to raise private funds. This period was supposed to be the golden opportunity to put the CLC's financial woes to rest once and for all. But Kay Collins was understaffed and overburdened with community obligations. More broadly, Collins and the younger staff who ran the CLC from 1969 to 1975 assumed, quite logically considering the unprecedented support for environmentalism from government agencies, that once they were able to secure funding from the state, it would continue into the foreseeable future. It was unimaginable to them that the government might pull the rug from beneath their feet as long as they were working hard and making progress. They simply thought that when the five years were up, the city and county of Denver, now aware of the important work of the CLC, would extend their budget into the future. They were wrong.

Prior to the announcement of the five-year development plan and the city and county funding appropriation, the CLC, in conjunction with the DPL Foundation, raised more than $100,000 from private foundations in a ten-year period. Between 1970 and 1975, only $35,000 in private grants was secured, and all this money went to cover expanded operating expenses.[95] The DPL Foundation was, according to the development plan, in charge of the fund-raising efforts. But with very little motivation from the leadership of the CLC, it made no attempt to reach the goal of $400,000, which was supposed to fund a permanent endowment fund by 1976.

At the end of the five-year period, the city officially announced that because of serious cutbacks and budget constraints, resulting primarily from the collapse of the oil and shale oil industry in Colorado, the Conservation Library would receive *no* funding from the city and county of Denver after December 31, 1975.[96] Further, Shearouse let the DPL staff know that, barring something extraordinary, the CLC would close permanently at that time, and the manuscripts, artifacts, and books would go to other departments within the DPL system.

The cuts in the CLC budget were part of a systemwide belt-tightening in the wake of massive municipal budget cuts. General library hours were shortened, DPL staff were laid off by the dozens, library hours were reduced, and services were sharply curtailed. Regardless of any support for the CLC within the DPL system, there was no chance that the funding of the previous five years could continue. Kay Collins was stunned. "The announcement to close the Conservation Library came as a great shock to me and the staff," she wrote. "When we heard about it in the open staff meeting we were all extremely upset."[97] Obviously, the DPL administration knew what was coming but did not feel obligated to inform Collins or any of the other CLC staff, yet another sign of the depth of the split between Collins and Shearouse.

In the wake of the announcement, Collins frantically wrote to friends and CLC counselors, trying to get support for continued funding. In southern California, Arthur Carhart fearfully viewed the events unfolding back at the CLC. He wrote embittered letters to Shearouse threatening to remove his materials and send them to the University of Iowa.[98] Small boxes containing reel-to-reel tapes arrived weekly from Carhart. On the tapes he sounded old and frail, his ghostly voice a plaintive plea for the significance of a life's work whose meaning appeared less assured in the confusion following the funding announcement.[99] The recordings and letters were carefully answered by Shearouse, who tried to convince the worried Carhart that nothing was going to happen to the CLC, and that his materials and hard work were still safe and secure at the Denver Public Library.[100] When Shearouse talked about the safety of the collections, he thought that even if they were not in one centralized place, they would still be part of the DPL. This situation, however, was what Carhart had feared all along: that somehow the CLC might be absorbed into the vortex of the DPL bureaucracy, never to surface again. Shearouse's letters did little to calm Carhart's fears, which were even more obvious in his correspondence with Kay Collins. After one such letter, she asked him to "just relax and take it easy." His frantic concern was not making her position any easier.[101]

In a desperate attempt to respond to this crisis, Collins and the supporters of the CLC formed the Conservation Library Advisory Committee (CLAC) to try to save the library from "extinction."[102] Significantly, CLAC was housed at the Rocky Mountain Center on Environment, a private environmental group organized by Ed Hilliard shortly before his death. Since Collins did not trust anyone within the DPL system, she reached out to the local environmental community instead. CLAC printed a brochure outlining the problem and mailed it to CLC supporters and counselors around the country. The title proclaimed, "The Conservation Library of the Denver Public Library, 1960–197?" Recipients of the brochure were asked to immediately send tax-deductible donations. "UNLESS your contribution is received NOW," the bold print screamed, "the Conservation Library will be closed."[103] Meanwhile, the advisory group established the Conservation Library Society to help raise funds.[104] Memberships in this organization ranged from a student rate of $5 to the donor category starting at $250. Members received a wildlife print "suitable for framing" and were entitled to discounts at a proposed lecture series sponsored by the Conservation Library Society. A second part of the plan to rescue the library involved a unique attempt to charge patrons for their use of the CLC. The service fee was $25 per half hour; students with a valid ID were charged only $15 per half hour. All computer and other services required an additional charge.[105]

The response to the brochure was gratifying. Hundreds of letters poured into the CLC from users upset about the impending closure. "I think that especially in our bicentennial year," one user wrote, "we should place greater emphasis upon preserving the quality of life that is left to us. The closing of the Conservation Library is in direct opposition to this feeling."[106] Many of the letters stressed the importance of the CLC as an unbiased resource for people searching for answers to difficult environmental questions during a period of great change. "Perhaps most importantly," wrote Joan Martin of the Thorne Ecological Institute, "no one has the unbiased credibility that the Conservation Library has. . . . there is no current institution or mechanism that could take its place."[107] The show of support was impressive. The letters came from a wide variety of users around the nation and demonstrated that the CLC was truly accomplishing a great deal despite ongoing managerial and financial problems.

As a result of this desperate attempt to save the CLC, the city and county of Denver and the DPL issued a temporary reprieve. The deadline for closure was pushed back to December 1976, and the CLC was given an $8,000 budget for the rest of the year. The money came along with a warning that nothing else was forthcoming. The CLC needed to secure outside funding from that point forward. This news gave Collins some breathing room but was not terribly encouraging. The idea of raising money by charging fees met with serious skepticism from many in the DPL and anger from the Denver community. Charging for services at a public library proved very unpopular with tax-paying library patrons. Nonetheless, the plan raised enough money to keep the library alive while alternatives were explored.

One of Collins's strongest arguments focused on the CLC's reputation as an unbiased and politically neutral meeting place for all sides of controversial issues. By 1976, the tenuous spirit of cooperation between business leaders, conservationists, preservationists, environmentalists, and prominent citizens in Colorado had all but vaporized. Antienvironmental activists began to borrow the grassroots organizing techniques of the wilderness movement and slowly began to regain power in western states.[108] Former allies gradually drifted apart. The conservation movement was always a coalition of shifting interests built around contingent situations. During the mid-1970s, the coalition began to dissolve.[109] The rural hunters and fishers who had played key roles in the conservation victories of the 1950s and the wilderness fight of the early 1960s clashed with the increasingly radical organized environmental movement.[110] By 1976, Carhart's rancher buddies had little in common with Boulderites whose vegetarian or environmentalist views were shaped by Francis Moore

Lappé's *Diet for a Small Planet*. New environmental issues and a changing political climate contributed to shifting demographics for the environmental movement.[111]

Environmental issues were a central concern for millions of Americans by 1976. In Colorado, concern about the environment was running at an all-time high. The debate over environmental issues, however, was degenerating into an acrimonious cycle of stalemates and gridlock. Despite this climate of distrust and antagonism, all sides of the environmental debate generally agreed that the CLC was a valuable resource and should be maintained. Commenting about the possibility of the library's closure, Linda Grace of the mining division of W. R. Grace and Company stated, "Given the potential resource development in the west with all of its many problems, the Conservation Library becomes more important as a source of unbiased information."[112] Collins tried to make the most of the perception of the CLC as a neutral meeting place, even recruiting Olin Webb of the Colorado Association of Commerce and Industry as a spokesman for the CLC. "In the past dozen years many of the old ways of doing business have been forced to change due to an emerging cornucopia of new environmental rules and regulations." The Conservation Library, he continued, "has become that source of environmental information essential to both business and business consultants . . . required to [survive] in business."[113] Despite Collins's success in generating strong endorsements from across the political spectrum, DPL administrators did not budge in their decision to stop all funding to the CLC. Endorsements such as those from Webb and Grace did little to convince Shearouse that Collins and her staff were not using the library to further their own liberal political agendas. By 1976, it was clear that no matter what Collins did, she and the CLC were on their own and possibly on their way out.

CONCLUSION

When the dust settled in mid-1976, Kay Collins found herself in charge of a temporarily floundering institution. All the promise of her early career and dreams for the future of the CLC lay in tatters around her. With many of the staff laid off, she spent several weeks virtually alone in the suddenly forlorn and eerily quiet CLC. As the country celebrated its bicentennial, there seemed to be little chance that the Conservation Library would survive into the next decade.

With hindsight, it is clear that Collins and the Conservation Library were caught up in an atmosphere of changing politics and ideological realignment. The environmental movement was evolving in many significant ways. Conservation organizations grew immensely in the late 1960s and early 1970s. Most opened or expanded offices in Washington, D.C., and made litigation, lobbying, and national fund-raising their primary focus. The grassroots emphasis of the conservation movement shifted toward new groups and new goals as bureaucratization and professionalization became the themes of the large established environmental organizations. At the same time, new grassroots coalitions formed to address local issues they felt the national groups were ignoring. As the head of the CLC during this tumultuous time, Kay Collins searched for ways to reconcile the grassroots heritage of the library with the structural changes in the environmental movement.

This period of change is often portrayed as a time of polarization, of blundering people taking unreasonably extreme positions. But, as the next chapter in the history of the CLC demonstrates, the story is more complicated. Collins and others in the environmental movement built on the grassroots traditions of the previous generation while looking to new technologies, new constituencies, and new funding strategies to move forward, simultaneously addressing the pressing social issues of the day. Many of the CLC's supporters viewed the funding crisis of the mid-1970s as evidence of the failure of the new generation to continue the traditions of the old. Why, they wondered, had Collins failed to capitalize on the five-year plan and generate new corporate and private funding? The funding crisis was, without question, a serious setback for the CLC. Still, it hardly signaled the end of the library or the failure of the new generation. As we shall see, the transformation of the CLC in the 1970s was a logical evolution within the context of the times, and ultimately Collins's change in focus proved far more successful than anyone had ever imagined.

In the aftermath of the 1975 funding crisis, Collins realized that, to survive, the CLC needed to capitalize on the growing popularity and support for environmentalism. More important, she understood that for the project of environmentalism to succeed, environmentalists would have to push the boundaries of information technology and move away from the antimodernism of previous generations. To do this, the CLC needed to dip into the vast new reserves of federal environmental agency money available from the Carter administration. In the coming years, Collins succeeded in arranging a marriage between the CLC and the federal government. This new partnership, which was the culmination of Carhart's dream of direct federal support, brought more money and more notoriety to the CLC than ever before. It also entailed significant bureaucratic responsibilities that threatened to obscure the original goals of the CLC and overwhelm Collins and the staff with red tape and paperwork. Most important, this new relationship with the federal government created an opportunity to transform the CLC from a museum of antimodernist thought into a laboratory for postscarcity environmentalism and alternative technology.

CHAPTER SIX

Soft Tech and Hard Facts

I like to think (and
the sooner the better!)
of a cybernetic meadow
where mammals and computers
live together in mutually
programming harmony
like pure water
touching clear sky

I like to think
(right now, please!)
of a cybernetic forest
filled with pines and electronics
where deer stroll peacefully
past computers
as if they were flowers
with spinning blossoms

I like to think
(it has to be!)
of a cybernetic ecology
where we are free of our labors
and joined back to nature,
returned to our mammal
brothers and sisters,
and all watched over
by machines of loving grace

Richard Brautigan, "All Watched
Over by Machines of Loving
Grace" (1967)

The shuffling of papers and hum of activity in the United States Senate chambers never seem to stop. The morning of September 26, 1980, was no different. Few noticed when a presidential secretary dropped a typed message from the president on the desk of Senator Howell Heflin of Alabama.[1] The report that landed on Heflin's desk that morning, the proceedings of the White House Conference on Libraries and Information

Sciences, was one of thousands required by the Washington bureaucracy, a minor report on yet another meeting. Still, it was a remarkable document in the history of the Conservation Library. In the report, President Jimmy Carter explained that libraries were the key to the nation's future environmental health and prosperity. The report was read into the record that morning in the Senate chambers as a matter of routine, with no comment. Even if the members of the Senate had noticed the delivery of the presidential message on libraries, few would have cared; relations between President Carter and Congress had reached an all-time low. Many Democrats no longer looked to Carter for leadership, and Republicans had long dismissed the hayseed from Georgia.

Four years earlier, Carter had ridden into the White House on his "outsider" status and high-minded rhetoric. For many Americans, Carter's dedication to morality in government seemed like a breath of fresh air after the tainted Nixon administration. His unprecedented walk through Washington after his inauguration seemed to confirm that with Carter in the White House, it would not be "business as usual." But the down-to-earth naïveté that voters found comforting irritated and ultimately alienated Carter from the Washington establishment and from many in his own party. Early on, it appeared that America was in for a rough ride with Carter at the wheel.[2]

Environmental issues became a focal point for animosity toward Carter early in his administration. Carter brought some strong ideas about the environment to the presidency. He appointed environmentalists to key positions and launched a campaign against costly reclamation projects that he believed wasted tax money and threatened America's landscape.[3] Carter appointees Gus Speth, who headed the Council on Environmental Quality, and Secretary of State Edmund Muskie worked to create the "Global 2000" report, a landmark study that evaluated global trends in population and environmental quality and projected how long-term trends in the international economy might play out in the future.[4] The bleak report seemed only to confirm that despite twenty years of intense environmental advocacy, America and the world were no nearer to any real solution to the environmental crisis.[5]

Although on paper Carter proved a friend of the environmental movement, he had a difficult time persuading Congress to support his ideas. Plagued with a serious economic downturn, one of the worst foreign policy nightmares of the postwar years, and an unprecedented energy crisis, Carter had his hands full. Still, he did try to champion environmental causes and was particularly supportive of creative links between the federal government, state and local agencies, and environmental groups and organizations. The paper that appeared on Senator Heflin's desk in September 1980, the "Report of the White House Conference on Libraries and

Information Sciences," outlined Carter's ideas about the role of libraries in shaping America's environmental future and the conclusions of the conference. "Since the beginning of our Nation," he wrote, "libraries have played an important role in providing citizens with the information they need to guide our destiny."[6] For Carter and the participants in the White House conference, libraries, as established information delivery centers, were a key part of the solution to increasingly complex environmental problems.

The Carter administration was not the only group beginning to think hard about the significance of the information revolution for environmentalism. By the late 1970s, a new generation of environmentalists and their organizations began to recognize links between explosive growth in new technologies and environmental activism. Many environmentalists began to eschew the technophobia of the postwar conservation and wilderness movements and look to new "appropriate technologies" and "soft-tech" renewable energy technologies as empowering tools for future activism.[7] Most notably, Stewart Brand and the staff of the *Whole Earth Catalog* and its successor, *Coevolution Quarterly*, began to graphically illustrate the connections between environmentalism, communications technology, and computers.[8] Brand started *Whole Earth* as a "movable education" for his counterculture friends "who were reconsidering the structure of modern life and building their own communes in the backwoods." Later, Brand and his followers were convinced that access to information and energy technology was a vital part of changing cultural perceptions that contributed to environmental decay.[9]

Although President Carter and his environmental advisers were coming from a very different point of view than the counterculture crew at *Whole Earth*, they were nonetheless moving in similar directions. Both hoped that expanded access to information might lead toward an environmentally sound future. In his endorsement of public libraries as centers of environmental information and environmental advocacy, Carter singled out the Conservation Library. The Conservation Library, Carter stated, "is an example of a library that is working closely with several agencies to make consumer and environmental information available. I encourage and support cooperation like this."[10] Starting in 1978, the Conservation Library and the Department of Energy worked together to create a ten-state Rocky Mountain regional environmental information network.[11] The agreement meant that the government agencies involved could utilize the resources and connections of the CLC to fill their information services needs.

For Kay Collins, Henry Shearouse, and the staff of the Denver Public Library, this lucrative partnership with the federal government meant that the CLC was snatched from the brink of collapse. In 1977, the Conservation Library was transformed into the Regional Energy/Environment Information Center (REEIC). With these changes, Kay Collins became the head of a well-funded regional institution with a newly expanded staff and the resources of the Department of Energy at her disposal. Once again the CLC received an eleventh-hour reprieve, and the transformation of the library from antimodernist museum to alternative technology laboratory began. This remarkable transformation was indicative of larger social and political changes within the American environmental movement. One of the most significant aspects of the change was the relationship between an evolving environmentalism and an explosive counterculture politics.

COUNTERCULTURE ENVIRONMENTALISM

There is strong evidence that by the mid-1970s there was a new group of environmental activists who were distinctly different from the previous generation and are best described as "counterculture environmentalists."[12] Counterculture environmentalism simultaneously encompassed both primitivism and technological innovation. Nowhere is this apparent contradiction more visible than in the pages of the *Whole Earth Catalog*, where primitive woodstoves and survivalist supplies for counterculture neo-Luddites share the page with personal computers, geodesic domes, and oscilloscopes. Inside the covers of the *Whole Earth Catalog*, just as in the equally eclectic collections of the Conservation Library, the neatly bipolar world of twentieth-century environmental politics becomes a messy mélange of seemingly incongruous philosophies and goals.

The relationship between the counterculture, technology, and the environment is complex. While this chapter relies on terms like "counterculture environmental movement," it would be a mistake to assume that all of those who considered themselves counterculturalists and environmentalists thought or acted alike. Even among those who rejected antimodernism and advocated the use of technology to solve environmental problems, there was rarely a clear program of action or thought. Often, it seemed as if countercultural environmentalists occupied separate but parallel universes defined by whether they considered technology to be the problem or the solution. Thus the relationship between the counterculture and technology was always one of fundamental ambivalence. Just as in the counterculture in general, counterculture environmentalists never constructed a unified philosophy that united like-minded individuals and organizations under one banner. They were instead a diverse group with a wide variety of perspectives, often pursuing opposed or mutually exclusive projects. Nevertheless, what differentiated counterculture environmentalists from

Clard Svenson of the Drop City Commune in southern Colorado stands in the nearly completed geodesic "theater for psychedelics," August 6, 1967. Denver Public Library, Western History Collection, Conservation Library Collection photos.

other environmental activists in the 1960s and 1970s was a shared desire to use environmental research, new technologies, ecological thinking, and environmental advocacy to shape a social revolution based on alternative lifestyles and communities, alternatives that would enable future generations to live in harmony with each other and the environment. The transformation of the CLC into the REEIC perfectly captures the enthusiasm and ambivalence that accompanied integration of a counterculture sensibility with environmentalism.[13]

The technology debate in the environmental movement dates to the beginnings of the nineteenth-century industrial revolution. While some Americans looked at advances in science and technology with a wary eye, many tended to view technology as beneficial and benign. This was particularly true for a generation of Progressive conservation advocates who believed that rational planning, expert management, science, and technology were the keys to perpetual abundance. From amateur conservation advocacy groups to the utilitarian U.S. Forest Service of Gifford Pinchot, American conservation advocates looked to science for solutions to waste and wanton destruction of scarce natural resources. For the better part of the twentieth century, most resource conservation advocacy grew from the notion that through science and the march of progress, humans could tame and control all elements of the natural world, stopping waste and maximizing productivity. This type of thinking inspired massive reclamation and irrigation projects and experiments with chemicals to rid the world of unwanted pests and predators. A steadfast faith in technology and the scientific worldview prevailed well into the 1950s.[14]

Despite this widespread faith in science, an early split between utilitarian conservationists and holistic preservationists characterized the rise of environmental advocacy in America. In contrast to conservationists, preservationists consistently rejected utilitarian and technological solutions. In the early decades of the twentieth century, John Muir, Aldo Leopold, Robert Marshall, and other preservationists worked to develop more ecologically sound alternatives to what they perceived as the materialism and hubris of the conservationists. This perceptive minority looked closely at the impact of unchecked industrial development on the environment, including attempts to regulate and conserve. For them, the technological advances of the modern world seemed anything but benign.

Intellectuals from a variety of backgrounds and ideological perspectives joined these preservationists in their distrust of modern industrial society and technological quick fixes for complex environmental problems. From the mid–nineteenth century on, a disparate collection of utopians, anarchists, back-to-the-landers, and antimodernists all contributed to a growing subcurrent in American culture aimed at rethinking the relationship between technology, society, and the environment. But through World War II, these voices of dissent remained a distinct minority.[15] The vast majority of Americans, including most conservation proponents, remained dedicated to the ideal of progress achieved through science and technology.

In the decades following World War II, attitudes toward technology gradually began to change. While never constituting a mainstream trend, more Americans began to question the dominant view of technology and progress. A catalyst for this reevaluation was the horrifying devastation caused by use of the atomic bomb in Japan. Once the patriotic fervor surrounding the end of the war subsided, many conservationists and intellectuals started discussing the environmental consequences of the godlike power of atomic weapons. Books like John Hersey's *Hiroshima*, first published in 1946, graphically depicted the awesome destructive power of nuclear weapons and inspired a growing segment of society to recognize the far-reaching implications of such technology.[16] Likewise, after years of turning out pro-war propaganda films, Hollywood, along with a legion of science fiction writers in the 1950s, started producing a steady stream of films and books that presented horrifying visions of technology run amok. A generation of Americans born after World War II grew up watching giant nuclear ants or other such mutants of technology destroying humanity in movies such as Gordon Douglas's *Them!* (1954). During the 1950s, there was a widening sense of genuine terror over the evil potential of science without a social conscience. By the mid-1960s, a growing segment of American society, particularly young Americans, evidenced an increasing ambivalence about technology. Arthur Carhart, along with many older members of the conservation movement, also found themselves increasingly alienated from the world of modern atomic science, massive reclamation projects, and postwar consumer technology. As the previous chapters demonstrate, within the conservation movement there was a growing ambivalence toward technology, which for many quickly grew into full-fledged antimodernism predicated on technophobia. For Carhart and his generation of conservationists, solutions for the future were found in the past. Nearing the end of their careers, this generation felt that Americans needed to remember simpler times, forsake technocracy, and rediscover nature. While their rhetoric was often strident, Carhart and his colleagues, in keeping with the Progressive spirit, were mainly aiming for compromise between technological progress and environmental protection.

Other critics of postwar society, including a growing contingent of more radical environmental preservationists and a group of prominent European and American intellectuals, were less inclined to search for compromise and more willing to propose far-reaching structural changes. The most stunning of these critiques came from biologist Rachel Carson, whose explosive *Silent Spring*, published in 1962, explained in frightening detail the ecological consequences of humanity's attempt to control and regulate the environment.[17] Carson became the first of many to warn of an impending environmental crisis. During the 1960s, a series of influential books warned of an apocalyptic future if the present course was not altered. One of Carson's fellow biologists, Barry Commoner, produced several best-sellers, including *The Closing Circle*, warning of the dangers of sacrificing the health of the planet for temporary material gain.[18]

Three other writers also provided inspiration for a new generation of Americans who were questioning the role of technology in the creation of social, economic, and environmental injustice. Jacques Ellul's *The Technological Society* asserted that "all-embracing technological systems had swallowed up the capitalistic and socialistic economies" and were the greatest threat to freedom in the modern world.[19] Ellul argued that there was "something abominable in the modern artifice itself." The system was so corrupted that only a truly revolutionary reorientation could stop social and environmental decay.[20] Like Ellul, Herbert Marcuse, in his popular *One Dimensional Man*, described a vast, repressive world technological structure that overshadowed national borders and traditional political ideologies.[21] Marcuse popularized the insights of the Frankfurt school of Marxian philosophers and sociologists.[22] Together he and Ellul provided a critical intellectual framework for Americans looking to construct alternatives to the scientific worldview.

Perhaps the most influential of the structural critics of technological society was Lewis Mumford, who began his career as a public intellectual as a strong proponent of science and technology. His 1934 classic, *Technics and Civilization*, influenced a generation and strengthened the popular belief that technology was moving human civilization toward a new golden age.[23] Like most Progressive thinkers of the industrial period, Mumford envisioned a modern world where technology helped correct the chaos of nature and brought balance to ecology. In *Technics*, he extolled the virtues of the machine and painted a positive picture of how technology could reshape the world to eliminate drudgery and usher in an unprecedented period in history where machines and nature worked together for human benefit. But this prophet of the machine age began to rethink his position in the 1960s. Like Marcuse and Ellul, Mumford became increasingly alarmed about the power of large technological systems. As he looked around at the world of the 1960s and 1970s, he worried that the ascendancy of the "megamachine" boded ill for human society.[24] The "machine," once the symbol of progress toward a more balanced world, began to emerge as a metaphor for describing a seemingly out-of-control capitalist system.[25]

The preoccupation with technology and its consequences became one of the central features of 1960s social and environmental movements, and of the counterculture in particular. In 1968, Theodore Roszak released his influential study of the youth movement, *The Making of a Counter Culture*. [26] Roszak maintained that the counterculture was a direct reaction to "technocracy," which he defined as a "society in which those who govern justify themselves by appeal to technical experts, who in turn justify themselves by appeals to scientific forms of knowledge."[27] The counterculture radicals of the 1960s, Roszak argued, were the only group in America capable of divorcing themselves from the stranglehold of 1950s technology and its insidious centralizing tendencies. Roszak's position on technocracy was similar to those of Ellul and Marcuse. For Roszak the most appealing characteristic of the counterculture was its rejection of technology and the systems it spawned. Charles Reich, in his best-seller *The Greening of America* (1970), also highlighted the youth movement's rejection of technology as a fundamental component of the counterculture ideology.[28] For both Reich and Roszak, what was evil about technocracy was its bureaucratic organization and complexity. From the perspective of these authors and a growing segment of the younger generation, the problem with America was that there was nothing small, nothing simple, nothing remaining on a human scale.

This mind-boggling bigness and bureaucratization likewise concerned British economist E. F. Schumacher, whose popular book *Small Is Beautiful* (1973) became a model for decentralized humanistic economics "as if people mattered."[29] Of all the structural critiques of technological systems, Schumacher's provided the best model for constructive action and was particularly influential in shaping an emerging counterculture environmentalism. Unlike more pessimistic critics of the modern technocracy, Schumacher provided assurance that by striving to regain individual control of economics and environments, "our landscapes [could] become healthy and beautiful again and our people . . . regain the dignity of man, who knows himself as higher than the animal but never forgets that *noblesse oblige*."[30] The key to Schumacher's vision was an enlightened adaptation of technology. In *Small Is Beautiful*, Schumacher highlighted what he called "intermediate technologies," those technical advances that stand "halfway between traditional and modern technology," as the solution to the dissonance between nature and technology in the modern world.[31] These technologies could be as simple as using modern materials to construct better windmills or more efficient portable water turbines for developing nations. The key to "intermediate technologies" was to apply advances in science to specific local communities and ecosystems. Schumacher's ideas were quickly picked up and expanded upon by a wide range of individuals and organizations, often with wildly different agendas, who came together under the banner of a loosely defined ideology that became known as "appropriate technology."

Appropriate technology emerged as a popular cause at a conference on technological needs for lesser-developed nations held in England in 1968.[32] For individuals and organizations concerned with the plight of developing nations, Schumacher's ideas about intermediate technologies seemed to provide a possible solution to the problem of how to promote a more equitable distribution of wealth while avoiding the inherent environmental and social problems of industrialization.[33] Appropriate technology quickly became a catchall for a wide spectrum of activities involving research into older technologies that had been lost after the industrial revolution and the development of new high- and low-tech small-scale innovations. The most striking thing about the move toward appropriate technology, according to historian Samuel Hays, was "not so much the mechanical devices themselves as the kinds of knowledge and management they implied." Appropriate technology represented a move away from the Progressive faith in expertise and professionalization and toward an environmental philosophy predicated on self-education and individual experience. [34]

The appropriate technology movement was also bolstered by ideas emerging from the New Left. Particularly influential were the writings of ecoanarchist Murray Bookchin, who situated the quest for alternative technologies within the framework of revolutionary New Left politics. In books such as *Our Synthetic Environment* (1962) and *Post-scarcity Anarchism* (1971), he argued that highly industrialized nations possessed the potential to create a utopian "ecological society, with new ecotechnologies, and ecocommunities."[35] From this perspective the notion of scarcity, a defining fear of the conservation movement, was a ruse perpetuated by "hierarchical society" in an attempt to keep the majority from understanding the revolutionary potentialities of advanced technology. More than most New Left critics, Bookchin also clearly linked revolutionary politics with environmentalism and technology. "Whether now or in the future," he wrote, "human relationships with nature are always mediated by science, technology and knowledge."[36] By explicitly fusing radical politics and ecology, New Left critics provided a model for a distinctly counterculture environmentalism. From the perspective of the New Left, pollution and environmental destruction were not simply a matter of avoidable waste but also symptoms of a corrupt economic system that consistently stripped both the environment and the average citizen of rights and resources.

Although the utopian program of Bookchin and the New Left ultimately failed to capture the hearts of most environmentalists, it did help establish a permanent relationship for many between environmental and social politics. This linking of the social, political, and environmental in the 1970s paved the way for new trends of the 1980s such as the environmental justice movement. For inner-city African-Americans and others who felt alienated from predominantly white middle-class environmental groups such as the Sierra Club or the Wilderness Society, the New Left vision of environmental politics provided inspiration. By connecting ecological thinking with a set of social politics, the New Left introduced environmentalism to a new and more diverse group of urban Americans who had felt little connection to the wilderness- and recreation-based advocacy of the conservation movement.

At the same time, the New Left helped bolster the growing technological fascination of many counterculture environmentalists. The appropriate technology movement represented a different direction for radical politics in the late 1960s and into the 1970s. By then the campus-based New Left was primarily a movement against the Vietnam War. New Left politics on college and university campuses focused on striking back at the Pentagon, IBM, AT&T, Dow Chemical Company, and other representatives of the technocratic power structure. Escalating violence, renewed scarcity fears, and a host of pressures both inside and outside the campus-based movement caused the New Left to fracture and ultimately collapse. Disillusioned by the failure of the revolution, many counterculturalists began to move away from radical politics. At the same time, proponents of appropriate technology in Europe and America were taking New Left–inspired politics in some different and unconventional directions. Individuals such as Stewart Brand (a former member of Ken Kesey's Merry Pranksters) and Kay Collins and organizations such as the CLC, ECOL, and the New Alchemy Institute began working to create an alternative society from the ground up by adapting science and technology for the people.

By the early 1970s, the neo-Luddites and antimodernists in the American environmental movement had ceded ground to a growing number of appropriate technologists. This new group of counterculture radicals, environmentalists, scientists, and social activists looked to new modes of protest that recognized the liberating power of decentralized individualistic technology. The CLC/REEIC, ECOL, and other public information projects fit perfectly with this new sensibility.

While appropriate technology was widely embraced as a new form of environmentalism, there was little consensus about what it was or should be. The appropriate technology movement was varied and diffuse, with much disagreement even among its adherents over how to define their ideology. The term meant different things to different groups, but broadly most agreed that an "appropriate" technology had the following features: "low investment cost per work-place, low capital investment per unit of output, organizational simplicity, high adaptability to a particular social or cultural environment, sparing use of natural resources, low cost of final product or high potential for employment."[37] In other words, an appropriate technology was cheap, simple, and ecologically safe. The proponents of appropriate technology also agreed on the basic idea that alternative technologies could be used to create more self-sufficient lifestyles and new social structures based on democratic control of innovation and communitarian anarchism. For supporters of appropriate technology, the most radical action one could take against the status quo was not throwing bombs or staging sit-ins but fabricating wind generators to unplug from the grid.

The move toward appropriate technology represented a significant break for the environmental movement. For younger environmentalists such as Kay Collins, the appropriate technology movement justified her project and elevated the mundane work of information management and dissemination to the highest calling of a vibrant social movement. Along with other young environmentalists, Collins and her colleagues in the Colorado environmental movement built on the ideas of Schumacher, Bookchin, Marcuse, and others to craft a very different political agenda from that of their technophobic predecessors. Access to environmental information and new green technologies became a valued commodity for counterculture environmentalists. *The Whole Earth Catalog* sold in the millions, and the CLC/REEIC moved to the forefront of a short-lived revolution in environmental information.

WITH STRINGS ATTACHED

One of the ironies of the new shift in the environmental movement in the 1970s was that it often required partnerships with the very federal bureaucracies that so infuriated counterculture critics. At the CLC the federal government partnership solved the immediate funding crisis but also raised many questions. During the 1970s, the Conservation Library, like many environmental institutions and advocacy groups, particularly those focused on alternative technology, established close ties with the Washington power structure and federal government agencies. This new relationship was a two-edged sword. On the one hand, it increased the political clout of environmentalists and gave them an unprecedented voice in the process of crafting environmental legislation and shaping federal environmental programs. It also provided a level of funding that was simply inconceivable without government support. In the case of the CLC, this funding provided virtually all the operating expenses and enabled Kay Collins to utilize the newest information technologies and to dramatically expand the constituency of the library. In fact, the linkage with the federal government made it possible for the Conservation Library to fulfill the promise of the early days and become a truly national center for environmental advocacy.

On the other hand, the marriage of the CLC to the federal agencies came with many strings attached. Federal government contracts specified how money could be spent and created a host of new responsibilities and tasks for the library staff. The specific focus on energy, law, and government program information moved the library farther and farther away from the original goal of constructing an archive with a foundation of manuscripts for amateur researchers. At the same time, this new relationship provided the means and the motivation to move the CLC closer than ever before to the pulse of contemporary environmental thought and action.

For a brief moment, the Conservation Library became a model for cutting-edge environmental advocacy and a leader in the appropriate technology and soft-path energy movement, a bustling center of activity where new ideas and new technologies for solving America's environmental crisis flowed freely. The reincarnation of the CLC as the REEIC proved to be short-lived, a final burst of energy before the big Reagan surprise conspired to temporarily end the dream. Although this last stage of the story of the CLC was brief, only three short years, it raises significant questions about the transformation of environmental thought in the late 1970s.

Histories of the post–World War II American environmental movement generally describe the transformation of environmental politics from a primarily local and amateur concern into a national movement represented by large professional and bureaucratic organizations. In fact, most historians view this shift as the most significant change in environmental politics after the 1960s. To some extent, the story of the CLC supports this argument. In the late 1970s, the Conservation Library was transformed from a primarily local, grassroots institution into a wing of a growing federal environmental bureaucracy.

The shift from local and amateur conservation to national and professional environmentalism is significant and worth the careful consideration it has received. Still, environmentalism was built on a constantly changing foundation of shifting imperatives, divergent goals, and unforeseen contingencies. Part of the problem with the traditional model of the environmental movement since the 1960s is the reliance on a bipolar model of change. As the example of the Conservation Library shows, there were many trends and agendas moving environmental advocacy in several directions at once. Ultimately the more interesting shift in American environmentalism, as epitomized by the transformation of the CLC into the REEIC, involved a subtle ideological change from an antimodernist juxtaposition of the unnatural versus the natural (technology versus wilderness) toward a postscarcity acceptance of appropriate technology, especially advances in computer and information technology, plus the realization that in the world of the late twentieth century preserving the environment meant expanding the boundaries of human awareness and embracing "that fearful brightness" that had so terrified Carhart and Eastlick.[38] For Collins and others like Stewart Brand, the "brightness" of the future and technology were not necessarily frightening; they could be comforting, like the warm glow of a computer screen linked to a world-wide web of information where counterculture pioneers could work to create a new world order.

There was, in the 1970s, a dawning realization that an informational "cyberecosystem" could more intimately link humans with each other and the world around them and help foster environmental awareness and social change. In the 1970s, technology suddenly became the friend, not the enemy, of many environmentalists. Computers, complex solar systems, geothermal and nuclear reactors (for some), and telecommunications and personal computers moved to the vanguard of environmentalist thought and action, while wilderness and forest history faded to the background. A new postscarcity perspective that ran toward technology, not away from it, joined the antimodernist strain of thought that dominated environmental thinking from the late 1800s right through the 1960s. There were still plenty of antitechnology environmentalists, and there was no consensus within the new movement about which technologies were acceptable and which were not. Also, the appropriate technology and soft-tech movements shared many of the same criticisms of modern industrial society with the antimodernists. Nevertheless, there was clearly something new in the air in the 1970s, and the Conservation Library was briefly at the center of a changing movement.[39]

DOWN THE SOFT PATH

The transformation of the CLC into the Regional Energy/Environment Information Center began with the energy crisis of the 1970s. This crisis spawned a heightened awareness of energy and environmental problems and led to the formation of several new, well-funded federal environmental agencies. Support for government agency development grew after the Arab oil embargo in the winter of 1973 and 1974 brought environmental problems home to millions of Americans.[40] It was hard to deny an energy crisis after sitting in a gas line for six or seven hours. Many people grasped for the first time the idea that America's seemingly limitless natural resources, such as petroleum, were finite and exhaustible. As concern over the depth of American dependence on foreign oil sparked searches for alternative sources of energy at home, the issue of energy quickly became politically charged. Environmentalists chided

President Gerald Ford for his slow response to the crisis, and energy became a key issue in the 1976 presidential election. Carter's promise to
make energy a priority gained him the support of America's environmentalists and the millions of average Americans who were shocked into
action by the Arab oil embargo.[41]

After the election, Carter set out to fulfill his promise to do something about the energy crisis. His rhetoric was forceful and uncompromising. "The energy shortage is permanent," he warned. "Live thriftily
and remember the importance of helping our neighbors."[42] Carter was
open to the exploration of alternative energy sources like shale oil, solar
power, wind energy, and geothermal power. When he took office, he began lobbying for the creation of a Department of Energy to administer
federal support for alternative energy exploration and to develop conservation programs. This new agency was a direct descendant of the Manhattan Project that would also manage the nation's nuclear capabilities
and problems, as well as conventional power sources like fossil fuels. Although Carter encouraged environmentalists with his strongly favorable
rhetoric about alternative energy and conservation, his actions did not
speak as loudly as his words.

Carter's political naïveté virtually ensured difficulty in shepherding
his energy and environmental legislation through a reluctant Congress.
When the president's energy program passed in 1978, it was greatly modified and included huge concessions to the major oil corporations. Nuclear energy was emphasized over more benign renewable alternative
sources favored by environmentalists.[43] Still, the DOE was created and
became a more efficient mechanism for dealing with energy issues than
the web of often conflicting agencies that had previously fulfilled that
role. All of these national developments had profound consequences for
the Conservation Library.

During the first year of the Carter administration, several federal energy agencies searched for new ways to disseminate information about
energy and the environment to the general public. The federal Non-nu-
clear Energy Research and Development Act of 1974 (P.L. 93-577), the Energy Reorganization Act of 1974 (P.L. 93-438), and the Energy Policy and
Conservation Act (P.L. 94-163) all mandated cooperation among federal
agencies to work toward solving the energy crisis.[44] In the spring of 1977,
representatives from the Environmental Protection Agency (EPA), the Energy Research and Development Administration, the Department of the
Interior, the Department of Commerce, and the Office of Heath, Education, and Welfare met and conceived the idea for a series of regional information centers.[45] Earlier that year, John Green, a regional administrator
of the EPA, approached the DPL about some type of a cooperative
arrangement between the agency and the Conservation Library.[46] Green

and others were familiar with the CLC and thought it might be the perfect solution to their information needs. The library also provided a ready opportunity to fulfill the cooperative mandate of the 1974 energy acts.[47]

An agreement was reached in June 1977, and the Conservation Library officially became the Regional Energy/Environment Information Center (REEIC). In August 1977, a ten-state energy and information conference was held in Denver to celebrate the opening of the REEIC. Governor Richard Lamm of Colorado addressed the crowd of 150 librarians, energy officials and experts, and federal agency heads from the Rocky Mountain West. The world was at a "hinge of history," he told the crowd. "New habits and mores and ways of dealing with things are being born."[48] Lamm was pleased that one of the new ways of dealing with things was right in his backyard.

Under the new agreement with the DOE, the REEIC was fully funded by the five federal agencies, the state of Colorado, and the city and county of Denver. The large government contracts, with big promises of more to come, were such a boon to the DPL that the city had reconsidered and agreed to continue funding the CLC as a part of the cooperative agreement.[49] Kay Collins and the supporters of the CLC had managed, once again, to gain a reprieve at the last minute.

The rechristened CLC/REEIC was supposed to serve as a western clearinghouse for government information on energy and environmental programs. Kay Collins and her staff were responsible for providing government program energy information services, including environmental impact statements and "Info-EES" forms, Energy Extension Services information sheets, for Colorado, Montana, Nebraska, Nevada, New Mexico, North Dakota, South Dakota, Utah, and Wyoming. The objective of REEIC was to provide a "centralized information system, accessible to the public."[50] All the federal agencies involved in the REEIC project were concerned with meeting the mandate for publicly available information as stipulated in the creation of the DOE. At several public "environmental evaluation" hearings, the central issue was "concern over public involvement at every stage of the energy/environmental decision making process."[51] Agency administrators viewed the REEIC as an efficient means of making this information available.

In its first year, the REEIC received strong support and direction from an interagency steering committee, which held regular meetings under the leadership of Joseph Smith of the regional office of the Department of the Interior.[52] Representatives of the other agencies involved regularly traveled to Denver from Washington and took a hands-on approach to helping Collins and the CLC staff organize the REEIC. Collins later remarked that in that first year "serious attention was given to the success of [the] cooperative initiative and to the responsibilities which these agencies shared for assuring its [REEIC] success."[53] It seemed as if the REEIC was off to a good start and that there was a decent chance that the program could succeed into the future. The strong support and the willingness of several key government officials to go to bat for the CLC/REEIC elated Collins and her staff.

The new REEIC agreement was the answer to Kay Collins's prayers and seemed like a perfect way to expand contacts between the library and the public. "A public library in the future will have to become a more active part of the community," she said; "we're looking for ways to develop the techniques for getting it [environmental information] into the hands of people who can use it."[54] Collins was also excited about new possibilities for using the latest information technology to further the environmental cause. "Libraries increasingly are trying to help solve social problems by taking available information and getting it into the hands of the people trying to find the solutions," Collins told reporters in 1979.[55] When speaking of technological advances, Collins displayed none of the ambivalence of Carhart or Eastlick. "Libraries are going to have . . . to join the revolution in information," she said, "or libraries aren't going to be as important in the community as they are now."[56] The DOE contracts brought all the latest information technology to the CLC. Almost overnight, the staff went from using file cards and typewriters to mainframe computers, databases, on-line computer links to government networks, and automated information storage systems. One of the best indicators that Collins and her staff were willing to tread where the older generation would not was the direct link established early on between the CLC and Oak Ridge. Instead of receiving a healthy dose of antimodernism from pamphlets and staff, patrons of the CLC could now go online to the nuclear establishment and learn about "our friend the atom." Surprisingly, neither Collins nor the staff seemed to notice this profound reversal of the atomic fears of the library founders. Flush with government cash, they reveled in their newfound national role.

In fact, Collins was so enthusiastic about the new direction of the CLC that she seemed to lose sight of the old problems. When asked about the scope of the collections of the REEIC, she commented that "the material collected is immense. We don't speak in terms of volumes but in tons." When pressed about the responsibilities of organizing this vast array of material, she was less enthusiastic. "Obviously we can't sit down and read all that," she said; "there are several tons of federal reports."[57] Collins knew that the huge responsibilities that accompanied the federal contracts would only exacerbate the persistent problem of organizing and managing the CLC. Nevertheless, because of the terrible pressure to secure funding from outside sources and the exciting possibilities of access to new technology, no government offers were refused. Understandably, it was very hard to turn away enthusiastic supporters after three years of little interest.

One of the strongest early supporters of the REEIC idea was Gerald Sophar, an executive director of technical information systems at the U.S. Department of Agriculture's Science and Education Administration. Sophar believed that "both libraries and bureaucracies might be revitalized or saved through a cooperative approach to information delivery."[58] In the coming years, the support of Sophar and other agency representatives became crucial for maintaining government funding of the CLC/REEIC. Collins realized that maintaining agency support required help from well-connected individuals in the bureaucratic structure. Unfortunately, dedicated administrators such as Sophar and the original members of the REEIC steering committee, who believed in the importance of public involvement and the regional center idea, seemed to be the exception rather than the rule.

Within the first year, a series of major agency reorganizations threw the REEIC funding into limbo once again. In 1978, energy agency reorganization resulted in a reconsideration of the long-term multiagency REEIC contract. As a result, Collins was forced to spend a great deal of her time working on new contracts. Negotiating and renegotiating government agency contracts became the abiding preoccupation of the CLC/REEIC management. Between 1976 and 1980, there was never a time when the administrators of the Conservation Library could relax. All government contracts were negotiated on an annual basis.

While the transfer of the REEIC to the exclusive control of the DOE threw things into temporary disarray in Denver, it also added a new base of support for the library. The reorganization program in 1977–78 included a provision to implement state energy conservation offices. In 1978, the Colorado Office of Energy Conservation (COEC) was established, with an information mandate similar to that of the national agencies. The administrators of the COEC turned to the REEIC for information services. The REEIC continued to serve the regional information needs of the DOE and also focused on providing local services as the Colorado Resource Center.

While the funding situation was temporarily resolved and the transfer of financial contracts completed without any major problems, the transfer of leadership was less successful.[59] The steering committee fell apart after 1978, and regular interagency meetings were abandoned. The steering committee had been responsible for "policy formation, budget approval, coordination of federal funds acquisition on an annual basis, performance reviews, etc."[60] These duties now fell to Collins and the staff of the Conservation Library, who after 1978 were on their own to manage the REEIC and work almost full-time to secure funding for the upcoming year. The federal government provided the money and set the requirements but gave little in the way of direction and management. The DOE reorganization undermined interagency cooperation and ultimately the REEIC project. With all the new federally mandated responsibilities, the staff was simply overwhelmed. Government red tape swallowed the days of the CLC administrators and left little time for attending to the needs of the library.

Between 1977 and 1981, federal and state agencies poured more than $574,000 into the REEIC project.[61] Collins and her staff earned every penny of the money, and activity at the CLC increased dramatically in 1977 and 1978. This was partly because a substantial chunk of the budget at the REEIC went toward advertising, allowing the REEIC to produce brochures and newsletters in large runs and then distribute them throughout the Rocky Mountain West. The volume of calls and visitors to the center increased by over 2,000 percent in the late 1970s.[62] The administrators of the REEIC served an expanded local clientele and answered requests for information from all over the nation. In 1977, requests for information rose to almost six hundred per month. By 1978, that figure had increased to more than seven hundred per month. With this level of public demand, cataloging and other activities related to maintaining and improving the CLC manuscripts stopped altogether. The focus at the CLC shifted completely to the REEIC activities.

The profile of the CLC/REEIC users changed and expanded along with the mission. Prior to 1977, most CLC users were private individuals, regional businesses, or environmentalists. The REEIC drew a more diverse crowd. Almost 30 percent of its patrons were federal, state, or local agency representatives.[63] Not surprisingly, most of the inquiries came from residents of the Denver metropolitan area, largely as a result of the explosion of energy research and energy projects in the state of Colorado.

In 1978, there were 141 energy projects "planned, proposed, or under construction" in the state of Colorado. Officials of the U.S. Bureau of Mines listed Colorado as the center of the national movement to explore alternative energy sources. "This [energy work] exceeds the number found in all other states," an official stated, "and represents more than 10 percent of the national total."[64] The energy crisis created a boom in exploration and development in Colorado during the late 1970s as shale oil, solar power, wind energy, and geothermal power projects sprung up all over the state. The REEIC benefited from this unusually high level of energy development. Business at the library was booming. More than at any time in its history, the CLC truly stood at the center of a national movement. The question was, which movement?

The new directions at the CLC would have baffled, and possibly horrified, Arthur Carhart. It is doubtful that he could have made the leap from conservation to energy technology as easily as Collins. In fact, many environmentalists in Colorado understandably looked at the alternative energy boom as a serious threat to the state's public lands and public health.[65] While most environmentalists could agree that solar power and other unambiguously "soft-path" solutions were a good thing, there was little agreement about synfuels, especially shale oil. For many, energy development was also "environmentalism" only to the extent that it did not involve permanent alteration of the landscape. For this group, shale oil development in Colorado appeared as a specter of doom. "If shale is commercialized," wrote Governor Richard Lamm and Michael McCarthy, "the consequences to the land will be harmful and extensive."[66] This ambivalence over alternative energy is indicative of the confusion and conflict within the environmental movement during the 1970s. The REEIC and other organizations were willing to embrace ideas like shale oil because they felt that in the long run these alternatives would prove more environmentally friendly. On the other hand, Lamm and other activists remained wary of depending on technology to solve the energy problem. These opposing viewpoints perfectly captured the split between a growing faction of technologically oriented postscarcity environmentalists and an equally vocal group of environmentalists who remained in the antimodernist camp.

The pro–alternative energy camp was very influential at this time, however, and Colorado was at the center of the movement. In September 1978, the REEIC signed on to help sponsor, along with a who's who of western and federal appropriate technology organizations, the University of Denver's "Energy Fest 1978."[67] Energy Fest featured a remarkable list of keynote speakers, including R. Buckminster Fuller, Amory Lovins, Congressman Morris K. Udall, and Worldwatch spokesman Denis A. Hayes. Fuller spoke on "Global Energy Strategies," Lovins on "Soft Energy Paths," and Hayes on the "Transition to a Post-petroleum World." The following day, workshops were conducted on solar technologies, gasohol, and wind energy. By all accounts the event was a huge success and a rare opportunity for enthusiasts to meet and listen to several of the most influential proponents of alternative technology. This remarkable event followed a successful alternative energy exhibit at the REEIC that was visited by an estimated fourteen hundred people.[68] Both events generated excellent press for the REEIC and seemed to confirm that the library was on the cutting edge of a rapidly changing environmental movement.

At the library Kay Collins and her staff worked daily to expand the information systems to reach a wider audience. In addition to the constant flow of visitors, thousands of calls came in from around the nation via the REEIC "Tel-Energy" system.[69] This was a rudimentary phone computer network, cutting-edge at the time, that allowed patrons to call

Colleen Cayton speaking at alternative energy fair with Kay Collins looking on and Henry Shearouse just visible in the background behind Collins, 1979. Denver Public Library, Western History Collection, Conservation Library Collection photos.

and listen to taped messages on a variety of energy topics and to connect to computer energy databases available through the DOE computers at Oak Ridge National Laboratory.[70] As an early "internet" experiment "Tel-Energy" was one of the first attempts to use the growing web of government computer networks to provide new methods of public information delivery. Services like "Tel-Energy" dramatically expanded the REEIC constituency. It was the centerpiece of the REEIC exhibit at the White House Conference on Library Information Systems. Collins and staff members Jim Arshem and Colleen Clayton went to Washington to represent the REEIC and worked throughout the conference with computers and phones linked to the REEIC back in Denver.[71] The event highlighted the innovative methods of environmental information delivery being developed in Denver, giving Collins and her staff a chance to show that their state-of-the-art services deserved federal support.

The staff of the CLC worked constantly to convince federal agencies that the library was an appropriate funding recipient. "The money budgeted to federal agencies does not carry an amount earmarked for information services and certainly not for public libraries," stated Colleen Cayton, director of development and public relations for the DPL. "What we do is package our product and our services in terms which relate to the current program priorities and budgets of a specific agency."[72] After the initial year, Collins and the rest of the staff realized that keeping federal money was harder than getting it the first time. The pressure to prove themselves was constant. Federal agencies wanted to see quantifiable results with a consistent upward trend. The CLC staff was in a state of near panic throughout the late 1970s.

The REEIC had different goals from each of its sponsors. For instance, the EPA funded a newsletter "designed to stimulate public awareness and participation in energy/environment decision making."[73] The U.S. Department of Agriculture funds helped cover operating expenses and provided for outreach and education programs. At the same time, in cooperation with the DOE Energy Extension Services (EES), the REEIC supplied services to the eight states of federal Region VIII (Arizona, Colorado, Montana, Nebraska, Nevada, New Mexico, North Dakota, Utah, and Wyoming). Answering EES requests for information and routing the appropriate documents soon consumed significant amounts of the staff's time.

The main thrust of the EES was the compiling and distribution of annotated bibliographies of energy information sources.[74] Compiling this information was time-consuming and required the attention of several staff members. State and federal agencies and DOE Regional Energy Extension agents from the ten-state region covered by the REEIC could request EES packets, which were updated and sent on a monthly basis. These publications covered topics ranging from "Conservation Concepts" to "Heating a House with Rolled Newspapers."[75] Even though the Info-EES system succeeded in providing a well-organized system of energy information that was disseminated to a wide readership in the Rocky Mountain region, it proved burdensome to the staff of the REEIC.

The year 1978 proved a very successful one for the REEIC. Overall, the fantastic response to the idea of using the public library to serve as the center of regional and community action seemed to vindicate Kay Collins's work in this direction for the past decade. Nevertheless, while things looked good on the surface, trouble was brewing underneath. The workloads and red tape associated with the REEIC pushed Collins and the staff to the limit. In addition, internal politics at the library increased. The huge initial success of the REEIC and the resurrection of the CLC were tainted by growing controversy over Collins's management and continued tensions between the CLC and the DPL administration. Even for those totally dedicated to the CLC/REEIC cause, the strain and uncertainty of relying on the government were beginning to take their toll. By the end of 1979, a change was inevitable.

AND THEN THERE WERE NONE

In November 1978, Arthur Carhart died. Worry and doubts about the Conservation Library marked his last years. Carhart left no immediate heirs. He had put his heart and soul into the building of the CLC, and he left what remained of his meager estate to the library. Carhart's death punctuated the end of an era of constant expansion, success, and national acclaim for the CLC. Many of Carhart's older friends had associated him so closely with the library that they often referred to it as the "Carhart Collection." They were saddened both by his death and by the tenuous state of the CLC; all of Carhart's hard work seemed threatened with financial failure. Although the federal funding for the REEIC had saved the CLC from complete collapse, many of those involved with the project over the years were skeptical about the REEIC and the politics behind this experiment. Carhart's death seemed to confirm that an era had passed and that the old goals and dreams of his generation no longer held sway with the leaders of the environmental movement.

Between 1973 and 1978, the CLC counselors had, for the most part, been out of the picture. Collins did not have the time to use this group to advise and direct the library, and she realized that many members of the group were unable or unwilling to accept the changes she had instigated. She did continue to look to certain members for financial help, but by 1978, when Carhart died, the counselors had ceased to play an important role in the collection. The generational shift at the CLC was complete. The old guard of elite conservationists who founded and shaped the early history of the place were swiftly fading from prominence. Over the past decade, many of Carhart's generation had died, and those who remained were less and less active.

It seemed as if the stage were set for Collins to assume her hard-won position as the matriarch of the CLC. But the death of her mentor hit her hard. Their friendship dated back to the early 1960s, when Collins was a master's candidate at the University of New Mexico. Carhart had been instrumental in almost every aspect of Collins's career, having helped her with her master's thesis research, advocated her candidacy for the DU librarianship program, nominated her for the AMCA, and engineered her move into his position as the head of the CLC when he left. The two became close friends, and Carhart profoundly shaped Collins's environmental ideology.[76] Even after his departure from Denver, Carhart continued to advise Collins through constant correspondence. As Carhart's health and mental state became more fragile, Collins continued to carefully answer his letters and spoke with him by phone on a regular basis.[77] She remained devoted to her friend and mentor long after he ceased making a contribution to the management of the CLC.

Although she worked for almost a decade to shape the CLC to fit her vision of environmental and social advocacy, Collins was, in some respects, one of those who thought of the CLC as the "Carhart Collection." His death seems to have caused her to reflect on the future of the CLC/REEIC and her role in that future.

In the late fall of 1979, Collins decided it was time to move on. She left the library to pursue a career as an environmental consultant in the expanding world of alternative energy and environmental information.[78] Collins's departure was caused by more than Carhart's death. During her last years, the tensions with Shearouse and the DPL management had increased, and relations between the CLC and the DPL administration went from bad to worse. Some of the conflict grew out of Collins's environmental advocacy. Because the library was a municipal entity supported by tax dollars, its employees were not supposed to use their public positions to advocate political views. Under Collins's leadership, however, the staff of the CLC often flouted this rule. By the late 1970s, Collins spent much of her time traveling to environmental meetings and speaking on controversial issues as the director of the Conservation Library. Eastlick tolerated this type of behavior. Shearouse, on the other hand, was not personally committed to the cause and had little sympathy with staff members who used the CLC as a platform for their personal ideology.[79]

There was a growing concern on the part of the DPL administration that the increased level of activism was jeopardizing the sound management of the CLC. By 1979, the conflict came to a head, and Collins resigned after fourteen years with the DPL. After years of working in the trenches of the Colorado environmental movement and building the CLC into a national center of advocacy, Collins quickly faded from the scene.

Kay Collins's environmental career, her rise to momentary national prominence, and her struggles to define a new leadership position for women in the library and environmental movement speak to the complex social and gender dynamics driving the political movements of the 1960s and 1970s. During her early years, she struggled against tradition to move into a leadership role in a movement led almost exclusively by men. The politics of librarianship in America made her challenge doubly difficult. Like many women of her generation, she paid the price for her politics. Her career suffered because she was unwilling to compromise her commitment to environmental politics to placate nervous colleagues and administrators. She also refused to play the subservient role expected of a young woman working in a very public capacity. Ultimately, this pathbreaking work stands as a model for other women looking to move into leadership roles in environmentalism and to use libraries as platforms for social advocacy, but for Collins the struggle to elevate herself to the top of her profession ended in disappointment and acrimony. By

Linda Cumming uses the "Tel-Energy" system in an early effort to use on-line technology to gather information, ca. 1979. Denver Public Library, Western History Collection, Conservation Library Collection photos.

1980, the situation at the DPL became unbearable, and she was forced to abandon the CLC.[80]

DOG AND PONY SHOWS

Collins was replaced by CLC staff member Linda Cumming, also a DU library school graduate who had worked as a librarian in the CLC since 1976.[81] Although personally sympathetic to the environmentalist cause, Cumming was not an activist. More than that, she had bad memories of her first experiences at the CLC under Collins's leadership.

When Cumming first came to work at the CLC—just after the city funding crisis and the reorganizations that financial catastrophe precipitated—she found a department in disarray. Cumming was shocked at the apparent lack of day-to-day management during this time. With Collins often gone for days attending environmental meetings or speaking to local groups, the CLC staff were left on their own. From Cumming's perspective, this type of management was disastrous.[82] Some of the staff members were simply incapable of handling the daily administration of the CLC without direct supervision, and rumors had spread through the library about strange goings-on in the Conservation Library.[83] This chaotic atmosphere was disturbing to the well-organized Cumming and left a long-lasting impression. When she was named head of the REEIC, she reorganized the staff and concentrated on the task of managing the CLC collections. She was dedicated to making the most of this opportunity and looked at the new position strictly from a librarianship point of view.

The task of managing the CLC/REEIC was complicated by the variety of agreements with federal agencies, each requiring a different product or service. Cumming had inherited a mass of bureaucratic administrative responsibilities and a system of federal contracts that boggled the mind. By 1979, the shift from several disparate environmental agencies to the consolidated management of the DOE changed the original mandates that resulted in the creation of the REEIC. The REEIC was "termed an 'anomaly' by one Washington DOE officer who explained that the service was outside the 'system' and programs of the DOE."[84] In Denver, CLC staffers and DPL administrators were perplexed and frustrated by this sudden lack of support for the REEIC. They found themselves once again scrambling to justify their existence and secure funding.

Users of the REEIC were quick to come to its defense. Collins, and then Cumming, urged users to express their support by writing to DOE officials. Many REEIC patrons expressed dismay that right at the moment when energy and environmental information was most needed, the government decided to stop funding one of the best sources in the nation for that information. For instance, geologist Eugene Ciancanelli wrote an angry letter to be forwarded to the DOE. "Kay Collins and the Denver Public Library have had, and are making, a direct contribution to energy exploration and development," he said, adding that if the REEIC closed, "library research . . . will suffer severely."[85] Other letter writers talked about the importance of the REEIC in light of the proliferation of complex environmental information. The professionalization of the environmental movement, coupled with the expanded environmental programs of the Carter administration, created a blizzard of energy and environmental information and regulations. The REEIC had proved itself a valuable agent in the management and distribution of this information, and it was inconceivable to many users, including officials of state and federal agencies that depended on the REEIC, that the DOE might stop funding the project.

In July 1979, the DPL sent representatives to the DOE Federal Regional Council meeting in Denver to make a case for continued funding of the REEIC.[86] At that meeting, the CLC called the attention of the DOE committee to the "Memorandum of Agreement" that initiated the REEIC project and asked that it simply follow through on this initial arrangement. The DPL representatives were apparently successful in their arguments because the DOE, along with the U.S. Department of Agriculture, agreed to continue funding on an annual basis. The victory was a hollow one, however. Cumming and her staff realized that the work required for annually renewable contracts would be constant. From 1979 forward, the REEIC staff lived on a "month to month basis as efforts to secure contract extensions and new contracts were undertaken."[87] In addition to this constant struggle over the federal contracts, Cumming realized that the manuscript collections of the CLC were in bad shape and needed immediate attention. "Many of the manuscript collections are less than available due to the shortage of staff and time to process them," she stated after taking over the CLC.[88] The manuscripts and artifacts that formed the bulk of the CLC holdings were a "diamond in the rough" in need of a thorough reorganization after the confusion of the final years of the Collins administration. Despite serious concerns about finances and the burdensome workload, Cumming and her newly reorganized staff remained enthusiastic about the project and were hopeful about the future of the Conservation Library.

One of the key issues for the REEIC under Cumming's leadership involved solar and renewable energy. Colorado was at the center of the movement to develop realistic and consumer-friendly alternative energy sources. Solar panels and windmills sprouted from the rooftops and backyards of fashionable Denver neighborhoods. These new energy devices were highly visible. They helped reduce Denver's famous winter "brown cloud," as did fuel additives like gasohol, MBTE, and ethanol, plus an expanded system of bike paths and walkways. Obviously, alternative energy was a hot topic, and the REEIC was the place to go to get information on the subject. Cumming hoped that there might be time to get the CLC collections back on track once the pressing issues of the energy crisis were resolved. If not, she was perfectly willing to close the archives to the public based strictly on the principles of library management and her view of the realities of the DPL system. "Of course we all wanted the CLC to continue," she commented, "but we had to be realistic."[89]

In its final two years, the REEIC reached a far larger audience than it ever had before the *Energy/Environment Information Newsletter,* edited by staff member Kathleen Parker, was sent out to a mailing list of over three thousand individuals and organizations across the eight-state region covered by the REEIC. By 1980, the REEIC was, without question, one of the centers of environmental action in the Rocky Mountain region and the nation.

Early in 1980, President Carter praised the CLC/REEIC and presented Congress with a plan for implementing a national system of environmental libraries based on the REEIC model.[90] Despite Carter's strong endorsement, the REEIC faced another crisis as national politics conspired to bring the honeymoon between the CLC and the federal government to an abrupt halt.

In December 1981, the last of a series of workshops on solar energy administered by the REEIC was completed. The workshops were part of a contract with Western Solar Utilization Network, a regional DOE solar energy program, which had hired the REEIC to produce a series of presentations around the region.[91] For almost a year, Linda Cumming and the CLC staff continued the work begun by Collins and spent virtually all their time traveling throughout Colorado and the Rocky Mountain region giving solar energy workshops.[92] The grueling schedule left little time for any other work at the REEIC. When the contracts ran out, Cumming, exhausted from a year on the road, was not interested in attempting to renew them. The contract was the last of the energy-related programs that the CLC was responsible for.[93] The Reagan administration was fulfilling its promise to the American voters to cut taxes. Energy programs were among the first victims, with their budgets radically slashed. With the federal money gone, CLC administrators once again faced a financial crisis. This one, however, proved worse than any of the previous ones.

Conclusion

All this while, the Ear reposes in its Pickling-Jar of Swedish lead Crystal, as if being withheld from Time's Appetite for some Destiny obscure to all.

Thomas Pynchon, Mason & Dixon

REAGANOMICS

Politics had built the CLC; politics would very nearly kill it. The Reagan administration was characterized by a "pervasive and determined commitment to turn the environmentalist tide."[1] Reagan and his conservative advisers assumed that environmental advocacy and the extensive environmental legislation of the past decade were harmful to American business and a direct threat to the American economy. Much of Reagan's antienvironmental ideology came straight out of Colorado.

Throughout the twentieth century, Colorado was a key state in almost every significant environmental debate. The success of the grassroots wilderness coalition in the 1960s, a series of environmental victories in the state, the growth and success of the CLC, and the solidification of a powerful state environmental lobby in the 1970s all hid a rising tide of environmental backlash in Colorado. Right-wing opposition to environmental politics ripened like cantaloupes in the San Luis Valley. Colorado became the center of the "Sagebrush Rebellion," a replay of the "land grab" of the 1940s, with ranchers, business leaders, and conservative politicians allying themselves to attempt to have public lands turned over to private individuals and companies.[2] Several graduates of the Sagebrush Rebellion and the Colorado environmental opposition became architects of the Reagan revolution.

Most prominent among these was James Watt, director of the Mountain States Legal Foundation, a right-wing organization financed by big business to combat government environmental regulation.[3] Mountain States had backing from Colorado businessmen such as Joseph Coors, who were willing to dig deep into their ample pockets to ensure that every environmental act and action received harsh scrutiny. More than any other single action, the appointment of Watt as secretary of the interior revealed the depth of Reagan's antipathy to environmentalism. This cynical, fox-in-charge-of-the-henhouse policy was extended to all federal environmental agencies. The EPA, one of the key support agencies for the REEIC, was taken over by another Coloradan, Anne Gorsuch, who was also a graduate of the Colorado environmental opposition. As a right-wing Colorado state legislator, she had used all her power and influence to undermine environmental legislation in the state and to prevent further development of the Colorado wilderness system. Finally, Robert Burford, a Colorado rancher and state legislator, became director of the Bureau of Land Management. For the directors of the CLC/REEIC, the ascendancy of these right-wing Colorado politicians to key positions in federal environmental agencies meant the death of their dream.

In the first two years of the Reagan administration, the EPA lost almost 30 percent of its funding.[4] The Department of Energy was slashed, and the REEIC was left completely without support. ECOL, the REEIC's sister library in Minnesota, suffered the same fate, although with internal library support and a smaller collection it was able to hang on until the late 1980s, when it closed. *Rocky Mountain News* columnist Sandy Graham lamented the fate of the REEIC: "The Denver Public Library's 'orphan child' . . . is up for adoption again. Uncle Sam has cut off its support."[5] Cumming and her staff were left with few options. The REEIC was exactly the type of government "waste" the Reagan administration had wanted removed.[6] Cumming expected action, but, like most federal dependents, she was caught off guard by the depth of antienvironmental sentiment that Reagan brought to Washington.

In the long term most of Reagan's appointees' plans to reduce the influence of environmentalists in Colorado and the West backfired; ironically, they did almost as much to reenergize the environmental movement as had the pro-environment Carter administration. In the first place, James Watt's open contempt for the environment and for the American people quickly made him a liability to the administration. His bizarre public statements were often so outrageous that millions of Americans, previously uninvolved in environmentalism, became terrified by his rhetoric and joined environmental organizations in unprecedented numbers. One environmentalist claimed that Watt "was the best organizer we ever had."[7] Watt was eventually forced to resign, as was Anne Gorsuch, after an EPA scandal left her disgraced and sent some of her deputies to jail.[8] Eventually this wave of antienvironmental sentiment proved too extreme for most Americans. Reagan and his advisers failed to understand the depth of pro-environmental sentiment among the general public. By the mid-1980s, the American environmental movement was deeply rooted in American society and culture. In the end, Reagan administration attacks on the environmental movement only "tested its strength and vitality and thereby demonstrated the degree to which it had become a broad and fundamental aspect of American public life."[9]

Unfortunately, the Conservation Library did not survive the initial steamroller of the Reagan revolution. In the aftermath of devastating budget cuts, Cumming turned once again to the idea of a fee-based system.[10] She enlisted the support of the Maxima Corporation, a private company that specialized in developing profit-making information systems.[11] Linda Cumming and Colleen Cayton, director of development for the library, worked closely with representatives of Maxima to develop a last-ditch plan to save the CLC/REEIC. DPL Commission members quickly voiced concerns about the tax status of the library if the cooperative venture were launched.[12] Cumming and Cayton received strong support from Henry Shearouse and the DPL administration, who saw the venture as a potential solution to a thorny problem. "If such a public/private partnership could be achieved," Shearouse wrote, it would "provide a solution to the year-to-year existence of the Conservation Library . . . and present the DPL with the potential for building a source of earned income."[13] Shearouse's hopes were bolstered by the positive attitude of the Maxima executives, who promised the DPL administration that they were "totally committed . . . to permanently establish the Conservation Library as one of the nation's foremost centers for energy and environmental information."[14]

For a few more months it seemed as if there was some hope that all would turn out well for the CLC. Sadly, it was not to be. The Maxima deal exploded in public controversy when CLC staff member Colleen Cayton announced that she had accepted a job with Maxima while she was working on securing the contract with the library. The local press cried "conflict of interest." Although the city attorney, Gerald Himelgrin, officially cleared Cayton of any wrongdoing, the deal with Maxima was essentially doomed.[15] Shearouse was forced to explain to Himelgrin why he allowed Cayton to continue working on the deal even after she informed him of her decision to accept a job with Maxima. The controversy seems to have solidified Cumming's resolve to cease working to save the CLC and begin planning for its demise. For Cumming, the decision to close the CLC was much easier than it would have been for either Collins or Carhart. Cumming was always a librarian first and an environmentalist second. The situation in the early 1980s demonstrated the contradictions inherent in using libraries as centers of social and ideological change. In Cumming's mind, the stability of the library was more important than any individual project, no matter how meritorious. Thus, in the end she was able to walk away from the CLC and move on to new opportunities in the library system without much regret.

During the four years that the CLC operated as the REEIC, the staff undertook virtually no private fund-raising. As one observer noted, "The Conservation Library has been near death a half-dozen times since the

1976 decision by the city to end its funding."[16] For five years, the CLC had relied on federal money and a tiny budget from the city and county of Denver. Keeping the federal agencies happy consumed all of the staff's fund-raising time. When the federal contracts were canceled, the minuscule budget from the city disappeared as well. In the aftermath of the Maxima scandal, the DPL administration decided that the CLC had reached the end of the road; after twenty years of development, it would be "discontinued."

The decision to discontinue the CLC was a difficult one, but in some sense it came as a relief.[17] Between 1979 and 1981, the staff juggled a mind-boggling tangle of federal paperwork and responsibilities.[18] Many of the federal contracts were obtained by promising the agencies more than the staff could deliver. So large were the demands that Linda Cumming and other staff members spent much of their time traveling around the region giving "dog and pony shows" for rural audiences in accordance with the contracts.[19] The pace of these commitments made management of the CLC impossible. All of those involved in the project realized that regardless of the funding situation, the REEIC had become unmanageable, its demise seemingly inevitable.

CLOSURE

In the spring of 1982, the staff of the DPL began to disperse the books of the Conservation Library to larger collections within the library system.[20] Special book collections, such as Howard Zahniser's private library, plus all manuscript materials were kept intact and moved to the Western History Collection. Other materials were sent to the science and politics sections. Most significantly, the space that had housed the CLC was reorganized. Rows of open stacks were moved in to replace the desks of the CLC staff and the manuscript areas. In other words, the CLC ceased to exist as a place. Just as Carhart had once feared, the material collections of the CLC were scattered into the void of the general library. The CLC's many awards and honors, which had once proudly graced the walls, were wrapped in brown paper and packed in boxes. All the material trappings that had marked the Conservation Library as an autonomous entity with a history and a future were removed.

Over the next five years, library administrators and staff erased all evidence of the CLC. By the late 1980s, few DPL staff were even aware of the existence of the manuscripts. The artifacts and prizes won during the 1960s were almost completely forgotten.[21] After the books, periodicals, pamphlets, and general material were dispersed to other parts of the library, the heart and soul of the CLC—the manuscripts, photos, and artifacts—were boxed and shipped to a warehouse in lower downtown Denver. Out in the musty Brighton Boulevard warehouse, just past Bud's Workingman's Café, tightly packed boxes began to gather dust, piled high in damp corners and on teetering narrow stacks. All the physical objects that had been so carefully collected, the objects that gave form and meaning to an ideology, were wrapped, tied, entombed, and forgotten.

For Carhart and his generation, the collection of material objects to represent a particular view of nature and society fit perfectly within a long-standing Western tradition. To a large extent "the modern world came to define itself, both communally and individually, largely in terms of ownership of goods."[22] Carhart, Eastlick, and all those involved in the early years of the Conservation Library project used, collected, and displayed material artifacts to stake a claim to a set of ideas and to a piece of history. For them, the meaning of their lives and work was encapsulated in the material of the CLC. From this point of view, the removal of the precious objects of the CLC to the obscurity of a warehouse was a nightmare. Since the power of artifacts as claims to history and intellectual property depends on public display, the removal of the treasures of the conservation movement to the warehouse represented the final blow to Carhart's dream of using the public library to further the environmental cause.

Kay Collins and the younger generation that inherited the CLC from Carhart and his cohort were less concerned with the physical artifacts and collections of past glories. They were more interested in using the power of the place as a platform for social and political advocacy. As a result, the artifacts and manuscripts of the CLC had languished, largely unused for many years before the official closure and removal to Brighton. Still, even though Collins's perspective was different from Carhart's, she, too, viewed the closure of the library as a tragedy.[23] For the 1970s staff, the CLC was a laboratory to push the limits of the public library as a center for environmental advocacy and politics. The CLC provided an excellent staging area for the mobilization of resources necessary for engineering social change: money, influence, and media. Collins was aware of the power of this public institution, sometimes using it to great effect. Ultimately, however, she was unable to reconcile the daily operation of the CLC as part of a library bureaucracy with the role of the CLC as a political and social platform.

The transformation of the CLC into the REEIC reflected in miniature what was happening to the environmental movement, both in Colorado and across the nation. In the 1970s, American environmentalists found themselves contemplating a much more complicated set of sometimes conflicting goals and political contingencies. Environmental politics were more confusing than ever before, and many of the central ideas of the previous generation came into question. By the 1970s, environmental issues affected so many people, in so many ways, that almost anyone could make some claim to "speak" for nature; everyone, from nuclear scientists and oil shale developers to geologists and DOE bureaucrats, began calling themselves "environmentalists." People like Kay Collins realized in the 1970s that, from an ecological point of view, we are all similarly paradoxically situated. Given this new awareness, Collins and many of her contemporaries in the environmental movement simply could not buy into the antimodernist ideology that had driven Carhart and most of his predecessors in the conservation movement. At the REEIC, Collins and her staff won the hearts of Colorado's oil geologists by giving them a fantastic research facility while also somehow managing to travel to Creede and Carbondale to show the folks how to put up solar panels and windmills. Collins and the staff of the REEIC did not view technology as unambiguously good, but they had moved away from the technophobia of Carhart and Eastlick and helped push environmentalism away from the old wilderness versus civilization dichotomy.

At the Conservation Library, this significant ideological shift was due partly to trends in environmentalism and partly to the unique position of the CLC within a changing system of public libraries. For obvious reasons, libraries quickly jumped on the computer and information technology bandwagon. Additionally, librarians were strikingly self-conscious about what new technologies meant for their way of doing business. Therefore, Collins and her staff were more prepared, and more willing, than most to fully grasp the significance of the information revolution for social movements in general and environmentalism in particular and to work to make the best use of new technology to further their project. Like many young environmentalists of her generation, Collins had accepted Stewart Brand's call to action: "We are as gods, and might as well get good at it." There was no reason to sit dreaming of far-off, pristine wilderness, when there were so many environmental problems right in the city—problems that required making the most of new technologies. Where Carhart and Eastlick had focused on material things as the best representatives for their ideology, Collins ultimately turned to bits and bytes as the artifacts most useful to her cause. She remained, in most senses, true to Carhart and his dream by carrying forward the notion that the CLC should be both a center for activism on behalf of nature and an environmental information clearinghouse. But the clientele, the media, and the messages had all changed.

The move toward "soft" environmental technology and openhanded grasping of new methods of information delivery and systems development highlights perhaps the most significant change in American environmental thinking in the late twentieth century. In the years following World War II, conservationists based their movement on a reaction against modernism and the rise of frightening new technologies. Throughout the twentieth century, environmental activists, from John Muir to Arthur Carhart, focused on the seemingly unbridgeable gulf between nature and humanity. In this ideological tradition, wilderness became the ultimate symbol of environmental purity, with the modern technological city as its antithesis. This bipolar, and fundamentally antimodernist, framework served conservationists well in the early fights to convince the American public to support the preservation of forestlands and spectacular natural treasures. But this simple dichotomy was less effective when applied to the increasing complexity of environmental politics and environmental science after the 1960s. Carhart realized early on the problems of creating false hierarchies of naturalness. Still, in the end he was unable to divorce his conservation philosophy from the prevailing antimodernist thought of his generation.

While Kay Collins carried on many of the ideas of her mentor, she moved beyond his antimodernism and attempted to make the Conservation Library an example of a postscarcity environmentalism more complex and flexible than that of the previous generation. On many levels she succeeded in this goal, but in the end she, too, failed to grasp the overlapping and contingent nature of environmental thinking during the tumultuous 1970s and 1980s. There could be no simple linear progression from one stage to the next. Each evolution involved a subtle blending of old ideas with new, of past imperatives with present politics—a dialectical change that never seemed to play out as the participants planned.

In retrospect, one must wonder if both Carhart and Collins, along with their many supporters, were realistic in thinking that somehow a public library could provide solutions to America's byzantine environmental landscape. The founders of the Conservation Library might have been a bit innocent, a bit naive to think that an archive within a public library could really change the world, but they were not alone. Americans have consistently placed great faith in public cultural institutions, especially libraries and museums, as agents for social and political change. As historian Mike Wallace recently put it in *Mickey Mouse History*, "I believe that they [museums] can serve as public forums, as spaces where citizens can come together to consider common concerns. They can help restore severed chronological connections—reknit our temporal fabric."[24]

Looking back at the wildly optimistic rhetoric of the early years of the Conservation Library, it is clear that Carhart's original vision of using it as a center for international environmental advocacy was somewhat naive. For Carhart and his generation, the library collections and artifacts had power because they represented a particular vision of the past. Like many older conservationists, he was unable to recognize that the early 1960s were the beginning of the end of his brand of environmental activism and that the new generation was less interested in preservation, of either history or wilderness, and more concerned with innovation. Carhart and his colleagues hoped that the library would become a storehouse of talismans to ward off technocracy. Like an anthropologist in a distant land, Collins carefully studied and tried to respect Carhart's talismans. Like a conscientious ethnographer, she became a participant observer and fellow traveler with the older men who surrounded her. Ultimately, however, she, like many in her generation, found that most of the cherished objects and ancient practices so valued by her elders were quaint at best and dangerous at worst in a rapidly changing world.

In many respects, Carhart's original vision of the library was not unrealistic. His hard work did succeed, if only briefly, in establishing a focal point for environmental research. During the REEIC period, the library even became, to a great extent, a national center for a new type of environmental advocacy. The question in the end was the same as at the beginning: How much can libraries or archives expect to influence larger social movements? The combined statistics of the CLC/REEIC are proof that the library did succeed in placing environmental information in tens of thousands of hands. Framed in terms of Carhart's bold dreams, the library essentially failed, but only because American society was changing in unanticipated ways. Collections as a means of legitimating a particular worldview and as a bulwark against frightening change carried less weight with a new generation.

The story of the rise and fall of the Conservation Library could be cast into the mold of previous histories of environmentalism in America: the rise of ideologically pure grassroots environmentalists and organizations, and the seemingly inevitable move toward faceless bureaucracy, polarization, and decline. In this model, the end of the Conservation Library story reads as a tragic failure, a noble dream crushed by the Reagan revolution and a sad dependence on federal bureaucratic funding. But the story of the CLC is more complicated than this scenario suggests.

In the end, the story of the Conservation Library suggests that behind most advocacy on behalf of the environment lies a rich tapestry of contradictory human history. When we set out to describe or represent nature, we often reveal more about ourselves, our fears, our politics, and our hopes than we do about the environment we propose to protect. As a result, the greatest legacy of the Conservation Library may be the story of the struggle to redefine environmental thinking to better fit the contingencies and paradoxes of the late twentieth century. Considering the significant transformations in environmental thinking during the crucial years between 1964 and 1982, it should come as no surprise that an institution like the Conservation Library might fail to weather the change.

Epilogue

Only from the extreme of comfort and leisure do we return willingly to adversity.

Yvon Chouinard, Climbing Ice

At fourteen thousand feet, the air is thin. Even in August, nighttime temperatures plunge below freezing. Mountaineers' cold fingers feel wooden as they grasp frosty aluminum carabiners and claw at stiff knots in kernmantel rope set like cement during the night. In the darkness before dawn, anxiety creeps upon even the most seasoned climber. Weeks of excitement—poring over maps, sorting gear, and planning each move—seem like a dream in the shadows of dark, looming cliffs that hide the sun and prolong the morning chill. Still, even with the fear, the excitement of the day's coming adventure prevails. Thoughts of doom fade as the first signs of dawn's glow brighten the horizon.

The state of Colorado is world renowned for the quality and quantity of its high mountains. There are more than fifty peaks that soar over 14,000 feet, and hundreds more at 12,000 or 13,000 feet. The "fourteeners" draw climbers from around the globe, people willing to endure punishing hikes, loose rock, unpredictable weather, and brutal descents to stand for a moment on the summit of one of these giants. Many Colorado residents dedicate their leisure time to the ultimate challenge of collecting the summits of the highest peaks in the state. For most climbers, bagging all the fourteeners is a lifetime goal, achieved slowly over the decades, often culminating with a celebration in a mountain meadow. Others, however, become obsessed with climbing each mountain over and over, compiling new records of ascents. Most of these adventurers return on Sunday evening, tired, sunburned, and happy, with another peak bagged, another weekend well spent away from the chaos and stress of the city. On any Sunday, however, the chance remains that some may not return.

In the predawn darkness of August 15, 1970, Edward Hilliard crawled out of his sleeping bag on the northeast side of North Maroon Peak near Aspen. The morning was clear, and all indications pointed toward a perfect day of climbing. Hilliard was on the mountain to act as guide for a party of friends. The ascent of North Maroon was to be Hilliard's second venture up the peak in less than five years. In addition to climbs in the Maroon Bells, Hilliard had racked up an impressive list of ascents in Colorado, Europe, and the Himalayas.[1] By all accounts, he was a thoughtful, experienced climber capable of leading an expedition in the treacherous Maroon Bells.[2]

Ed Hilliard knew the risks involved in the Maroon Bells. As he sorted gear in the early morning light, he paid special attention to safety. All the climbers in the party wore helmets to protect them from deadly projectiles spilling down from the summit. In addition, Hilliard carefully prepared his climbing hardware and inspected his ropes. The party that day consisted of Hilliard and three family friends: Ann Fowler, an avid and experienced climber, Rodney Aller Sr., and Rodney Aller Jr. The Allers were also experienced climbers but not as expert as Hilliard or Fowler. The main purpose of the outing was to help Ann Fowler achieve her goal of climbing all of Colorado's fourteeners by her fortieth birthday. North Maroon was the second to last on her list, and the birthday was only two days away.[3] Fowler never reached the summit of North Maroon, or her fortieth birthday.[4]

At 7:00 A.M. the climbers started their ascent from the bench at timberline, below the dam on the northeast side of the mountain. Even though Hilliard had climbed the mountain before, by the same route, he was not certain how far they should traverse across the south face of the mountain before heading up to the summit route. The crumbling rock made it particularly difficult to find a route; everywhere they turned, the rock seemed too steep and broken. After hours of searching, the climbers were unable to find the elusive summit pitches.[5] Moreover, the danger from loose rock became apparent early on and worsened as the day progressed. While searching for the route, the climbers, even though they exercised utmost caution, dislodged several large rocks that crashed down the face of the mountain, sending ominous echoes out across the valley below.

Finally Hilliard decided to ascend the couloir above and to the north of the main snowfield on the east face. As the four climbers approached the top of the couloir, the rock steepened, so they stopped and tied into their ropes. Hilliard led the first two roped pitches, but on a ledge below the last pitch before the top of the couloir, he stopped. The rock above him towered precariously, becoming nearly vertical toward the top. The forty-eight-year-old Hilliard felt the strain of the climb. He complained of some weakness in his arm and decided to let the younger of the Allers lead the last pitch. The two Allers reached the top of the couloir without incident and set up a belay for Hilliard and Fowler to follow.

After situating themselves on a comfortable ledge, the Allers called down to Hilliard and Fowler waiting below. A moment passed, and they called again. There was no response, only the far-off sound of rocks clattering down the cliff. Worse, the rope was slack. Tense moments passed slowly as the two repeated their calls. Still no answer. Inching to the edge of the cliff, they carefully scanned the ledges below. There was no sign of either Hilliard or Fowler; they were simply gone. Later, both bodies were found resting on the side of the mountain. Rocks apparently dislodged from above knocked the pair off their precarious perch after Hilliard inexplicably untied them from the ropes. Fowler fell approximately six hundred feet, Hilliard almost twice that distance. Both were killed instantly.

The tragic accident that day silenced one of the strongest voices of the grassroots environmental movement. Hilliard's untimely death ended one of the most promising attempts to reconcile conservative and liberal conservationists in the state of Colorado. Although Hilliard was little known outside Colorado, his career as a moderator between opposing political factions made him an important player in several key environmental battles of the 1960s. He not only helped to reconcile individuals and groups with environmental interests but also helped to bridge the gap between an older generation of conservationists and a younger generation of environmentalists.

The tragic accident in Aspen that day also proved a harbinger of problems for environmentalism in Colorado and the still young Conservation Library. Hilliard's untimely death symbolized for many the beginning of the end of a very productive and powerful environmental coalition in Colorado, with the Conservation Library at its center. The unity of purpose and thought that characterized environmental advocacy in the early 1960s, which Edward Hilliard epitomized, suffered throughout the 1970s. Work on behalf of the environment became entangled with the complex social dynamics of the 1960s and 1970s.[6] By the 1980s, the situation deteriorated to the point that virtually all forms of environmental issues in the state wound up in the courts. It was during these dark days that Colorado environmentalists missed the moderating voice of Ed Hilliard.

During his coalition-building days in the 1960s and 1970s, Hilliard depended on the support of his wife, who played a less public but significant role in the Colorado environmental movement and especially in the history of the Conservation Library. An enthusiastic mountaineer, world-class sport fisher, pioneer supporter of Planned Parenthood, and thoughtful philanthropist, Joy Hilliard picked up the baton from her fallen husband. In many respects, the Conservation Library owes as much to Joy Hilliard as to any other individual. The CLC in its current incarnation depends on an endowment she supplied—a fitting tribute to a man who considered coalition building to be his greatest accomplishment. Hilliard, who understood the difficulty of uniting diverse groups and generations behind a common cause, would have been pleased that his money went to a place that was defined by similar issues.

During the period from 1982 to 1995, the Conservation Library did not completely fade from view. A few researchers continued to use the manuscripts in systematic ways, while others stumbled upon various pieces of the CLC strewn throughout the larger DPL collections.[7] While most people quickly forgot the library, a group of environmentalists and concerned community members began working to restore it a few years after the official closure. The DPL Acquisitions Committee, under the direction of Barbara Walton, became involved and actively worked to locate new sources of funding and to secure new collections. Many of Carhart's surviving old friends, devastated by the closure of the CLC, worked with Walton to formulate a plan to reinstate the library. Among these, Theodore Swem, a past president of the Wilderness Society and former assistant director of the Department of the Interior, became a driving force. Throughout the thirteen-year dormant period, there was never a time when the CLC was completely forgotten, although many had given up hope that it would ever be reestablished. Small groups often gathered at Dozen's Restaurant across from the library to mull over the resurrection of the library while having club sandwiches and pitchers of iced tea. The rising popularity of environmental history during the late 1980s and early 1990s brought a new generation of researchers to Denver in search of the former Conservation Library. By the mid-1990s, requests for use of the CLC had grown significantly, prompting the DPL administration to search for ways to expand accessibility and possibly work toward organizing the content of the CLC collections. The archives remained locked away in the warehouse, but it was becoming clear that they would need to be brought back downtown, where they could be opened to the public. The resolution to the Conservation Library's long term in purgatory came in the form of a generous gift from Joy Hilliard.

During the years since her husband's death, Joy worked to use his money in ways that symbolized his dedication to the environmental movement. The Hilliards personally funded several of Colorado's most successful grassroots environmental organizations during the 1960s and 1970s. Joy thought that the Conservation Library was a perfect representation of her husband's commitment to cooperation and the open flow of ideas.[8] She hoped that her gift would enable the Conservation Library to once again become a center for grassroots environmental action, if perhaps, this time, on a more realistic scale. She also realized that historians might want to look at the rich records of the Conservation Library to search for the players in the story, like her husband, who did not quite fit into traditional histories of the movement.

Joy Hilliard's gift dramatically changed the fortunes of the Conservation Library. The shrine is reopened. The artifacts are reassembled, though less accessible, and the books are finding their way home from the science and technology stacks. At least at this writing, the CLC is once again open to researchers, with many of the original CLC rare books gathered together in a new room bearing Ed Hilliard's name. The Hilliard family gift made possible future growth of the library by providing research and materials-processing facilities, funds for acquisition of additional materials, and trained staff to manage the collections. The staff members this time around are librarians and archivists, not activists.

Although the Conservation Library is a much quieter place than it once was, it is, in many respects, closer now to what Carhart and Eastlick had originally intended. The manuscripts have been weeded, cleaned, and organized. Researchers can use the manuscripts and perhaps uncover some new insights into the complex history of American relations with the environment. Activists who wish to study past history of their movement will find easy access to rich documents that will reveal the daunting challeges facing those who choose to speak for nature. In many ways the CLC has reverted to its earliest stages, yet its current shape also admirably reflects the work of Kay Collins and her generation of environmentalists. Researchers who come to gaze at John Muir's artifacts or to read about pioneer nature advocates will also have to confront the artifacts of alternative technology and try to puzzle out the links between woodstoves, personal computers, and wilderness. Arthur Carhart's conservation icons and Kay Collin's alternative technology relics rest side by side as they should. The environmental movement has always created strange bedfellows.

NOTES

PREFACE

1. During the course of its development, the Conservation Library was known by several names. In the 1960s, it was called variously the Conservation Library Center of North America, the Conservation Library, the Conservation Library Center, and the Conservation Library Collection. All these names imply an actual physical space in addition to the archival collections. In its current incarnation it is known simply as the Conservation Collection. In this study I will use "Conservation Library" or "CLC" to refer to the physical space that evolved and changed over time, as well as the archival collections that constitute the past and current holdings of the Denver Public Library related to the environment and the conservation movement.

2. John Eastlick, "Proposed Collection of Conservation of Natural Resources," CLC Archive, box 4, FF-51.

PROLOGUE

1. DPL/WHC, AHC Papers, James Cagney Correspondence, box 1:200.
2. "Toughie Cagney Fights Pollution," *Rocky Mountain News*, December 13, 1968; Ron Offen, *Cagney* (Chicago: Henry Regnery, 1972).
3. Ibid.
4. James Cagney to Kenneth Porter, December 28, 1968, DPL/WHC, CLC Archive, box 8, f.2.
5. Offen, *Cagney*, 169.
6. Aldo Leopold, *A Sand County Almanac and Sketches Here and There* (New York: Oxford University Press, 1987).
7. Offen, *Cagney*, 168.
8. James Cagney to Arthur Carhart, June 22, 1956, DPL/WHC, CLC Archive, box 8, f.2. See also James Cagney–Arthur Carhart correspondence, DPL/WHC, AHC Papers, box 1:200.
9. American Motors Conservation Awards press release kits, DPL/WHC, American Motors Awards Collection, box 14.
10. "Remarks by R. E. Long, Denver Zone Manager, American Motors Corporation, Before the National Watershed Congress Banquet," June 9, 1970, DPL/WHC, American Motors Awards Collection, box 15.
11. Nash press release, DPL/WHC, American Motors Awards Collection, box 1, f.1.
12. "Remarks by R. E. Long," 5.
13. "American Motors Corporation: Conservation Awards, Our Objective," DPL/WHC, American Motors Awards Collection, box 1, f.1.
14. "Resource Library Lauded as Source," *Denver Post*, December 17, 1968.
15. "City Library Recognized," *Denver Post*, December 13, 1968.
16. Ibid.

CHAPTER 1. COLLECTING HISTORY

1. I owe a great debt to historian Donna Haraway for providing an innovative conceptual framework for the type of analysis I attempt here. Her wonderful essay "Teddy Bear Patriarchy: Taxidermy in the Garden of Eden, New York City, 1908–1936," in her book *Primate Visions: Gender, Race, and Nature in the World of Modern Science* (New York: Routledge, 1989), provided the original inspiration for using a collection as the starting point for an analysis of gender, nature, and the cultural politics of environmentalism. Parts of this chapter are derived from an essay, "Human Nature in the Vault," in *Human/Nature: Biology, Culture, and Environmental History,* ed. John P. Herron and Andrew G. Kirk (Albuquerque: University of New Mexico Press, 1999), 121–34.

2. Carleton Knight, "What Is Post-modernism, Anyway?" *Travel and Leisure* 15, no. 5 (May 1985): 28–32. Knight provides a good overview of Graves and the postmodern architecture movement in American public cultural buildings.

3. Henry Petroski, *The Pencil: A History of Design and Circumstance* (New York: Knopf, 1992).

4. The Carter quotation is from "Conservation Library Energy/Environment Information Center: Foundation Report," November 15, 1981, DPL/WHC, CLC Archive, box 3. Other examples of how the CLC influenced library development and design can be found in the following: John Eastlick, "The Conservation Library Center of North America," *Special Libraries* 54 (December 1963): 637–38; Joan Hinkemeyer, "Energy/Environment Information Center," *Colorado Libraries,* March 1979, 18–19; Colleen Cayton, "The Denver Public Library's Regional Energy/Environment Information Center: An Uncommon Cooperative Venture," *Library Journal* 106 (January 1981): 21–25.

5. The only other published sources on the development and significance of the collection are by this author. See Andrew G. Kirk, *The Gentle Science: A History of the Conservation Library* (Denver: Denver Public Library, 1995); and Kirk, "Human Nature in the Vault." An indication of how fast the CLC faded from view is the striking omission of any reference to the collections in the otherwise very complete *Encyclopedia of American Forest and Conservation History.* This two-volume set even includes a section titled "Historical Sources," where one might assume to find at least brief mention of the CLC. But by 1983, when the encyclopedia project was completed, the CLC had already faded to obscurity. Richard C. Davis, ed., *Encyclopedia of American Forest and Conservation History,* 2 vols. (New York: Macmillan, 1983).

6. Conservation historian Stephen Fox is the *single* exception to this rule. He includes a very brief reference to the CLC in his history of the American conservation movement. Stephen Fox, *The American Conservation Movement: John Muir and His Legacy* (Madison: University of Wisconsin Press, 1981), 269.

7. See especially Jennifer Price, "Looking for Nature at the Mall: A Field Guide to the Nature Company," in *Uncommon Ground: Toward Reinventing Nature,* ed. William Cronon (New York: Norton, 1995); and Price, "A Natural History of the Plastic Pink Flamingo," in *The Nature of Nature: New Essays from America's Finest Writers on Nature,* ed. William H. Shore (New York: Harcourt Brace, 1994). See also Donna Haraway's essay, "Teddy Bear Patriarchy." Ethnographers have also explored this subject. See especially James Clifford, *The Predicament of Culture: Twentieth-Century Ethnography, Literature, and Art* (Cambridge, Mass.: Harvard University Press, 1988); and James Clifford and George E. Marcus, eds., *Writing Culture: The Poetics and Politics of Ethnography* (Berkeley: University of California Press, 1986).

8. Haraway, "Teddy Bear Patriarchy."

9. Clifford, *The Predicament of Culture*, 218.

10. Museology tends to focus on analytical study of museum culture and all its social implications, drawing heavily on the work of other cultural studies and the social sciences, as opposed to the more practical museography, which focuses on the practice of museum work and design. The literature of museum studies is extensive. The following are some of the works by authors in museum studies and history that I found most useful for this study. Dillon Ripley, *The Sacred Grove: Essays on Museums* (London: Victor Gollancz, 1970). Although sometimes elitist and outdated, this classic study contains real gems on collecting and collectors. The single best study of museum theory and material culture, in my opinion, is Susan M. Pearce, *Museums, Objects, and Collections* (Washington, D.C.: Smithsonian Institution Press, 1992). Another fine study is Stephen E. Weil, *A Cabinet of Curiosities: Inquiries into Museums and Their Prospects* (Washington, D.C.: Smithsonian Institution Press, 1995). Eileen Hooper-Greenhill, ed., *Museum, Media, Message* (London: Routledge, 1995); Jo Blatti, *Presenting the Past: Essays on History and the Public* (Philadelphia: Temple University Press, 1986); Edward P. Alexander, *Museums in Motion: An Introduction to the History and Function of Museums* (Nashville, Tenn.: American Association for State and Local History, 1979). See Michael Kammen, *Mystic Cords of Memory: The Transformation of Tradition in American Culture* (New York: Vintage, 1991), a weighty tome that is indispensable for anyone interesting in the cultural history of museums and collecting placed in the larger context of evolving manifestations of tradition in popular culture. David Lowenthal's *The Past Is a Foreign Country* (Cambridge: Cambridge University Press, 1985) has a good chapter on material culture and history. Ivan Karp and Steven D. Lavine, eds., *Exhibiting Cultures: The Poetics and Politics of Museum Display* (Washington, D.C.: Smithsonian Institution Press, 1991); Simon J. Bronner, ed., *Consuming Visions: Accumulation and Display of Goods in America, 1880–1920* (New York: Norton, 1989); Jean Baudrillard, *Le Systéme des objects* (Paris: Gallimard, 1968); Jane R. Glaser and Artemis A. Zenetou, eds., *Gender Perspectives: Essays on Women in Museums* (Washington, D.C.: Smithsonian Institution Press, 1994); Steven Conn, *Museums and American Intellectual Life, 1876–1926* (Chicago: University of Chicago Press, 1998). Also very useful is David Jenkins, "Object Lessons and Ethnographic Displays: Museum Exhibitions and the Making of American Anthropology," *Comparative Studies in Society and History* 36 (April 1994): 242–70.

11. Roderick Nash, *Wilderness and the American Mind*, rev. ed. (New Haven, Conn.: Yale University Press, 1973); Samuel P. Hays, *Conservation and the Gospel of Efficiency: The Progressive Conservation Movement, 1890–1920* (Cambridge, Mass.: Harvard University Press, 1959); Hays, *Beauty, Health, and Permanence: Environmental Politics in the United States, 1955–1985* (Cambridge: Cambridge University Press, 1987); and Hays, *Explorations in Environmental History: Essays by Samuel P. Hays* (Pittsburgh: University of Pittsburgh Press, 1998); Donald Worster, *Nature's Economy: A History of Ecological Ideals*, 2d ed. (Cambridge: Cambridge University Press, 1994). See also Michael P. Cohen, *The Pathless Way: John Muir and the American Wilderness* (Madison: University of Wisconsin Press, 1984); Robert C. Paehlke, *Environmentalism and the Future of Progressive Politics* (New Haven, Conn.: Yale University Press, 1989); Fox, *The American Conservation Movement;* Fromme, *Battle for the Wilderness* (New York: Praeger, 1974); Richard D. Lamm and Michael McCarthy, *The Angry West: A Vulnerable Land and Its Future* (Boston: Houghton Mifflin, 1982); Kirkpatrick Sale, *The Green Revolution: The American Environmental Movement, 1962–1992* (New York: Hill and Wang, 1993); Philip Shabecoff, *A Fierce*

Green Fire: The American Environmental Movement (New York: Hill and Wang, 1993); Hal Rothman, *The Greening of a Nation?* *Environmentalism in the United States Since 1945* (New York: Harbrace, 1997); and Rothman, *Saving the Planet: The American Response to the Environment in the Twentieth Century* (Chicago: Ivan R. Dee, 2000); Bob Pepperman Taylor, *Our Limits Transgressed: Environmental Political Thought in America* (Lawrence: University Press of Kansas, 1992).

12. Many recent works attempt to move beyond the models established by Nash and Hays. See especially Max Oelschlaeger, *The Idea of Wilderness: From Prehistory to the Age of Ecology* (New Haven, Conn.: Yale University Press, 1991); and Oelschlaeger, ed., *The Wilderness Condition: Essays on Environment and Civilization* (Washington, D.C.: Island Press, 1992).

13. William Cronon's *Uncommon Ground* is a notable example of this trend. This book came out of a semester-long interdisciplinary conference explicitly exploring cultural constructions of the idea of "nature." The New Mexico Environmental Symposium, April 1996, expanded on this theme by examining how ideas of "nature" and "human nature" operate within environmental discourse to inform the work of environmental historians and environmentalists.

14. Vera Norwood, *Made from This Earth: American Women and Nature* (Chapel Hill: University of North Carolina Press, 1993); Carolyn Merchant, *Ecological Revolutions: Nature, Gender, and Science in New England* (Chapel Hill: University of North Carolina Press, 1989); Joni Seager, *Earth Follies: Coming to Feminist Terms with the Global Environmental Crisis* (New York: Routledge, 1993); Virginia Scharff, "Are Earth Girls Easy? Ecofeminism, Women's History and Environmental History," *Journal of Women's History* 7 (summer 1995): 164–75.

15. One of the key aspects of this story is the role of the Conservation Library, and libraries in general, as avenues for social empowerment. The development of the library hierarchy during the 1960s and 1970s mirrored changing race and gender dynamics in society at large. Some of these issues of race and gender within the framework of the library are explored in the following literature: Laurel Ann Grotzinger, *The Power and the Dignity: Librarianship and Katherine Sharp* (New York: Scarecrow Press, 1966); James Thorpe, *Henry Edwards Huntington: A Biography* (Berkeley: University of California Press, 1994); Ismail Abdullahi, ed., *E. J. Josey: An Activist Librarian* (Metuchen, N.J.: Scarecrow Press, 1992); Phyllis Dain, "Ambivalence and Paradox: The Social Bonds of the Public Library," *Library Journal* 100 (1975): 261–66; Joanne E. Passet, "The Literature of American Library History, 1991–1992," *Libraries and Culture* 29 (fall 1994): 415–39.

16. Glaser and Zenetou, *Gender Perspective.*

CHAPTER 2. A CLEAN-CUT OUTDOOR MAN

1. Some may find this biography of Carhart too detailed for this study. I think, however, that to understand the place, you need to understand the man who conceived it. Carhart's life story is an outstanding example of the transformations in conservation thinking that ultimately led to the creation of the CLC. His struggles to define a viable environmental philosophy and reconcile it with a dramatically changing social landscape are emblematic of his generation and crucial to this story.

2. Virtually all conservation histories include at least some small reference to Carhart. Most historians acknowledge that he was a central figure in the early Forest Service debates about wilderness, but few go beyond a paragraph about

his role in the early wilderness debate. Even a careful review of the literature leaves one with the impression that Carhart appeared on the scene in 1919 and disappeared completely in 1921.

3. Donald N. Baldwin, *The Quiet Revolution: The Grass Roots of Today's Wilderness Preservation Movement* (Boulder, Colo.: Pruett, 1972); Roderick Nash, "Arthur Carhart: Wildland Advocate," *Living Wilderness* 44 (December 1980): 32–34; Nash, *Wilderness and the American Mind*, rev. ed. (New Haven, Conn.: Yale University Press, 1973), 185–88; Erik J. Martin, "A Voice for the Wilderness: Arthur H. Carhart," *Landscape Architecture* 76, no. 4 (July/August 1986): 71–75.

4. A recent notable exception to the trend is Paul S. Sutter, "'A Blank Spot on the Map': Aldo Leopold, Wilderness, and U.S. Forest Service Recreational Policy, 1909–1924," *Western Historical Quarterly* 29 (summer 1998): 187–214. Sutter revisits the old Carhart-Leopold story but does a much better job of contextualizing the wilderness-recreation debate in the Forest Service and the philosophical differences between the two men. The wilderness purity test is still present, but overall Sutter's description of the debate and Carhart's position in it is much more balanced than previous accounts.

5. Carhart was a contemporary of Bernard DeVoto and Aldo Leopold and knew almost every significant American environmentalist personally. Among others, Wallace Stegner credited Carhart as one of the people who "galvanized" his personal environmental thinking. Richard Etulain and Wallace Stegner, *Conversations with Wallace Stegner on Western History and Literature* (Salt Lake City: University of Utah Press, 1983), 170.

6. In addition to Donna Haraway's work, listed earlier, see, in particular, Gail Bederman, *Manliness and Civilization: A Cultural History of Gender and Race in the United States, 1880–1917* (Chicago: University of Chicago Press, 1996); Andrew Ross, "The Great White Dude," in *Constructing Masculinity*, ed. Maurice Berger, Brian Wallis, and Simon Watson (New York: Routledge, 1995); Harvey Green, *Fit for America: Health, Fitness, Sport and American Society* (Baltimore: Johns Hopkins University Press, 1986); E. Anthony Rotundo, *American Manhood: Transformations in Masculinity from the Revolution to the Modern Era* (New York: Basic Books, 1993); Vera Norwood, *Made from This Earth: American Women and Nature* (Chapel Hill: University of North Carolina Press, 1993); Norwood, "Constructing Gender in Nature: Bird Society Through the Eyes of John Burroughs and Florence Merriam Bailey," in *Human/Nature: Biology, Culture, and Environmental History*, ed. John P. Herron and Andrew G. Kirk (Albuquerque: University of New Mexico Press, 1999), 49–62, and, in the same volume, Virginia Scharff, "Man and Nature! Sex Secrets of Environmental History," 31–48; Carolyn Merchant, *Ecological Revolutions: Nature, Gender, and Science in New England* (Chapel Hill: University of North Carolina Press, 1989).

7. Bederman, *Manliness and Civilization*, 172. Bederman convincingly uses Roosevelt to demonstrate the dualistic quality of American manliness. For more on the tradition of violence, hunting, and manhood in American culture, see Richard Slotkin, *Gunfighter Nation: The Myth of the Frontier in Twentieth-Century America* (Norman: University of Oklahoma Press, 1998), 33–35, 50–52.

8. Gail Bederman and Donna Haraway both effectively use Teddy Roosevelt as the ultimate example of the attempt to reconcile the violent and civilized sides of American masculinity.

9. Arthur Carhart, "Biographical Sketch," DPL/WHC, AHC Papers, box 482. There are several good sources, in addition to the preceding, on Carhart's early life. See Roscoe Flemming, "The Story of Arthur Carhart," *Rocky Mountain*

News, December 29, 1941, 2; McClellan Melville, "A Conservationist Conserves Learning," *American Forests* 79 (January 1973): 15, 60–63; Nash, "Arthur Carhart: Wildland Advocate," 32–34. More important are the manuscript materials contained in the CLC collections. An unpublished book manuscript (c. 1974) by Carhart, entitled "This Way to Wilderness," DPL/WHC, box 75, envelope 1, details Carhart's personal journey toward a recognition of wilderness values. A document entitled "Arthur Carhart, America's Pioneer Wilderness Planner," printed by the U.S. Forest Service (March 14, 1973), is also useful. One of the best concise sources is a letter from Arthur Carhart to John Devlin of the *New York Times,* December 12, 1962, DPL/WHC, AHC Papers, box 699.

10. Carhart, "Biographical Sketch," 2.

11. Carhart's relationship with his father is frustratingly difficult to document. When Arthur was an adult, they corresponded regularly and seemed to have a good relationship. Earlier correspondence indicates that there was a great deal of tension between them. It is, admittedly, difficult to gauge the degree to which the elder Carhart's talk of becoming a man had to do with a desire for his son's future financial health or fears about his son's perceived lack of masculinity.

12. Carhart, "This Way to Wilderness," 6.

13. Carhart, "Biographical Sketch," 3.

14. John Davey, *The Tree Doctor: A Book on Tree Culture* (New York: Saalfield Publishing Company, 1904).

15. Iowa State yearbooks, 1914–1916, DPL/WHC, AHC Papers, box 432.

16. Carhart to Devlin, December 12, 1962, 1.

17. Ibid., 2.

18. Carhart, "This Way to Wilderness," 7.

19. Carhart to Devlin, December 12, 1962, 2.

20. Arthur Carhart, *Water or Your Life* (Philadelphia: Lippincott, 1951), 260–63.

21. Suellen Hoy, *Chasing Dirt: The American Pursuit of Cleanliness* (New York: Oxford University Press, 1995), 134–38.

22. Carhart, "Biographical Sketch," 2.

23. Harold K. Steen, *The U.S. Forest Service: A History* (Seattle: University of Washington Press, 1976).

24. Anne Whiston Sprin, "Constructing Nature: The Legacy of Frederick Law Olmsted," in *Uncommon Ground: Toward Reinventing Nature,* ed. William Cronon (New York: Norton, 1995), 91–113.

25. Nash, "Arthur Carhart: Wildland Advocate," 32.

26. Arthur Carhart, *Timber in Your Life* (Philadelphia: Lippincott, 1955), 138.

27. On April 12, 1973, the Forest Service hosted a banquet in honor of Arthur Carhart. The proceedings from this event provide good information on Carhart's Forest Service career. In addition to Donald Baldwin's *The Quiet Revolution,* many newspaper articles profiling Carhart's early career appeared in the Colorado press, where he was something of a local celebrity. One of the best of these is Roscoe Flemming's short article "The Story of Arthur Carhart," 2.

28. Carhart, "This Way to Wilderness," 15.

29. Carhart's accomplishments in the Forest Service have been the source of considerable historical controversy. During the 1960s, he was recognized as a national leader of the conservation movement. Most Americans knew him as the author of successful conservation books and articles and as one of the leading opponents of the Echo Park dam. Few, however, remembered his early career in the Forest Service, which is ironic considering that now few know him for any-

thing else. This situation changed with the appearance of a dissertation on the origins of the wilderness movement by Donald Baldwin, "Historical Study of the Western Origin, Application and Development of the Wilderness Concept" (Ph.D. diss., University of Denver, 1965), which presented a surprising thesis. Baldwin argued, in no uncertain terms, that contrary to most historians and the Forest Service, Carhart, not Aldo Leopold, was the "father" of the wilderness concept in the United States. Baldwin reached this conclusion after researching Carhart's early career. He argued that based on the timing of events in the early 1920s the first application of something that could be called a "wilderness policy" within the Forest Service took place in Colorado at a remote area of the Routt National Forest. This line of reasoning ran contrary to the generally accepted history of the wilderness movement that focused on Leopold's work in the Gila National Forest of New Mexico, which became America's first official wilderness area in 1924. Baldwin maintained that the first wilderness designation actually occurred four years earlier in Colorado. This boring debate about wilderness paternity has had a surprisingly long life that hopefully will end soon.

30. Ibid.

31. Arthur Carhart, "Historical Development of Outdoor Recreation," in *Outdoor Recreation Literature: A Survey*, Outdoor Recreation Resources Review Commission Study Report 27, Washington, D.C., 1962, 111.

32. Ibid.

33. In addition to Baldwin's version of the story, many accounts have appeared in print over the years. Carhart told the story himself in a number of publications. The most complete version can be found in *Timber in Your Life*. Also useful are John C. Hendee, George H. Stankey, and Robert C. Lucas, *Wilderness Management* (Washington, D.C.: U.S. Department of Agriculture, Forest Service, 1978), 35; Carl J. Stahl, "The Recreational Policy of the Forest Service," *Trail and Timberline*, no. 17 (January 1920): 7; Steen. *The U.S. Forest Service*, 154; Nash, *Wilderness and the American Mind*, 185–86.

34. Arthur Carhart, "General Working Plan, Recreational Development of the San Isabel National Forest, Colorado, December 1919," DPL/WHC, AHC Papers, box 2: 111.

35. Arthur Carhart, "Recreation Plan, Superior National Forest, Minnesota, 1921," DPL/WHC, AHC Papers, box 2: 111.

36. Despite Baldwin's claims to the contrary, Leopold clearly controlled the discussion and influenced Carhart's thinking rather than the other way around. Throughout his years with the Forest Service, Carhart struggled with these issues and never reached any firm conclusions about wilderness. Leopold, on the other hand, had developed some fairly sophisticated plans by the time of the meeting in Denver.

37. Arthur Carhart to Estella Leopold, April 24, 1964, DPL/WHC, CLC 585, box 1.

38. Arthur Carhart, "Memorandum to Aldo Leopold," December 10, 1919, DPL/WHC, CLC, box 696.

39. *Webster's New Riverside University Dictionary* (Boston: Riverside, 1984), 984.

40. Arthur Carhart, "A Memo to My Friends," DPL/WHC, CLC, box 699.1.

41. Carhart, *Timber in Your Life*, 137.

42. Carhart, "A Memo to My Friends," 2.

43. Carhart, *Timber in Your Life*, 148.

44. The San Isabel and Mount Evans regional plans are good examples of

Carhart's abilities as a land planner. Both of these studies encompassed large geographic regions with myriad management problems.

45. Carhart, "This Way to Wilderness," 42.

46. Carhart, "Biographical Sketch," 1.

47. Steen, *The U.S. Forest Service*, 158.

48. Carhart, ORRRC Study Report 27, 113.

49. Steen, *The U.S. Forest Service*, 157–58.

50. Carhart, "Biographical Sketch," 4.

51. Ibid.

52. In *The Quiet Revolution,* Baldwin points to the Superior plan as the key to Carhart's wilderness preservation ideology, hailing it as the "second and largest application of the wilderness concept" in America, with the "third" application coming in 1924 with Leopold's plan for the Gila. Using strident and uncompromising rhetoric, Baldwin argues emphatically for the centrality of Carhart's role in the genesis of the wilderness movement in the Forest Service. "In the interest of historical accuracy, let the record be corrected to reflect that the wilderness concept was the brain-child of Arthur Carhart *not* Aldo Leopold" (6). This reinterpretation of Carhart's role in the founding of the wilderness movement became, surprisingly, the standard interpretation for a number of years after the publication of *The Quiet Revolution* with several key books accepting and reiterating Baldwin's argument. Especially important in establishing the legitimacy of Baldwin's interpretation was Nash's *Wilderness and the American Mind.* See also Steen, *The U.S. Forest Service;* and R. Newell Searle, *Saving Quetico-Superior: A Land Set Apart* (St. Paul: Minnesota Historical Society Press, 1977).

53. "Arthur Carhart, America's Pioneer Wilderness Planner," U.S. Forest Service, DPL/WHC, CLC Archive, box 75.

54. "Recognition Ceremony for Arthur Carhart, Forest Service's First Landscape Architect," U.S. Forest Service, DPL/WHC, CLC Archive, box 75.

55. "Charter and Program," Arthur Carhart National Wilderness Training Center. See also Hendee, Stankey, and Lucas, *Wilderness Management,* 13, 34–35, 222. Although the Baldwin thesis initially met with a warm reception in the Forest Service and the historical community, recent evaluations have tended to question the nature of Carhart's role. Historian Roderick Nash accepted Carhart as a pioneer wilderness planner but questioned Baldwin's attempt to establish Carhart as the sole intellectual parent of the wilderness concept. As he states in "Arthur Carhart: Wildland Advocate," "Baldwin's tribute seems overstated. . . . Carhart appears to have been a rather reluctant preservationist" (33). Nash gives credit to Carhart's role as a pioneer of large-scale land planning and broad thinking about wildland use and management while questioning his role as a wilderness prophet along the lines of Aldo Leopold. A more critical analysis of the Baldwin thesis may be found in David Backes's dissertation on the Quetico-Superior Wilderness. See Backes, "The Communication-Mediated Roles of Perceptual, Political, and Environmental Boundaries on Management of the Quetico-Superior Wilderness of Ontario and Minnesota, 1920–1965" (Ph.D. diss., University of Wisconsin-Madison, 1988). Backes seriously questions Baldwin's assertions and raises critical questions about Carhart's wilderness philosophy in the dissertation and in a later article: "Wilderness Visions: Arthur Carhart's 1922 Proposal for the Quetico-Superior Wilderness," *Forest and Conservation History* 35 (July 1991): 128.

56. Backes, "Wilderness Visions," 132.

57. The 1922 plan contained numerous suggestions for cabins, motorboat

launches, and other structures as part of a management plan to distribute visitors and facilitate travel. Backes points to these inclusions in as evidence of Carhart's lack of a "true" wilderness vision. In some ways Backes falls into the same lumping and splitting trap that he criticizes Baldwin for. In his attempts to prove that Carhart was not a *real* preservationist, he tends to simplify the debate about differing perceptions of wilderness.

58. William Cronon, ed., *Uncommon Ground: Toward Reinventing Nature* (New York: Norton, 1995), 69.

59. Ibid., 136.

60. Arthur Carhart, *Planning for America's Wildlands: A Handbook for Land-Use Planners, Managers and Executives, Committee and Commission Members, Conservation Leaders, and All Who Face Problems of Wildland Management* (Harrisburg, Pa.: Telegraph Press, 1961), 20.

61. Carhart, "Biographical Sketch," 5.

62. Most of Carhart's writings during this time dealt with outdoor recreation and his ideas for change within the Forest Service. The best of these articles appeared in local Denver magazines. For example, Arthur Carhart, "Going to the Glaciers: New Road Planned to Arapaho Peaks to Bring Ice Rivers Within Sixty Miles of Denver by Automobile," *Municipal Facts,* March–April, 1922, 7–10. Another good example of this early recreation writing is "The Lure of the Land Above the Trees: A Story for the Lover of Mountains, of the Land Where the Jagged Monarchs of the High Ranges Defiantly Challenge Devotees of Hazardous Sport," *American Forests and Forest Life* 30 (June 1924): 352–58. During the Forest Service years, he published similar articles about recreation in *Parks and Recreation, American Forestry, Vacation Magazine, Country Gentleman, Northern Sportsman,* and other periodicals.

63. "Partial List of Published Material by Arthur Hawthorne Carhart," December 1931, DPL/WHC, CLC box 75.

64. Arthur Carhart, *The Ordeal of Brad Ogden: A Romance of the Forest Rangers* (New York: J. H. Sears, 1929).

65. Arthur Carhart, "The Sacrifice of Centipede Ranch," *Five Novels Monthly,* June 1931, 393–424; Carhart, "Through the Red Dusk," *Blue Book Magazine,* March 1926, 7–33.

66. Carhart, *Ordeal of Brad Ogden,* 74–76; Arthur Carhart, *Son of the Forest* (Philadelphia: Lippincott, 1952).

67. Although I mention only four particular stories, Carhart wrote over thirty with this theme. "Partial List of Published Material," 5.

68. Carhart, "Through the Red Dusk," 33.

69. There are several good sources on pulp fiction and dime novels. See, for example, Henry Nash Smith, *Virgin Land: The American West as Symbol and Myth* (Cambridge, Mass.: Harvard University Press, 1950); Russell Nye, *The Unembarrassed Muse: The Popular Arts in America* (New York: Dial Press, 1970). There is also a widening body of writing on western pulp fiction and western fiction in general. See John A. Dinan, *The Pulp Fiction Western: A Popular History of the Western Fiction Magazine in America* (San Bernardino, Calif.: Borgo Press, 1983); Richard Etulain, *Re-imagining the Modern American West: A Century of Fiction, History, and Art* (Tucson: University of Arizona Press, 1996); and Etulain, *Telling Western Stories: From Buffalo Bill to Larry McMurtry* (Albuquerque: University of New Mexico Press, 1999).

70. Arthur H. Carhart and Stanley P. Young, *The Last Stand of the Pack* (New York: J. H. Sears, 1929).

71. Aldo Leopold, *A Sand County Almanac and Sketches Here and There* (New York: Oxford University Press, 1987), 130.

72. Most conservationists in the early part of the century firmly believed in predator control. Carhart was not alone, especially among hunters, in his desire to see wolves and other "pests" eliminated.

73. Carhart and Young, *Last Stand of the Pack*, xix–xx.

74. Ibid., 3.

75. In 1930, Carhart sent a copy of *Last Stand* to Swedish Arctic explorer Vilhjalmur Stefansson, ironically inscribed "To Vilhjalmur Stefansson, who understands the courage of the wolf." This copy is in the collection of the author.

76. John F. Reiger, *American Sportsmen and the Origins of Conservation* (Norman: University of Oklahoma Press, 1986).

77. Mary Austin, review of *Last Stand of the Pack, Saturday Review of Literature*, December 21, 1929, 587.

78. This is, admittedly, a hard thing to gauge. Based on the published reviews, sales of his books, and personal correspondence he received about his publications, one can, I would argue, make the claim that his fiction was well received. Another useful source for determining Carhart's success as an author may be found in his royalty statements, which seem to verify that he not only was able to survive as an author but actually made a considerable amount of money for the 1930s. DPL/WHC, AHC Papers, box 2:112, royalty statements, two folders.

79. Carhart, "Biographical Sketch," 5.

80. Carhart to John Devlin, 3.

81. Ibid.

82. See the following, all by Carhart: *Colorado* (New York: Coward-McCann, 1932), *How to Plan the Home Landscape* (Garden City, N.Y.: Doubleday Doran, 1935), *Trees and Shrubs for the Small Place* (Garden City, N.Y.: Doubleday Doran, 1935), *Drum Up the Dawn* (New York: Dodd, Mead, 1937). In addition to these books, Carhart published two westerns written under the pen name Hart Thorne: *Bronc Twister* (New York: Dodd, Mead, 1937); and *Saddle Men of the C Bit Brand* (New York: Dodd, Mead, 1937).

83. Carhart to Devlin, 3.

84. This sensitivity is most evident in the transcript of a radio broadcast titled "Writing in the Western Scene," KOA radio, Denver, Colorado (February 7, 1933), DPL/WHC, AHC Papers, box 2: 111. Particularly stinging were the comments of one eastern editor who referred to western writers as "oafs" and "hayseed-scribblers."

85. Ibid.

86. Carhart's one-man onslaught against the Colorado cattlemen began in March 1947 with "Raiders on the Range," *Trail and Timberline*, no. 339 (March 1947): 39–43, followed by "Who Says—Sell Our Public Lands in the West?" *American Forests* 53 (April 1947): 153–60, "Land Grab: Who Gets Our Public Lands?" *Atlantic Monthly* 182 (July 1948), 57–62; "Our Public Lands in Jeopardy," *Journal of Forestry* 46 (June 1948): 409–13; "Don't Fence Us In!" *Pacific Spectator* 1 (summer 1947): 251–64. Carhart's best statement of his philosophy can be found in *Timber in Your Life*. See also "The Politics of Public Lands: A Radio Discussion by Arthur Carhart, Meredith Wilson and William Wright," *University of Chicago Round Table* 541 (August 1, 1948).

87. Carhart, *Drum Up the Dawn*, 96.

88 Arthur Carhart, "A Memo to My Friends," November 25, 1948, DPL/WHC, AHC Papers, box 1:101.

89. The actual number of women involved in outdoor sports is hard to determine. During much of Carhart's life, women's participation would have been more limited than in recent decades. Still, mountain clubs, bird-watching clubs, garden clubs, and other outdoor organizations counted women as one of their key constituencies even during the early part of the century. As auto camping opportunities expanded, even more women participated in outdoor activities, and many assumed leadership roles in outdoor and conservation groups.

90. Robert Gottlieb, *Forcing the Spring: The Transformation of the American Environmental Movement* (Washington, D.C.: Island Press, 1993), 212–18. Gottlieb highlights a separate trend in environmental thinking for women that evolved alongside the male-dominated major organizations and clubs.

91. Arthur Carhart, *The Outdoorsman's Cookbook* (New York: Macmillan, 1945).

92. Arthur Carhart, *Hunting North American Deer* (New York: Macmillan, 1946); Carhart, *Fresh Water Fishing: Bait and Fly Casting, Spinning, Lures and Equipment* (New York: A. S. Barnes, 1949); and Carhart, *Fishing in the West* (New York: Macmillan, 1950).

93. Jim Bond to Arthur Carhart, August 23, 1960, DPL/WHC, AHC Papers, box 1:102.

94. Carhart to Devlin, 4.

95. The best example of Carhart's work with the timber industry is the widely circulated pamphlet "Trees and Game—Twin Crops" (Washington, D.C.: American Forest Products Industries, c. 1950).

96. Arthur Carhart, *Hi, Stranger! The Complete Guide to Dude Ranches* (Chicago: Ziff-Davis, 1949), 1.

97. The "land grab" was an attempt by western stockmen to use their political influence to purchase federal lands at giveaway prices. Carhart-DeVoto correspondence, DPL/WHC, AHC Papers.

98. Carhart wrote numerous articles against the dam. Two of the best are "State Must Not Toss Away Scenic Dinosaur Park" *Denver Post*, April 7, 1954, 41; and "The Menaced Dinosaur National Monument," *National Parks Magazine* 26 (January/March 1952): 19–30.

99. Arthur Carhart to Citizens Committee on Natural Resources, October 31, 1961, Bancroft Library, Sierra Club Records, 71/103c, 63:1.

100. Arthur Carhart to Martin Litton, August 8, 1953, Bancroft Library, Sierra Club Records, 71/103c, 87:33; "Lower Colorado River, Fact Sheet," October 1960, Bancroft Library, Sierra Club Records, 71/103c, 63:1

101. Mark W. T. Harvey, *A Symbol of Wilderness: Echo Park and the American Conservation Movement* (Albuquerque: University of New Mexico Press, 1994).

102. Arthur Carhart, *Conservation Please! Questions and Answers on Conservation Topics* (New York: Garden Club of America, 1950). Also, *Water or Your Life, Timber in Your Life, The National Forests* (New York: Knopf, 1959), and *Planning for America's Wildlands*.

103. Carhart, *Timber in Your Life*, 23.

104. *Water or Your Life* was criticized by some as inaccurate and alarmist, but it generally received good notices. See, for example, *New York Times,* July 29, 1951, 7, and the *Chicago Sunday Tribune*, August 26, 1951, 6.

105. Carhart, *Conservation Please!* 10.

106. Ibid.

107. Ibid., 13.

108. Ibid., 58.

109. Arthur Carhart, "Poisons: The Creeping Killer," *Sports Afield*, November 1959, 1–5.

110. Carhart, *Conservation Please!* 58.

111. Rachel Carson to Arthur Carhart, January 16, 1963, AHC Papers, box 1:200.

112. Nash, "Arthur Carhart: Wildland Advocate," 34.

113. Carhart, *Planning for America's Wildlands*, 19.

114. William Cronon is the most eloquent proponent of this position; see "The Trouble with Wilderness; or, Getting Back to the Wrong Nature," in *Uncommon Ground*, 69–90.

115. Carhart, *Planning for America's Wildlands*, 19.

116. For information on Carhart's position on the wilderness bill, see Cal Queal, "Ah, Wilderness," *Denver Post*, December 23, 1958, 18. In this interview Carhart speaks about his ambivalence toward the wilderness bill on the grounds that it could open the door to exploitation of less remote and scenic areas: "I recognize that the bill may be necessary to protect the wilderness, but it is only a portion of the all-inclusive plan we need for the recreational use of all our public land."

117. It is unclear where this reference originated, possibly with Carhart himself, but not all of Carhart's peers would have agreed with this grand title. It was popularized by Baldwin's *Quiet Revolution* and picked up by the Forest Service; the CLC used the title in much of its early literature.

118. Even those who worried about Carhart's lack of zeal for the wilderness bill and his close association with the timber industry applauded his arguments about land planning. Howard Zahniser turned to Carhart for advice on wilderness planning and tips on dealing with the timber industry and cattlemen's associations. Although the two men never agreed on the specifics of the wilderness bill, they respected each other's viewpoints and often worked together. See especially Howard Zahniser's foreword to *Planning for America's Wildlands*, and correspondence between Carhart and Zahniser, DPL/WHC, AHC Papers, box 83.

119. Carhart was concerned enough with conservation advocacy education to write a guidebook to educate potential leaders in the field. The unpublished manuscript, "The Home-Town Conservationist," DPL/WHC, AHC Papers, box 83, was a blueprint for grassroots environmental advocacy.

CHAPTER 3. COLLECTING NATURE

1. Thomas Jefferson, "Notes on the State of Virginia" in *The Life and Selected Writings of Thomas Jefferson*, ed. Adrienne Koch and William Peden (New York: Random House, 1993), 186.

2. Michael P. Cohen, *The History of the Sierra Club, 1892–1970* (San Francisco: Sierra Club Books, 1988), 242–46.

3. Jonas Frykman and Orvar Löfgren, *Culture Builders: A Historical Anthropology of Middle-Class Life*, trans. Alan Crozier (New Brunswick, N.J.: Rutgers University Press, 1987), 55.

4. "List of Counselors," DPL/WHC, CLC Archive, box 4, f.54.

5. Stephen Fox, *The American Conservation Movement: John Muir and His Legacy* (Madison: University of Wisconsin Press, 1981), 333–57.

6. Vera Norwood, *Made from This Earth: American Women and Nature* (Chapel Hill: University of North Carolina Press, 1993), 143–47.

7. Ibid., 144.

8. Ibid., 223; Horace M. Albright and Frank J. Taylor, *Oh, Ranger! A Book About the National Parks* (New York: Dodd, Mead, 1937).

9. Arthur Carhart to Dick Bratterton, August 31, 1961, DPL/WHC, "vault" box 2, f.1.

10. Ibid.

11. Ibid.

12. Arthur Carhart to Dr. Paul B. Sears, September 16, 1961, DPL/WHC, CLC Archive, box 7, Carhart file.

13. Ibid.

14. Ibid.

15. For more on the OWAA and the rift between sportsmen and environmentalists, see Ted Williams, "Natural Allies," *Sierra* 81, no. 5 (September/October 1996):46–53.

16. Arthur Carhart to Homer Circle, February 2, 1967, DPL/WHC, OWAA Papers, CLC Archive, 585, box 2.

17. "We Would Like You to Meet . . . the Counselors of the Conservation Library Center," DPL/WHC, CLC Archive, box 4, f.54.

18. *Denver Post*, May 22, 1961.

19. Ibid.

20. Arthur H. Carhart, "The Lore and Learning of Conservation," *American Forests* (January 1963).

21. Carhart and Eastlick never clearly defined their goals for creating a center for "constructive action." Obviously, the CLC, as part of a municipal department, could not advocate politically controversial positions. The hope remained, however, that by providing a centralized location the collection would aid the environmental movement.

22. Walter A. McDougall, *The Heavens and the Earth: A Political History of the Space Age* (New York: Basic Books, 1985).

23. Olaus J. Murie, as quoted in Fox, *The American Conservation Movement*, 268.

24. Ibid., 266.

25. The best source dealing with the strange ways that cold war politics influenced popular perceptions of American history and spawned a wave of interest in preserving particular versions of the past in exhibits and collections can be found in Michael Kammen, *Mystic Cords of Memory: The Transformation of Tradition in American Culture* (New York: Vintage, 1991), 571–617.

26. Arthur H. Carhart, draft of proposal for conservation education, DPL/WHC, CLC Archive, box 4, f.51.

27. John Eastlick, "The Conservation Library Center of North America," *Special Libraries* 54 (December 1963): 638.

28. Similar antimodernist arguments against technology can be heard today from critics of "virtual reality." N. Katherine Hayles, "Simulated Nature and Natural Simulations: Rethinking the Relation Between the Beholder and the World," in *Uncommon Ground: Toward Reinventing Natur,* ed. William Cronon (New York: Norton, 1995). Carhart's notions of human nature are remarkably similar to those expressed by proponents of Biophilia, notably, E. O. Wilson. "What . . . will happen to the human psyche when such a defining part of the human evolutionary experience [contact with wild nature] is diminished or erased?" E. O. Wilson, "Biophilia and the Conservation Ethic," in *The Biophilia Hypothesis,* ed. Stephen R. Kellert and Edward O. Wilson (Washington, D.C.: Island Press, 1994), 35.

29. T. J. Jackson Lears, *No Place of Grace: Antimodernism and the Transformation*

of American Culture, 1880–1920 (New York: Pantheon, 1981). In this book I use the term "antimodernism" to group individuals and organizations who defined themselves in opposition to the prevailing twentieth-century belief in progress through *technological innovation.* Antimodernists in the conservation and preservation movements rarely rejected the modernist/Progressive ideal that societies are improvable; they simply rejected the notion that improvement required looking forward to new technologies to solve old problems.

30. A nice, concise discussion of the renewal of scarcity fears during the postwar period may be found in Hal K. Rothman, *Saving the Planet: The American Response to the Environment in the Twentieth Century* (Chicago: Ivan R. Dee, 2000), 113–17.

31. Most environmental historians have generally ignored the role of antimodernism in the conservation movement. The exception is Stephen Fox's *The American Conservation Movement.* Fox highlights Muir's antimodernist rhetoric as evidence that the conservation movement had, from the beginning, two distinct strains of thought: one, progressive and modern, focused on efficiency and reform; and the other, antimodernist, focused on the aesthetic and spiritual values of wilderness. A more complete discussion of these ideas can be found in philosopher Max Oelschlaeger's *The Idea of Wilderness: From Prehistory to the Age of Ecology* (New Haven, Conn.: Yale University Press, 1991). He convincingly argues against Fox's idea of John Muir as antimodernist and proposes instead that Muir and his conservation philosophy be viewed as the "leading edge of postmodernism" (203). The idea of a deconstructive antimodernist philosophy in constant tension with the modernist status quo may not ring true for a visionary like Muir, but it does provide a useful framework for analyzing Carhart and his cohorts in the 1950s.

32. Oelschlaeger, *The Idea of Wilderness* 201–2.

33. Fox, *The American Conservation Movement,* 352.

34. John Eastlick, "Proposed Collection of Conservation of Natural Resources," CLC Archive, box 4, FF-51.

35. James Clifford, *The Predicament of Culture: Twentieth-Century Ethnography, Literature, and Art* (Cambridge, Mass.: Harvard University Press, 1988), 218.

36. David Lowenthal, *The Heritage Crusade and the Spoils of History* (Cambridge: Cambridge University Press, 1998), 10–11.

37. David Jenkins, "Object Lessons and Ethnographic Displays: Museums Exhibitions and the Making of American Anthropology," *Comparative Studies in Society and History* 36 (April 1994): 242.

38. Susan M. Pearce, *Museums, Objects, and Collections* (Washington, D.C.: Smithsonian Institution Press, 1992), 46–66.

39. Andrew G. Kirk, "Conservationists and Wilderness Preservation in Colorado" (M.A. thesis, University of Colorado Denver, 1992). Although strong, the tradition of conservation advocacy in Colorado remained, as in other western states, an undercurrent in a river of discontent centered on federal land policies. Opponents of conservation outnumbered proponents for at least the first half of the state's history. For more on this subject, see G. Michael McCarthy, *Hour of Trial: The Conservation Conflict in Colorado and the West, 1891–1907* (Norman: University of Oklahoma Press, 1977).

40. Carhart, "The Lore and Learning of Conservation," 2.

41. Olaus J. Murie to Arthur Carhart, January 16, 1961, DPL/WHC, CLC Archive, box 4, f.54.

42. Bernard L. Orell to Arthur Carhart, January 9, 1961, DPL/WHC, CLC Archive, box 4, f.54.

43. Other responses can be found in DPL/WHC, CLC Archive, box 4, f.51–54.

44. Oelschlaeger, *The Idea of Wilderness*. In addition to Oelschlaeger's work, a number of good sources exist on the shift from conservation to environmentalism. See, for example, Samuel P. Hays, "From Conservation to Environment: Environmental Politics in the United States Since World War II," *Environmental Review* 6:2 (fall 1982): 14–29; Michael McCloskey, "Wilderness Movement at the Crossroads, 1945–1970," *Pacific Historical Review* 41 (1972): 346–61; Mark Harvey, "Echo Park, Glen Canyon, and the Postwar Wilderness Movement," *Pacific Historical Review* 60 (1991): 43–67.

45. Pearce, *Museums, Objects and Collections*, 48–66.

46. Arthur Carhart, *Water or Your Life* (Philadelphia: Lippincott, 1951), 17.

47. William Vogt, *Road to Survival* (New York: William Sloan, 1948), 18.

48. Arthur Carhart, *Planning for America's Wildlands* (Harrisburg, Pa.: Telegraph Press, 1961).

49. Several good sources in the CLC collections speak to the challenges of defining conservation. See especially "Criteria and Classifications in the Material Uses of Natural Resources" and "Proposed Collection on Conservation of Natural Resources," both in DPL/WHC, CLC Archive, box 4, f.51. See also "Basic Books on Conservation," DPL/WHC, CLC Archive, box 4, f.40; and "To Meet a Critical Need," DPL/WHC, CLC Archive, box 4, f.54. In addition to these documents, much of the correspondence from the years 1960–61 in CLC box 4 highlights the debate over the definition of the conservation ideology.

50. Eleanor Gehres, interview with author, Denver, Colorado, July 8, 1995.

51. This is the definition that Carhart and Eastlick concocted and circulated to the CLC counselors in the fall of 1960, DPL/WHC, CLC Archive, box 4, f.51.

52. Arthur Carhart, "Trees and Game—Twin Crops," (Washington, D.C.: American Forest Products Industries, c. 1950), 4.

53. Richard Smith to Arthur Carhart, August 8, 1963, DPL/WHC, CLC Archive, box 4, f.54.

54. Ibid.

55. Ibid.

56. Walter P. Taylor to Arthur Carhart, August 23, 1963, DPL/WHC, CLC Archive, box 4, f.51.

57. Ibid.

58. Olaus Murie to Arthur Carhart, January 16, 1961, DPL/WHC, CLC Archive, box 4, f.54.

59. The classic work on this subject is Samuel P. Hays, *Conservation and the Gospel of Efficiency: The Progressive Conservation Movement, 1890–1920* (Cambridge, Mass.: Harvard University Press, 1959).

60. Donald Worster, *Nature's Economy: A History of Ecological Ideas*, 2d ed. (Cambridge: Cambridge University Press, 1994), 209–20.

61. A good source on shifting environmental ideologies in the postwar period is M. Jimmie Killingsworth and Jacqueline S. Palmer, *Ecospeak: Rhetoric and Environmental Politics in America* (Carbondale: Southern Illinois University Press, 1992).

62. Taylor to Carhart, August 23, 1963.

63. "Criteria and Classifications in the Material Uses of Natural Resources," 2.

64. E. F. Shumacher, *Small Is Beautiful: Economics as If People Mattered* (New York: Harper and Row, 1973), 15.

65. "Conservation Unit Set Up at Library," *Rocky Mountain News*, May 13,

1961; "World Conservation Center Opening at Denver's Public Library," *Denver Post,* May 21, 1961; "Conservation Library Gets $25,000 Grant," *Rocky Mountain News,* January 12, 1962; "A Treasury of Conservation Lore," *Rocky Mountain News,* September 10, 1962; "Conservation Center Grows," *Denver Post,* November 10, 1962; "Conservation Center Given Rare Records," *Rocky Mountain News,* March 25, 1962; "Denver, Washington to Join in Providing Library Service," *Denver Post,* September 16, 1965; "City Conservation Center Booming," *Denver Post,* August 22, 1965; "Conservation Library Knows the Answer," *Denver Post,* September 9, 1967; "Conservation Asset to Denver," *Denver Post,* December 13, 1968; "Public Land Use Facts at Library," *Denver Post,* July 18, 1969; "Storehouse for Conservation," *Denver Post,* October 4, 1970.

66. Carhart, "The Lore and Learning of Conservation," 2.

67. Ibid.

68. Ibid.

69. There were several donations of Zahniser materials, some before his death and some after.

70. Mary Douglas, *Purity and Danger: An Analysis of Concepts of Pollution and Taboo* (London: Routledge, 1980). Whether some of these artifacts were intentionally gathered or just happened to be thrown together in the chaotic rush to find a home for the ceaseless onslaught of new collections is impossible to determine. Regardless of how they found themselves occupying the same space, the juxtaposition raises interesting questions.

71. Stephen J. Leonard and Thomas J. Noel, *Denver: From Mining Camp to Metropolis* (Niwot: University of Colorado Press, 1990), 190–202; Kathleen M. Blee, *Women of the Klan: Racism and Gender in the 1920s* (Berkeley: University of California Press, 1991); Robert Alan Goldberg, *Hooded Empire: The Ku Klux Klan in Colorado* (Urbana: University of Illinois Press, 1981).

72. Goldberg, *Hooded Empire,* 118.

73. Paul R. Ehrlich, *The Population Bomb* (New York: Ballantine, 1968).

74. Fox, *The American Conservation Movement,* 307.

75. Vogt, *Road to Survival,* 46.

76. Fox, *The American Conservation Movement,* 307.

77. In addition to Vogt, CLC counselor and Carhart friend Olaus Murie wrote some of the most pointed critiques of postwar population problems. See, in particular, Olaus Murie to John M. Spencer, April 2, 1953, Bancroft Library, Sierra Club Records, 71/103c, 63:18.

78. Vogt, *Road to Survival,* 145.

79. John P. Herron and Andrew G. Kirk, eds., *Human/Nature: Biology, Culture, and Environmental History* (Albuquerque: University of New Mexico Press, 1999).

80. *Cape Times,* March 25, 1963; *El Mensajero Forestal,* January 1963.

81. Carhart, "The Lore and Learning of Conservation."

82. "The Denver Public Library Foundation," brochure explaining organization and goals of the group, DPL/WHC, CLC Archive, box 3.

CHAPTER 4. WILDERNESS, BIRTH CONTROL, AND CARD CATALOGS

1. Tam Mossman, ed., *The Best of Robert Service* (Philadelphia: Running Press, 1983), 14.

2. Kirkpatrick Sale, *The Green Revolution: The American Environmental Movement, 1962–1992* (New York: Hill AND Wang, 1993); Samuel P. Hays, *Beauty,*

Health, and Permanence: Environmental Politics in the United States, 1955–1985 (Cambridge: Cambridge University Press, 1987); Hays, *Explorations in Environmental History: Essays by Samuel P. Hays* (Pittsburgh: University of Pittsburgh Press, 1998); Hal Rothman, *Saving the Planet: The American Response to the Environment in the Twentieth Century* (Chicago: Ivan R. Dee, 2000);. Theodore Roszak, *The Making of a Counter Culture: Reflections on the Technocratic Society and Its Youthful Opposition* (Garden City, N.Y.: Doubleday, 1969); Todd Gitlin, *The Sixties: Years of Hope, Days of Rage* (New York: Bantam, 1987); Irwin Unger, *The Movement: A History of the American New Left, 1959–1972* (Lanham, Md.: University Press of America, 1988); David R. Farber, *The Age of Great Dreams: America in the 1960s* (New York: Hill and Wang, 1994); Farber, *The Sixties: From Memory to History* (Chapel Hill: University of North Carolina Press, 1994).

    3. Sale, *The Green Revolution*, 12–14.

    4. Murray Bookchin, *Post-scarcity Anarchism* (Berkeley: Ramparts Press, 1971).

    5. Ibid., 12.

    6. Ibid., 11.

    7. Ibid., 12.

    8. Michael McClosky, "Wilderness Movement at the Crossroads, 1945–1970," *Pacific Historical Review* 41 (1972): 346–61; Samuel P. Hays, "From Conservation to Environment: Environmental Politics Since World War Two," *Environmental Review* 6:2 (fall 1982): 14–41;. Mark W. T. Harvey, "Echo Park, Glen Canyon, and the Postwar Wilderness Movement," *Pacific Historical Review* 60 (1991): 43–67.

    9. There is a large body of literature on wilderness and wilderness preservation. See, for example: Max Oelschlaeger, *The Idea of Wilderness: From Prehistory to the Age of Ecology* (New Haven, Conn.: Yale University Press, 1991); Max Oelschlaeger, ed., *The Wilderness Condition: Essays on Environment and Civilization* (San Francisco: Sierra Club Books, 1992); Roderick Nash, *Wilderness and the American Mind*, rev. ed. (New Haven, Conn.: Yale University Press, 1973); Michael Fromme, *Battle for the Wilderness* (New York: Praeger, 1974); William L. Graf, *Wilderness Preservation and Sagebrush Rebellions* (Savage, Md.: Rowman and Littlefield, 1990); Craig W. Allin, *The Politics of Wilderness Preservation* (Westport, Conn.: Greenwood Press, 1982); Mark W. T. Harvey, *A Symbol of Wilderness: Echo Park and the American Conservation Movement* (Albuquerque: University of New Mexico Press, 1994); Alfred Runte, *Yosemite: The Embattled Wilderness* (Lincoln: University of Nebraska Press, 1990); David Brower, ed., *Wilderness: America's Living Heritage* (San Francisco: Sierra Club Books, 1961); Arthur H. Carhart, *The National Forests* (New York: Knopf, 1959); Donald N. Baldwin, *The Quiet Revolution: The Grass Roots of Today's Wilderness Preservation Movement* (Boulder, Colo.: Pruett, 1972); James P. Gilligan, "The Development of Policy and Administration of Forest Service Primitive and Wilderness Areas in the Western United States" (Ph.D. diss., University of Michigan, 1954); McCloskey, "Wilderness Movement at the Crossroads," 346–61.

    10. Harvey, *A Symbol of Wilderness;* Susan Rhoades Neel, "Irreconcilable Differences: Reclamation, Preservation, and the Origins of the Echo Park Dam Controversy" (Ph.D. diss., University of California–Los Angeles, 1990); Owen Stratton and Phillip Sirotkin, *The Echo Park Controversy* (Indianapolis: Bobbs-Merrill, 1959); Wallace Stegner, ed., *This Is Dinosaur: Echo Park Country and Its Magic Rivers* (New York: Knopf, 1955).

    11. Michael P. Cohen, *The History of the Sierra Club, 1892–1970* (San Francisco: Sierra Club Books, 1988), 142–49.

12. See, for example, Howard Zahniser's foreword to Arthur H. Carhart, *Planning for America's Wildlands* (Harrisburg, Pa.: Telegraph Press, 1961). Zahniser articulated the new direction in the wilderness fight. "There is little hope for preserving wilderness by simply resisting here and there the . . . projects that would destroy it. Rather it must be defended in recognized, designated areas in accordance with a preservation policy and program that *positively* protect *it,* rather than by opposing, *negatively,* the forces threatening wilderness" (xii).

13. Stephen Fox, *The American Conservation Movement: John Muir and His Legacy* (Madison: University of Wisconsin Press, 1981), 269–72; Brower, *Wilderness,* 155–62. Sale, *The Green Revolution,* 14–15.

14. Fox, *The American Conservation Movement,* 269.

15. Correspondence between Carhart and Zahniser can be found in DPL/WHC, CLC Archive, the Wilderness Society files, 1–3.

16. As quoted in Fox, *The American Conservation Movement,* 269.

17. "Howard Zahniser to The Wilderness Committee of Colorado," DPL/WHC, Hilliard Papers, box 402; Howard Zahniser, "Transcript of Presentation to the House Public Lands Subcommittee, Hearing in Montrose, Colorado," November 1, 1961, DPL/WHC, Hilliard Papers, box 402.

18. Andrew Kirk, "Conservationists and Wilderness Preservation in Colorado" (M.A. thesis, University of Colorado Denver, 1992), 95–120.

19. DPL/WHC, transcript of meeting between Edward Hilliard, Wayne Aspinall, and Peter Dominick, Washington, D.C., April 5, 1962, Hilliard Papers, box 402. See also Carhart-Aspinall correspondence, DPL/WHC, AHC Papers, box 1:200.

20. Arthur Carhart to Edward Hilliard, April 13, 1962, DPL/WHC, Hilliard Papers, box 402. This important letter outlines Carhart's concerns about environmental advocacy and the tricky politics of the CLC as a public institution.

21. Ibid.

22. Ibid.

23. G. Michael McCarthy, *Hour of Trial: The Conservation Conflict in Colorado and the West, 1891–1907* (Norman: University of Oklahoma Press, 1977). McCarthy makes a convincing argument for the preeminence of anticonservation politics in the state of Colorado, demonstrating that from the beginnings of the Forest Reserve system Coloradans who favored environmental preservation faced well-organized resistance from within the state. See also James H. Baker and LeRoy R. Hafen, eds., *History of Colorado* (Denver: Linderman, 1927), 2:757–83.

24. Earl Pomeroy, *In Search of the Golden West: The Tourist in Western America* (Lincoln: University of Nebraska Press, 1978); Hal Rothman, *Devil's Bargains: Tourism in the Twentieth-Century American West* (Lawrence: University Press of Kansas, 1998).

25. Hugh E. Kingery and Elinor Eppich Kingery, *The Colorado Mountain Club: The First Seventy-five Years of a Highly Individual Corporation, 1912–1987* (Evergreen, Colo.: Cordillera Press, 1988); Janet Robertson, *The Magnificent Mountain Women: Adventures in the Colorado Rockies* (Lincoln: University of Nebraska Press, 1990); Robertson, *The Front Rangers: A History of the Boulder Group of the Colorado Mountain Club* (Boulder: Colorado Mountain Club, 1971). *Trail and Timberline,* the CMC's monthly magazine, is an excellent source on grassroots environmentalism among Colorado's outdoor sports community.

26. Kingery and Kingery, *The Colorado Mountain Club,* 78.

27. "Redfield Gun Sight Co.," DPL/WHC, CLC Archive, box 586.

28. Joy Hilliard, interview with author, July 9, 1995. Ernest Thompson Seton was chief scout of the Boy Scouts of America. His stories generally dealt with

brave young scouts and their anthropomorphized animal friends. See, for one example out of many, Ernest Thompson Seton, *Rolf in the Woods: The Adventures of a Boy Scout with Indian Quonab and Little Dog Skookum* (New York: Grosset and Dunlap, 1911).

29. DPL/WHC, Hilliard Papers, Edward Hobbs Hilliard résumé 1962, box 1, f.1.

30. "Redfield Gun Sight Co." DPL/WHC, CLC Archive, box 586.

31. Ibid.

32. "Personal and Civic," DPL/WHC, Hilliard Papers, box 1, f.1.

33. "Memorial Award Recipient Praises Late Conservationist," *Denver Post,* February 10, 1978, 32.

34. Ibid.

35. Roger P. Hanson, "Eulogy for Edward Hilliard," courtesy of Joy Hilliard.

36. Ibid.

37. "Edward H. Hilliard, Jr.," *Living Wilderness* 34 (autumn 1970): 4.

38. "Wilderness Committee of Colorado" and "Conservation Council of Colorado," DPL/WHC, Hilliard Papers, box 404.

39. This was the philosophy voiced by many of the leaders of the American environmental organizations. Hilliard, Olaus Murie, and others in the Wilderness Society consistently pointed to population as the crux of the environmental crisis. See, for example, Olaus Murie to John Spencer, April 2, 1953, Bancroft Library, Sierra Club Records, 71/103c, 63:18. Especially influential were William Vogt, *Road to Survival* (New York: William Sloane, 1948); and Paul Ehrlich, *The Population Bomb* (New York: Ballantine, 1968). For a thorough discussion of population and environmental politics, see Bob Pepperman Taylor, *Our Limits Transgressed: Environmental Political Thought in America* (Lawrence: University Press of Kansas, 1992), 27–50.

40. Joni Seager, *Earth Follies: Coming to Feminist Terms with the Global Environmental Crisis* (New York: Routledge, 1993), 213–19.

41. Ibid., 216.

42. Historian Linda Gordon argues that Planned Parenthood, and the conservation movement in general, contributed to the decline of a women-centered popular birth control movement focused not only on controlling population but also on elevating the status of women. Linda Gordon, *Women's Body, Women's Right: Birth Control in America* (New York: Penguin, 1990), 394–96. See also James Reed, *The Birth Control Movement and American Society: From Private Vice to Public Virtue* (Princeton, N.J.: Princeton University Press, 1983).

43. Ibid.; Betsy Hartmann, *Reproductive Rights and Wrongs* (New York: Harper and Row, 1987); Christa Wichterich, "From the Struggle Against 'Overpopulation' to the Industrialization of Human Production," *Reproductive and Genetic Engineering* 1 (1988): 1.

44. Like many women of her generation, Joy Hilliard is reluctant to take credit for her advocacy work. When asked about her role, she consistently downplays her participation and gives the credit for anything positive to her husband. Although she may be unwilling to acknowledge her role in the subtle transformations of the environmental coalition in Colorado, the record seems to indicate otherwise.

45. Richard Lamm, phone interview with author, June 12, 1992.

46. Edward Hilliard to Nanine Hilliard Greene, May 1, 1964, DPL/WHC, Hilliard Papers, box 1, f.2.

47. "Transcripts of Colorado House Public Lands Subcommittee Wilderness Hearings, 1963," DPL/WHC, Hilliard Papers, box 402; Hugh Kingery to John

Saylor, April 14, 1964, DPL/WHC, Hilliard Papers, box 401, Wilderness Committee file. This important letter thanks Saylor for his "pointed remarks regarding the value of citizen testimony at the hearings" and verifies Colorado wilderness supporters' claims that the Colorado hearings had a substantial impact on the ultimate passage of the wilderness bill.

48. Edward Hilliard to "Coloradoans Interested in Wilderness," February 14, 1964, DPL/WHC, Hilliard Papers, box 402, Wilderness Committee of Colorado file.

49. "Summary Financial Report, Conservation Library Center, January 1, 1961–December 31, 1966," DPL/WHC, CLC Archive 68, box 1.

50. In many cities the local papers began, in the 1960s, to feature regular columns dealing with environmental issues. For example, the *Denver Post* ran a weekly column, called "Man and His World," that regularly featured stories about the Conservation Library.

51. "Summary Financial Report," DPL/WHC, CLC Archive, LAC 68, box 1, f.2.

52. Sources on the Pittman-Robertson program include the following: Marion Clawson and Burnell Held, *The Federal Lands: Their Use and Management* (Baltimore: Johns Hopkins University Press, 1957); Dorothy Childs Hogner, *Conservation in America* (Philadelphia: Lippincott, 1958); Samuel P. Hays, *Conservation and the Gospel of Efficiency: The Progressive Conservation Movement, 1890–1920* (Cambridge, Mass.: Harvard University Press, 1959); Fox, *The American Conservation Movement*.

53. Hogner, *Conservation in America*, 132–33.

54. "Report of the Library Research Committee on the Library Reference Service Project," September 1969, DPL/WHC, DPL Archive, box 99, f.26

55. Ibid.

56. Arthur Carhart to Homer Circle, February 7, 1967, DPL/WHC, CLC Archive, box 2.

57. "Denver, Washington to Join in Providing Library Service," *Denver Post*, September 16, 1965.

58. Cooperative Agreement with the Department of the Interior, Bureau of Sport Fisheries and Wildlife, A Proposal for The Conservation Library Center of North America," DPL/WHC, CLC Archive, box 4; Transcripts of International Association of Game, Fish and Conservation Commissioners, Fifty-fourth Annual Meeting, Atlantic City, New Jersey, September 18, 1964, "Resolution #7," and "Resolution #16," DPL/WHC, DPL Archive, box 99, f.26.

59. "International Association of Game, Fish, and Conservation Commissioners," DPL/WHC, DPL Archive, box 99, f.25.

60. "Conservation Library Designated Official Depository," press release issued by the Colorado Game, Fish and Parks Department, October 18, 1964, DPL/WHC, DPL Archive, box 99.

61. "Conservation Library Knows Answer," *Rocky Mountain News*, September 19, 1965; "Denver, Washington to Join in Providing Library Service," *Denver Post*, September 16, 1965.

62. John Eastlick and Arthur Carhart to Board of Trustees, Max C. Fleischmann Foundation, October 16, 1964, DPL/WHC, DPL Archive, box 99, f.14.

63. "Conservation library Center: An Evaluation and Statement of Goals," July, 1966, DPL/WHC, CLC Archive, LAC 68, box 1, f.2.

64. "A Conference on Methods of Evaluation," November 11, 1965, DPL/WHC, CLC Archive, box 1, f.2.

65. Ibid., 3.

66. Ibid.

67. Ibid., 5.

68. Arthur H. Carhart, "Trees and Game—Twin Crops" (Washington, D.C.: American Forest Products Industries, 1953), 3.

69. "AFPI Contributor to AHC Papers," *AFPI Report* 2 (June 1966): 1.

70. "A Proposal for the Conservation Library Center of North America," prepared by the Denver Public Library Foundation, 1966, DPL/WHC, CLC Archive, box 4.

71. Ibid.

72. Thomas Currigan to Gerald Peters, President of the Denver Public Library Foundation, August 26, 1965, DPL/WHC, CLC Archive, box 4.

73. "A Proposal for the Conservation Library Center of North America."

74. "Memo for the Record," transcript of conference, Monroe Bush's Office, Washington, D.C., August 8, 1965, DPL/WHC, CLC Archive, box 7.

75. Ibid.

76. Ibid., 3. Carhart tacked a "personal commentary" onto the transcript of this disturbing meeting in which he explained his feelings after the meeting.

77. Roberta Winn to Department Head, January 10, 1966, DPL/WHC, DPL Archive, box 98, Department Head File.

78. Ibid., 5.

79. Ibid., 4.

80. David Fischer résumé, DPL/WHC, CLC Archive, box 1, f.2.

81. David Fischer, "The Broadened Concept of Conservation at the CLC," August 1, 1966, DPL/WHC, CLC Archive, box 1, f.2.

82. Ibid.

83. "Conservation Library Center: An Evaluation and Statement of Goals Submitted to the American Conservation Association, Inc." (July 1966), DPL/WHC, CLC Archive, box 135.

84. "A Proposal for the Conservation Library Center of North America."

85. Fischer, "The Broadened Concept of Conservation at the CLC."

86. In discussing librarianship and conservation, one encounters a terminology problem. The term "conservation librarian" existed before Eastlick and Carhart dreamed up their idea. Traditionally, however, the title applied to librarians trained in the conservation of artifacts, manuscripts, and books. The CLC effort was the first attempt to create a program for environmental conservation in a graduate librarianship program.

87. Fox, *The American Conservation Movement*, 309–10.

88. DPL/WHC, DPL Archive, box 99, f.16.

89. Kay Collins, "The Transmountain Diversion of Water from the Colorado River: A Legal-Historical Study" (M.A. thesis, University of New Mexico, 1965).

90. Kay Collins, interview with author, June 7, 1995.

91. Fischer, "The Broadened Concept of Conservation at the CLC," 1.

92. Angela Medbery, "Twenty-six Year Old CEC Seeks Tax Exemption Status," *Colorado Environmental Report*, May–June 1991, 20–21.

93. Roger Fuehrer, "CMC Conservation: The History Unfolded," *Trail and Timberline*, no. 759 (April 1982): 87–90. See also "Some Comments on a Quality Colorado Environment," COSCC Policy Statement, DPL/WHDC, Hilliard Papers, box 401; "COSCC Organization," DPL/WHC, Hilliard Papers, box 401; "Proposed Organizational Structure: Colorado Open Space Council," October 31, 1964, DPL/WHC, Hilliard Papers, box 401.

94. Fuehrer, "CMC Conservation," 89.

95. Richard Lamm, phone interview with author, July 16, 1992.

96. Nanine Hilliard Greene to Roger Hansen and John Wells, 1970, courtesy of Joy Hilliard.

97. Hanson, "eulogy for Edward Hilliard."

98. John Eastlick to "All the Counselors of the Conservation Library Center," September 14, 1966, DPL/WHC, CLC Archive, box 4, f.52.

99. Ibid.

CHAPTER 5. A LIBRARY OF HER OWN

1. John Eastlick to All the Counselors of the Conservation Library Center, September 14, 1966, DPL/WHC, CLC Archive, box 4, f.52.

2. Bob Pepperman Taylor, *Our Limits Transgressed: Environmental Political Thought in America* (Lawrence: University Press of Kansas, 1992), 52. Taylor provides an excellent overview of the historiography of environmentalism and the subtle political and philosophical differences of individuals within the environmental movement who have sometimes been lumped together as representatives of a particular monolithic viewpoint.

3. Examples of this view are expressed, to a greater and lesser degree, in the following: Samuel P. Hays, *Beauty, Health, and Permanence: Environmental Politics in the United States, 1955–1985* (Cambridge: Cambridge University Press, 1987); Philip Shabecoff, *A Fierce Green Fire: The American Environmental Movement* (New York: Hill and Wang, 1993); Kirkpatrick Sale, *The Green Revolution: The American Environmental Movement, 1962–1992* (New York: Hill and Wang, 1993); Robert Gottlieb, *Forcing the Spring: The Transformation of the American Environmental Movement* (Washington, D.C.: Island Press, 1993).

4. Darlene E. Weingand, ed., *Women and Library Management: Theories, Skills, and Values* (Ann Arbor, Mich.: Pierian Press, 1982). For statistics, see Kathleen M. Heim, "Factors Contributing to a Continued Status Differentiation Between Male and Female Librarians" in the same volume. Heim notes that although women constitute more than 90 percent of the workforce in libraries, they hold only a tiny percentage of management positions.

5. Kenneth A. Porter to Conservation Library Center Personnel, "Responsibilities and Lines of Authority for Conservation Library Center Programs," July 15, 1968, DPL/WHC, CLC Archive, box 6. Porter's policies are also outlined in a document entitled "Policy of the Conservation Library," DPL/WHC, DPL Archive, box 99.

6. DPL/WHC, DPL Archive, box 99, f.14.

7. "Annual Report: Conservation Library Center, 1966," CLC Archive, box 8.

8. Kenneth A. Porter to Roger Hansen, COSC, March 14, 1968, DPL/WHC, CLC Archive, box 7. This letter outlines Porter's ideas about collaboration between the CLC and the local environmental community and demonstrates his emphasis on advocacy over librarianship.

9. Kenneth A. Porter to Kay Collins, July 24, 1968, "Conservation Library Center Clientele," DPL/CLC, CLC Archive, box 6.

10. Stuart Baillie to Arthur Carhart, June 25, 1962, DPL/WHC, CLC Archive, box 9. This letter laid out the concept for the "conservation librarianship" program at DU and provided guidelines for suitable candidates.

11. "The University of Denver Graduate School of Librarianship," 1962–64, DPL/WHC, CLC Archive, box 9.

12. Carhart also recorded his recollections on reel-to-reel tapes and convinced many of his older friends to do the same. Among the most interesting items in the CLC today are the four boxes of tapes that constitute a significant oral history of the American conservation movement. DPL/WHC, vault boxes.

13. The yard at the Eudora Street house was literally Carhart's landscape architecture laboratory. When he and Vera bought the house new, the yard was completely barren. He spent decades carefully planting trees and fostering gardens on the large corner lot. The experience he gained was captured in two books, *Trees and Shrubs for the Small Place* (Garden City, N.Y.: Doubleday, Doran, 1935), and *How to Plan the Home Landscape* (Garden City, N.Y.: Doubleday, Doran., 1935).

14. A couple of years later, Carhart realized that he should not have disposed of the book collection and tried to have a nephew retrieve the books from Denver stores. Unfortunately, it was too late. The two novels written under the pen name Hart Thorne are particularly scarce. If anyone has an extra copy of *Saddle Men of the C-Bit Brand*, I would love to have it!

15. Carhart's correspondence from California to the CLC from 1968 until his death was located in the file cabinet in the rare book room and in the vault. Now this series of letters is located in the "vault" boxes in the DPL/WHC, AHC Papers.

16. John T. Eastlick and Willard O. Youngs, *A Survey of the Pikes Peak Regional District Library* (Chicago: American Library Association, 1967); John Eastlick, ed., *The Changing Environment of Libraries* (Chicago: American Library Association, 1971); John Taylor Eastlick and Robert D. Stewart, *Library Management* (Littleton, Colo.: Libraries Unlimited, 1977).

17. Eastlick, *The Changing Environment of Libraries*, 2.

18. Kay Collins to the author, March 16, 1997.

19. "Lines of Authority," DPL/WHC, CLC Archive, box 6.

20. "Conservation Library Center Reference and Information Service," section 5, C.2, DPL/WHC, DPL Archive, box 99, f.14.

21. Kay Collins résumé, DPL/WHC, CLC Archive, box 8.

22. The literature on women in librarianship is rich indeed. The redefinition of women's roles in librarianship during the 1960s inspired a rash of introspective literature on the history and status of women in the field. Much of the best of this strain of inquiry came from women librarians themselves, who began publishing monographs and collections of essays on the issue in the late 1960s and early 1970s. See, for example, Laurel Ann Grotzinger, *The Power and the Dignity: Librarianship and Katharine Sharp* (New York: Scarecrow Press, 1966); Dee Garrison, *Apostles of Culture: The Public Librarian and American Society, 1876–1920* (New York: Free Press, 1979); Kathleen Weibel, Kathleen M. Heim, and Dianne J. Ellsworth, eds., *The Role of Women in Librarianship, 1876–1976: The Entry, Advancement, and Struggle for Equalization in One Profession* (Phoenix, Ariz.: Oryx Press, 1979); Weingand, *Women and Library Management*; Kathleen M. Heim, ed., *The Status of Women in Librarianship: Historical, Sociological, and Economic Issues* (New York: Neal-Schuman, 1983); Lori A. Goetsch and Sarah B. Watstein, eds., *On Account of Sex: An Annotated Bibliography on the Status of Women in Librarianship, 1987–1992* (Metuchen, N.J.: Scarecrow Press, 1993); Joanne E. Passet, *Cultural Crusaders: Women Librarians in the American West, 1900–1917* (Albuquerque: University of New Mexico Press, 1994); Abigail A. Van Slyck, *Free to All: Carnegie Libraries and American Culture, 1890–1920* (Chicago: University of Chicago Press, 1995); Suzanne Hildenbrand, ed., *Reclaiming the American Library Past: Writing the Women In* (Norwood, N.J.: Ablex, 1996). Another excellent source for information on women in American librarianship is the *Journal of Library History*, which over

the years has devoted substantial space to articles by and about women in libraries. See, for example, Laurel Grotzinger, "The Proto-feminist Librarian at the Turn of the Century: Two Studies," *Journal of Library History* 10 (July 1975): 195–213; Mary Niles Maack, "Toward a History of Women in Librarianship: A Critical Analysis with Suggestions for Further Research," *Journal of Library History* 17 (spring 1982): 164–85; Mary Biggs, "Librarians and the 'Woman Question': An Inquiry into Conservatism," *Journal of Library History* 17 (fall 1982): 407–28; Phyllis Dain, "Women's Studies in American Library History: Some Critical Reflections," *Journal of Library History* 18 (fall 1983): 450–63.

23. *Cultural Crusaders.*

24. Ibid., 151.

25. Garrison, *Apostles of Culture,* 173.

26. Ibid.

27. Passet, *Cultural Crusaders,* xiv.

28. Kathleen Weibel, "Towards a Feminist Profession," in *The Role of Women in Librarianship, 1876–1976,* 287. The meanings and interpretation of the "feminization" of librarianship remain a hotly contested subject. Pioneer researchers like Dee Garrison argued that the process of feminization contributed to the marginalization of libraries as cultural institutions. Later historians and students of librarianship dispute this assumption and argue, to the contrary, that the high percentage of women in libraries contributed to the rise of the library as a center of American culture and learning. For an overview of differing interpretations of women in librarianship, see Maack, "Toward a History of Women in Librarianship," 164–85.

29. Abigail A. Van Slyck, *Gender and Space in American Public Libraries, 1880–1920* (Tucson: Southwest Institute for Research on Women), 4.

30. For more on this theme, see Abigail A. Van Slyck's excellent study of Carnegie libraries, *Free to All.*

31. Grotzinger, *The Power and the Dignity.*

32. There is a growing body of literature on the subject of activism and librarianship in the twentieth century. See, for example, Mary Lee Bundy and Frederick J. Stielow, *Activism in American Librarianship, 1962–1973* (New York: Greenwood Press, 1987); David Shauit, *The Politics of Public Librarianship* (New York: Greenwood Press, 1986); Patricia Glass Schuman, ed., *Social Responsibilities and Libraries* (New York: Bowker, 1976); Sidney L. Jackson, Eleanor B. Herling, and E. J. Josey, *A Century of Service: Librarianship in the United States and Canada* (Chicago: American Library Association, 1976); Michael F. Winter, *The Professionalization of Librarianship* (Champaign: University of Illinois Press, 1983); Ismail Abdullahi, ed., *E. J. Josey: An Activist Librarian* (Metuchen, N.J.: Scarecrow Press, 1992).

33. Bundy and Stielow, *Activism in American Librarianship,* 174.

34. African-American civil rights activists within America's libraries pioneered the movement to open the library hierarchy to underrepresented peoples and use the ALA as a forum for political and social advocacy. Notable among black library activists was E. J. Josey, founder of the ALA Black Caucus. Josey and others argued that libraries were centers of democracy and should form the vanguard of any social movement. He worked to open up the conservative ALA to liberal and nontraditional points of view and helped pave the way for women activists, who joined him and then began to work on their own behalf. Abdullahi, *E. J. Josey.*

35. Bundy and Stielow, *Activism in American Librarianship,* 170.

36. Ibid.

37. Bundy and Stielow, *Activism in American Librarianship*, 175.

38. Apparently this career change had been Porter's original goal when he moved to Denver from Arizona, where he received a teaching certificate from the University of Arizona. Porter's biographical material is in a report, "Conservation Library Center Reference and Information Service," DPL/WHC, DPL Archive, box 99, f.14.

39. "Paper Tiger May Devour U.S., Environmentalist Warns," *Denver Post*, June 26, 1970, 25. In the months leading up to and following Earth Day, traffic at the CLC expanded by over 50 percent, and a series of articles about the library appeared in the papers around the same time.

40. Sale, *The Green Revolution*, 24–25.

41. "Women Are Winners of Eight of Twenty American Motors Conservation Awards," AMCA Press Release, May, 1970, DPL/WHC, American Motors Awards Collection, box 15.

42. Ibid., 1.

43. The full text of Collins's award reads: "Because, in her unique capacity as librarian of the Conservation Library Center in Denver, she ranks as the first Conservation Librarian in North America. . . . Because she maintains the official library for records of more than a dozen major organizations, including the International Association of Game, Fish and Conservation Commissioners, the Wildlife Management Institute, and Outdoor Writers of America. . . . Because she is one of the most effective speakers in the Denver area on natural resources conservation, and serves as chairman of the information and education workshop of the Colorado Open Spaces Council. . . . Because in these and other ways she exemplifies the finest traditions of the professional conservationists in America. . . . Therefore, it is the privilege and pleasure of American Motors Corporation to present one of ten professional awards for 1970 to Miss Kay Collins of Denver, Colorado, for her important contributions to the cause of conservation." "Remarks of R. E. Long," DPL/WHC, American Motors collection, box 15, 5–7.

44. Stephen Fox, *The American Conservation Movement: John Muir and His Legacy* (Madison: University of Wisconsin Press, 1981), 175–77.

45. "Eight Women Are Selected as Winners of American Motors Awards," press release from American Motors, May 22, 1970, American Motors Awards Collection, Collins file, box 69.

46. "Paper Tiger May Devour U.S."

47. Ibid.

48. Arthur Carhart to Ed Zern, January 19, 1970, American Motors Awards Collection, Collins File, box 69.

49. Monroe Bush to Ed Zern, January 25, 1970, DPL/WHC, American Motors Awards Collection, box 15.

50. "Paper Tiger May Devour U.S."

51. Ibid.

52. Kay Collins to author, February 28, 1997.

53. Bush to Zarn, January 25, 1970, 2.

54. Ibid.

55. The relationship between Shearouse and Collins is admittedly hard to track. The politics of the library dictated that animosities remain below board, so both worked hard to maintain a civil relationship for the public and the rest of the staff. Memos between the two, however, reveal the tension and radically different perspectives. See, for example, DPL/WHC, CLC Archive, box 6, ff.2–28.

56. "Environmental Ecology and the Library, Pre-conference Seminar, Col-

orado Library Association Conference, September 30, 1970, Antlers Hotel, Colorado Springs, Colorado," DPL/WHC, CLC Archive, box 7.

57. Ibid., 1.

58. Ibid.

59. "Program: Environmental Crisis and the Library," DPL/WHC, CLC Archive, box 7.

60. Ibid.

61. "Old Dominion Foundation Annual Report, 1968," DPL/WHC, DPL Archive, box 99.

62. Old Dominion Foundation correspondence and contracts, DPL/WHC, DPL Archive, box 99, f.15.

63. Ibid.

64. Theodore Swem, interview with author, January 4, 1995, Denver, Colorado.

65. Ted Swem was a central figure in the restoration of the CLC in the early 1990s. For more than four years, he worked to secure funding and researched and cataloged the holdings of the CLC. His careful notes on the various players and organizations in the CLC story proved an invaluable resource for this study.

66. At the time of this writing, the Wilderness Society Papers were the only individual collection within the CLC under the care of an archivist.

67. CLC Annual Report, 1968, DPL/WHC, CLC Archive, box 3, f.23.

68. "Comments from Users," an appendix compiled for the "Proposal for Support," Conservation Collection/REEIC, 1979, CLC Archive, box 5.

69. "Conservation Library Guest Book," DPL/WHC, CLC Archive, box 5. See also information on Roderick Nash, Arthur Carhart, and the CLC in chapter 2.

70. "Annual Report: Conservation Library Center, 1966–1970."

71. "Comments from Users."

72. Kay Collins, phone interview with author, June 26, 1995.

73. Ibid.

74. "Policy of the Conservation Library Center," March 14, 1969, DPL/WHC, CLC Archive, box 6.

75. A 1968 report to the Fleischmann Foundation outlines the CLC connection to the local grassroots environmental movement and its plans for helping the movement by providing information systems support. DPL/WHC, DPL Archive, box 99, f.14.

76. Kay Collins, phone interview with author, June 10, 1995.

77. Ibid.

78. The five-year development plan is outlined in, DPL Archive, box 98, ff-4.

79. "Fund-Raising Dinner Set," *Denver Post*, February 28, 1971, 40. The dinner was organized to raise money (tickets cost fifteen dollars per person), and to introduce the "Five Year Development Plan" to as many potential contributors from the Denver area as possible. Peter Farb, author of the best-selling *Face of North America: The Natural History of a Continent* (New York: Harper and Row, 1963), was a longtime supporter of the CLC and agreed to come to Denver to speak at the banquet. Mayor McNichols hosted the event, with Henry Shearouse presenting the five-year plan to the audience. Farb then took the stage and gave a rousing speech praising the work of the Conservation Library and calling the five-year plan and the support from the city "long over due." The event generated a considerable amount of money but failed to start a trend in local donations as hoped.

80. "Annual Reports, 1968–1972."

81. The openness of the 1970s evidenced itself, ironically, in darker ways at the CLC during this time. Some of the staff were known to indulge in fairly open substance abuse while on the job. Reports of pot smoke drifting out of bathroom stalls were not unheard of. In one infamous case a staff member brought a large suitcase full of liquor to work each day to fuel multiday drinking binges. The free flow of ideas and politics that characterized the CLC in the 1970s allowed staff members a level of leeway that some clearly could not handle. This atmosphere resulted in some lively debates that, according to one staff member's recollection, degenerated into screaming matches, fistfights, and chair-throwing incidents. Linda Cumming, interview with author, June 10, 1995.

82. Ibid.

83. "Kay Collins: Internal Memos, Leave Requests," DPL/WHC, CLC Archive, box 6, ff.2–16.

84. Kay Collins to Arthur Carhart, November 17, 1975, DPL/WHC, CLC Archive, acquisitions cabinet, Carhart file.

85. Hays, *Beauty, Health, and Permanence*, 143.

86. The sources available for public use during this period were, as they are now, extensive yet diffuse. For environmental information, researchers could turn to several federal archival repositories such as the National Archive and the Library of Congress in Washington, D.C., which contain the papers of many leading figures in the environmental movement, and the records of the Forest Service and other federal agencies concerned with land management and conservation. Some state archival repositories also collect environmental information of various types. Specifically, the state historical societies of Wisconsin and Minnesota contain the records of lumber companies and some conservationists. The Minneapolis Public Library's Environmental Conservation Library was the only comparable institution to the CLC. It never was as large, however, and emphasized secondary literature over archival collections, and mainly regional in scope. For information on other sources of conservation information, see Richard C. Davis, ed., *Encyclopedia of American Forest and Conservation History* (New York: Macmillian, 1983), 1:290–93.

87. The best overview of the history of ECOL is a brief article. "Environmental Library of Minnesota," *North Country Anvil*, December–January 1973–74, 72–73. Also useful is the *ECOL News*, a newsletter published by the library between 1973 and 1987. Information on ECOL is housed as part of an informal collection of documents at the Minneapolis Public Library.

88. *ECOL News*, 6, no. 2 (February 1982).

89. Ibid.

90. See Carhart-Olson correspondence, DPL/WHC, AHC Papers, box 1:103.

91. *ECOL News*, 2, no. 4 (October 1974), 1.

92. William L. Johnson to the author, January 12, 2000. Johnson was the last of the ECOL librarians working with the project between 1986 and 1993, when the library ceased to exist as an autonomous enterprise.

93. "Environmental Library of Minnesota," 73.

94. For more on ECOL's decline and closure, see the conclusion of this book.

95. "Conservation Library/Energy Information Center: Foundation Report," November 15, 1981, DPL/WHC, CLC Archive, box 3.

96. Ibid.

97. Kay Collins to Arthur Carhart, November 17, 1975.

98. "Shearouse Correspondence, 1973–1979," DPL/WHC, DPL Archive, box 99, f.1. Carhart had already donated copies of manuscripts to the University of Iowa after it requested that he join the university's collection of "Iowa Authors."

99. The CLC oral history collection is in flux at the time of this writing. Most of the tapes can be found in the "vault" collections, along with several boxes of tapes in the Carhart Papers. The condition of many of the oral histories was very poor, some may be unrecoverable.

100. Conservation Library Oral History Collection, Carhart Correspondence, CLC Archive, box 7.

101. Kay Collins to Arthur Carhart, November 17, 1975.

102. "The Conservation Library of the Denver Public Library, 1960–197?, DPL/WHC, CLC Archive, box 2.

103. Ibid.

104. "Conservation Library Society: The Conservation Library Needs Our Help," December 10, 1976, DPL/WHC, CLC Archive, box 2.

105. DPL/WHC, DPL Archive, box 99, f.1.

106. "Comments from Users," Jill Boisclair, Librarian of Limnetics Environmental Consultants to the Conservation Library, January 1976, DPL/WHC, DPL Archive, box 99.

107. "Comments from Users," Joan Martin, Director of Education of the Thorne Ecological Institute, to Kay Collins, January 1976.

108. William L. Graf, *Wilderness Preservation and the Sagebrush Rebellions* (Savage, Md.: Rowman and Littlefield, 1990).

109. The best discussion of the shifting politics and alliances during this time is found in Hays, *Beauty, Health, and Permanence*. Hays tends to draw too sharp a distinction between conservation and environmentalism in the 1950s, but he does a good job of explaining how and why the movement shifted during the late 1960s and 1970s.

110. Ted Williams, "Natural Allies," *Sierra* 81, no. 5 (September/October 1996): 46–53; John F. Reiger, *American Sportsmen and the Origins of Conservation* (Norman: University of Oklahoma Press, 1986).

111. Hays, *Beauty, Health, and Permanence*, 54–55.

112. "Comments from Users," a letter mailed with Conservation Library Society brochures, 1976, CLC Archive, box 4.

113. "Comments from Users," Olin Webb, Colorado Association of Commerce and Industry, to Kay Collins, January 1976, CLC Archive, box 4.

CHAPTER 6. SOFT TECH AND HARD FACTS

1. *Congressional Record*, S13621, 126:151, September 26, 1980.

2. Michael Schaller, Virginia Scharff, and Robert D. Schulzinger, *Present Tense: The United States Since 1945* (Boston: Houghton Mifflin, 1992), 455–68.

3. Philip Shabecoff, *A Fierce Green Fire: The American Environmental Movement* (New York: Hill and Wang, 1993), 203.

4. *Environmental Quality: The Eleventh Annual Report of the Council on Environmental Quality* (Washington, D.C.: U.S. Government Printing Office, 1980).

5. Kirkpatrick Sale, *The Green Revolution: The American Environmental Movement, 1962–1992* (New York: Hill and Wang, 1993), 47.

6. *Congressional Record,* S13622, September 26, 1980.

7. Thomas P. Hughes, *American Genesis: A Century of Invention and Techno-logical Enthusiasm* (New York: Penguin, 1989), 453–59; David Dickson, *Alternative Technology and the Politics of Technical Change* (Glasgow: Fontana/Collins, 1974); Nicholas Jéquier, ed., *Appropriate Technology: Problems and Promises* (Paris: Development Centre Studies, 1976); Amory B. Lovins, "Energy Strategy: The Road Not Taken?" *Foreign Affairs* 55 (October 1976): 77–96; Lovins, *The Energy Controversy: Soft Path Questions and Answers* (San Francisco: Friends of the Earth, 1979); Jim Harding, ed., *Tools for the Soft Path* (San Francisco: Friends of the Earth, 1979); Franklin A. Long and Alexandra Oleson, eds., *Appropriate Technology and Social Values: A Critical Appraisal* (Cambridge, Mass.: Ballinger, 1980); Mathew J. Betz, Pat McGowan, and Rolf T. Wigand, eds., *Appropriate Technology: Choice and Development* (Durham, N.C.: Duke University Press Policy Studies, 1984);. Marilyn Carr, *The AT Reader: Theory and Practice in Appropriate Technology* (New York: Intermediate Technology Development Group of North America, 1985); Ron Westrum, *Technologies and Society: The Shaping of People and Things* (Belmont, Calif.: Wadsworth, 1991).

8. *The Whole Earth Catalog* has had many incarnations. Because of the editor's iconoclastic style and alternative publishing methodology, *Whole Earth* is maddeningly difficult to properly cite. The first edition was published in 1968 as *The Whole Earth Catalog: Access to Tools,* edited by Stewart Brand and published by the Portola Institute, with distribution provided by Random House. Several new versions followed between 1969 and 1971, all with Brand as the lead editor. *The Last Whole Earth Catalog* (Menlo Park, Calif.: Portola Institute), appeared in 1971 and won the prestigious National Book Award in 1972. All of the books were reprinted many times, and often there were seasonal editions. Between 1972 and 1999, there were several notable editions. See, especially, Stewart Brand, ed., *The Next Whole Earth Catalog: Access to Tools* (San Rafael, Calif.: Point Foundation, 1980), by Rand McNally in the United States and Random House in Canada. This particular edition is notable for its sheer size (608 oversized pages) and breadth of coverage. There were also several *Whole Earth*–type companion volumes, such as J. Baldwin and Stewart Brand, eds., *Soft-Tech* (New York: Penguin, 1978); and Kevin Kelly, ed., *Signal: Communication Tools for the Information Age, A Whole Earth Catalog* (New York: Harmony Books, 1988), that focused on particular issues. Brand relinquished the editorship in the 1980s, and several editors have since shepherded the perennially popular publication through several more editions. Most notable among these are Howard Rheingold, ed., *The Millennium Whole Earth Catalog* (San Francisco: HarperSanFrancisco, 1994); and Peter Warshall, ed., *Thirtieth Anniversary Celebration: Whole Earth Catalog* (San Rafael, Calif.: Point Foundation, 1999). The thirtieth-anniversary edition includes a wonderful collection of alternative technology and counterculture essays by leaders from the 1960s to the 1990s.

9. Warshall, *Thirtieth Anniversary Celebration: Whole Earth Catalog,* 3.

10. *Congressional Record,* September 26, 1980.

11. "Lamm Urges Energy Saving at Regional Center Opening," *Rocky Mountain News,* August 9, 1977, 105.

12. The best overview of the New Left, the counterculture, and environmentalism can be found in Robert Gottlieb's excellent book *Forcing the Spring: The Transformation of the American Environmental Movement* (Washington, D.C.: Island Press, 1993), 81–114. For a very different point of view from Gottlieb's and from that in this book, see Samuel Hays, *Beauty, Health, and Permanence: Environmental*

Politics in the United States, 1955–1985 (Cambridge: Cambridge University Press, 1987), 259–65. Hays argues that there were only superficial similarities between the "negative" counterculture and the "positive" environmental alternative lifestyle movement. The evidence of the CLC and the alternative technology movement in general seems to suggest that the counterculture and environmentalism converged in significant ways that transcend Hay's model of "negative" and "positive."

13. This section on counterculture environmentalism is partially derived from an essay I wrote for a forthcoming edited collection on the counterculture: "Machines of Loving Grace: Appropriate Technology, Environment, and the Counterculture," in *Imagine Nation: The American Counterculture of the 1960s and 1970s*, ed. Michael Doyle and Peter Braunstein (New York: Routledge, 2001).

14. The classic study of the conservation movement is Samuel P. Hays, *Conservation and the Gospel of Efficiency: The Progressive Conservation Movement, 1890–1920* (Cambridge, Mass.: Harvard University Press, 1959). Also useful is Stephen Fox, *The American Conservation Movement: John Muir and His Legacy* (Madison: University of Wisconsin Press, 1981).

15. Lewis Mumford, *Technics and Civilization* (New York: Harcourt, Brace and World, 1962).

16. John Hersey, *Hiroshima* (New York: Knopf, 1985).

17. Rachel Carson, *Silent Spring* (Greenwich, Conn.: Fawcett, 1962).

18. Barry Commoner, *The Closing Circle: Nature, Man, and Technology* (New York: Knopf, 1971).

19. Jacques Ellul, *The Technological Society*, trans. Joachim Neugroschel (New York: Continuum, 1980), first published in French in 1954 and in English in 1964. Quotation is from Hughes, *American Genesis*, 450.

20. Quotation is from Langdon Winner, "Building a Better Mousetrap: Appropriate Technology as a Social Movement," in *Appropriate Technology and Social Values: A Critical Appraisal*, ed. Franklin A. Long and Alexandra Oleson (Cambridge, Mass.: Ballinger, 1980), 33.

21. Herbert Marcuse, *One Dimensional Man: Studies in the Ideology of Advanced Industrial Society* (Boston: Beacon Press, 1964).

22. Hughes, *American Genesis*, 445.

23. Mumford, *Technics and Civilization*.

24. Hughes, *American Genesis*, 446–50; Lewis Mumford, *The Myth of the Machine: The Pentagon of Power* (New York: Harcourt Brace Jovanovich, 1970).

25. For an in-depth look at the "machine" in American culture, see Leo Marx, *The Machine and the Garden: Technology and the Pastoral Ideal in America* (New York: Oxford University Press, 1964). This classic study remains the best source on the strange relationship between technology and nature in American culture. See also Richard White, *The Organic Machine* (New York: Hill and Wang, 1995).

26. Theodore Roszak, *The Making of a Counter Culture: Reflections on the Technocratic Society and Its Youthful Opposition* (Garden City, N.Y.: Doubleday, 1969).

27. Ibid., 8.

28. Charles A. Reich, *The Greening of America: How the Youth Revolution Is Trying to Make America Livable* (New York: Random House, 1970).

29. E. F. Schumacher, *Small Is Beautiful: Economics as If People Mattered* (New York: Harper and Row, 1973).

30. Ibid., 124.

31. A useful taxonomy of technologies can be found in Carr, ed., *The AT Reader*, 6–11.

32. Witold Rybczynski, *Paper Heroes: A Review of Appropriate Technology* (Garden City, N.Y.: Anchor Books, 1980), 1–4.

33. Dickson, *Alternative Technology and the Politics of Technical Change*, 148–73.

34. Hays, *Beauty, Health, and Permanence*, 262.

35. Lewis Herber [Murray Bookchin], *Our Synthetic Environment* (New York: Knopf, 1962); Murray Bookchin, *Post-scarcity Anarchism* (Berkeley: Ramparts Press, 1971); quotation is from *Post-scarcity Anarchism*, 22. See also Ulrike Heider, *Anarchism: Left, Right, and Green* (San Francisco: City Lights Books, 1994); and Arthur Lothstein, ed., *"All We Are Saying . . .": The Philosophy of the New Left* (New York: Capricorn Books, 1970).

36. Bookchin, *Post-scarcity Anarchism*, 21.

37. Ibid., 9. There are many fine sources on the development of appropriate technology. See, for example, Dickson, *Alternative Technology*; Jéquier, *Appropriate Technology*; Long and Oleson, *Appropriate Technology and Social Values*; Witold Rybczynski, *Taming the Tiger: The Struggle to Control Technology* (New York: Penguin, 1985); Betz, McGowan, and Wigand, *Appropriate Technology*; Westrum, *Technologies and Society*; and Theodore Roszak, *Where the Wasteland Ends: Politics and Transcendence in Postindustrial Society* (Garden City, N.Y.: Anchor, 1973).

38. "Soft tech" originated in the 1960s to describe adaptive, earth-friendly technology. It was replaced in the early 1970s with "appropriate technology" but was resurrected by Stewart Brand and others, who thought that the word "soft" was more indicative of the goals and ideals of environmentalists. Baldwin and Brand, *Soft-Tech*, 4–5.

39. Social theorist Anthony Giddens argues that the "humanization" of technology is the final transformation of modern environmentalism into postmodern environmentalism. Early environmentalism arose as a response to the ecological degradation that resulted from industrialization. Antimodernism and a fear of technology were logical components of this response from the turn of the century through the 1960s. Once the basic concepts of environmental thinking became established in the 1960s, environmentalists were able to reconsider their antimodernism and technophobia. Giddens identifies this reevaluation and humanization of technology as the final stage in the transformation of the modern into the postmodern. Stuart Hall, David Held, Don Hubert, and Kenneth Thompson, eds., *Modernity: An Introduction to Modern Societies* (Cambridge, Mass.: Blackwell, 1996), 453–54.

40. Schaller, Scharff, and Schulzinger, *Present Tense*, 463–65.

41. Hays, *Beauty, Health, and Permanence*, 240–45.

42. As quoted in Schaller, Scharff, and Schulzinger, *Present Tense*, 464.

43. Hays, *Beauty, Health, and Permanence*, 241.

44. "Regional-Energy Environment Information Center Steering Committee Memorandum of Agreement," REEIC, Proposal for Support, August 1979, DPL/WHC, CLC Archive, box 3.

45. Ibid.

46. "City Library Holds 'Tons' of Environmental References," *Denver Post*, September 13, 1979.

47. "Cooperative Agreement to Assist in Public Awareness, Dissemination, and Evaluation of EIA Publications/Services," CLC Archive, box 3, f.4.

48. "Lamm," *Rocky Mountain News*, August 9, 1977, 105; Denver Public Library, *The Inkling* 8, no. 8 (August 1977): 1–2.

49. The best guide to REEIC funding and contracts can be found in "Conservation Library/Energy Information Center Foundation Report, Appendix 4: Funding History, 1961–1981," November 15, 1981, DPL Archive, box 98, f.2.

50. REEIC, "Proposal for Support," 1979, 3.

51. Ibid., 1.

52. Ibid., 4.

53. Ibid.

54. "Unique Energy Data Center in Denver," *Denver Post,* September 14, 1979, 25.

55. "City Library Holds 'Tons' of Environmental References."

56. Ibid.

57. "Unique Energy Data Center in Denver."

58. Colleen Cayton, "The Denver Public Library's Regional Energy/Environment Information Center: An Uncommon Cooperative Venture," *Library Journal* 106 (1981): 22.

59. REEIC, "Proposal for Support," 5.

60. Ibid, 6.

61. "Conservation Library/Energy Information Center Foundation Report," section 4.

62. REEIC, "Proposal for Support," 10–14.

63. Ibid., 12.

64. Ibid., 13.

65. Richard D. Lamm and Michael McCarthy, *The Angry West: A Vulnerable Land and Its Future* (Boston: Houghton Mifflin, 1982), 24–50; "Synfuels: Unrealistic Goal," *Denver Post,* August 26, 1979; Kevin Markey, "Why Colorado Isn't Ready for the Shale Boom," *Denver Magazine,* spring 1981; "Seeking Answers to Shale Oil Hazards," *Denver Post,* August 21, 1981.

66. Lamm and McCarthy, *The Angry West,* 31.

67. "Energy Fest 1978," Program, DPL/WHC, CLC Archive, box 5.

68. "Library Has Exhibit on Energy Future," *Denver Post,* August 3, 1977.

69. Kathleen Parker, "Energy Facts?" *Colorado Country Life,* February 1981, 12–13.

70. Ibid., 12.

71. "First White House Conference," Denver Public Library Annual Report to the People, January 1980, DPL/WHC, CLC Archive, box 3.

72. "EIC Environmental Outreach Award," December 24, 1980, DPL/WHC, CLC Archive, box 3.

73. Cayton, "Uncommon Cooperative Venture," 22.

74. "Info EES Project—DOE Grant no. DE/FG48/81R80/019," DPL/WHC, CLC Archive, box 3, f.6.

75. "Info-EES Order Form," DPL/WHC, CLC Archive, box 3, f.6.

76. Kay Collins, interview with author, July 10, 1995.

77. Ibid.

78. Kay Collins résumé, August 1979, "Appendix F, Proposal for Support." Collins was founder and president of an environmental consulting firm, Applied Information and Documentation. From 1972 until her departure in the summer of 1979, she worked on private projects ranging from hazardous materials research to environmental information systems.

79. Linda Cumming, interview with author, July 10, 1995.

80. Collins hardly left the CLC a broken women. She traded troubles of the library for excellent opportunities in California. Later she returned to librarianship, where she continued to work at the time of this writing.

81. "Cumming New RE/EIC Head," *Energy/Environment Information* 1, no. 1 (November 1980): 2.

82. Kay Collins requests for days off, travel, and time off to attend meetings, DPL/WHC, DPL Archive, boxes 98–99.

83. Cumming interview with author, July 10, 1995.

84. REEIC, "Proposal for Support," 6.

85. Eugene V. Ciancanelli to Henry Shearouse, May 9, 1979, DPL/WHC, CLC Archive, box 3, f.2.

86. REEIC, "Proposal for Support."

87. "Conservation Library/Energy Information Center Foundation Report," 2.

88. Ibid., 3.

89. Cumming interview with author, July 10, 1995.

90. Ibid.

91. "Proposal: Western Solar Utilization Network," September 19, 1980, DPL/WHC, CLC Archive, box 3, f.22.

92. Western Solar Utilization Network, "Policy Agreement Between Denver Public Library and Colorado Office of the Western Solar Utilization Network," DPL/WHC, CLC Archive, box 3, f.22.

93. "Conservation Library/Energy Information Center Foundation Report," 3.

CONCLUSION

1. Samuel P. Hays, *Beauty, Health, and Permanence: Environmental Politics in the United States, 1955–1985* (Cambridge: Cambridge University Press, 1987), 491.

2. William L. Graf, *Wilderness Preservation and the Sagebrush Rebellions* (Savage, Md.: Rowman and Littlefield, 1990).

3. Ibid., 494.

4. Kirkpatrick Sale, *The Green Revolution: The American Environmental Movement, 1962–1992* (New York: Hill and Wang, 1993), 50.

5. "DPL's Energy Center Faces Collapse," *Rocky Mountain News*, December 9, 1981, 11.

6. Ibid.

7. As quoted in Sale, *The Green Revolution,* 53.

8. Ibid., 52.

9. Hays, *Beauty, Health, and Permanence,* 492.

10. "Annual Report: Conservation Library Regional Energy/Environment Information Center," January 20, 1981, DPL/WHC, CLC Archive, box 3, f.23.

11. "Unique Partnership Proposed to Save Denver's Unique Library Collection," DPL/WHC, DPL Archive, box 99; "Information Memo 22–82: The Future of the Conservation Library," March 1, 1982, DPL/WHC, DPL Archive, box 99.

12. "Library Commission minutes," May 5, 1982, DPL/WHC, DPL Archive, box 99.

13. "Information Memo 22–82," 1.

14. Joshua Smith, President, Maxima Corporation, to Henry Shearouse, April 9, 1982, DPL/WHC, DPL Archive, box 99.

15. "Outgoing DPL Aide Cleared on Pact," *Denver Post,* May 12, 1982.

16. Ibid.

17. "Annual Report: REEIC," DPL/WHC, CLC Archive, box 3, f.23. The tone of this last report is one of relief at the prospect that, after five years, the staff could move on to new projects within the library. Compared with the meticulous detail and cautious optimism of previous reports, this final effort pales. Cayton concludes by saying, "Actually, the above problems are inconsequential when

weighted against the problem of determining the future of the Conservation Library."

18. The primary responsibilities of the REEIC were to organize federal energy information sources and make them available to the public. This required the staff to construct elaborate annotated bibliographies that were very time-consuming to produce. In addition, it operated the Tel-Net system, and fielded information inquiries from across the ten-state area. Finally, CLC staff traveled around the region giving energy information talks to rural and small-town audiences.

19. Cumming interview with author, July 10, 1995.

20. Georgiana Tiff to Linda Cumming, August 29, 1984, "Conservation Library Closure Proposal," DPL/WHC, DPL Archive, box 99.

21. When I began the research for this book in 1995, only three DPL staff had any knowledge of the CLC and its history. Most of the staff members interviewed had never even heard of the Conservation Library.

22. Susan M. Pearce, *Museums, Objects, and Collections: A Cultural Study* (Washington, D.C.: Smithsonian Institution Press, 1992), 3.

23. Kay Collins, interview with author, June 13, 1995.

24. Mike Wallace, *Mickey Mouse History and Other Essays on American Memory* (Philadelphia: Temple University Press, 1996), 35.

EPILOGUE

1. The Hilliards were financial contributors to the American Everest expedition of 1963, the first American ascent of the world's highest mountain. Because of their connections with the expedition, they were invited to trek up to the base camp, which they did as part of a six-week Himalayan expedition. James Ramsey Ullman, *Americans on Everest: The Official Account of the Ascent Led by Norman G. Dyhrenfurth* (Philadelphia: Lippincott, 1964), 424.

2. Among the most recognizable mountains in the world, the Maroon Bells are situated just northwest of the town of Aspen. Their unusual geology, characterized by huge gullies and slanting horizontal ledges that collect and hold snow in stunning patterns, makes them popular targets for photographers and painters. But the same qualities that make them so aesthetically pleasing for artists make them dangerous for climbers. Not only do the snow-filled gullies present immense danger, the Maroon Bells are also notorious for deadly loose rock. Even for the well-seasoned veteran of Colorado's other fourteeners, the Maroon Bells present a daunting challenge.

3. "Climbing Victim Avid Sportswoman," *Rocky Mountain News*, August 18, 1970, 6.

4. "Report to Sheriff Whitmire," DPL/WHC, Hilliard Papers, box 1, ff-1. The incident on North Maroon was widely covered by the local press. See, for example, "Noted Ecologist, Woman Die in Fall on Peak Near Aspen," *Rocky Mountain News*, August 17, 1970, 1; "Two Denverites Die in Fall Off Peak," *Denver Post*, Monday August 17, 1970, 1. Hilliard's death was also widely reported in the conservation community. See especially "Edward Hilliard, Jr.," *Living Wilderness* 34 (autumn 1970): 4.

5. Climbers use the term "pitch" as a unit of measurement roughly equivalent to a single rope length, or about fifty meters. Technical climbs are measured in pitches instead of feet or meters. The term "couloir" is another climbing reference, used to describe a steep, narrow gully.

6. A letter from Hilliard's sister to his colleagues at the Rocky Mountain Center for Environment shortly after the accident outlines Hilliard's position on generational problems in environmental advocacy. Nanine Hilliard Greene to John Wells and Roger Hansen, fall 1970, courtesy of Joy Hilliard. Copies may also be found in the CLC, Hilliard Papers.

7. Historian Mark Harvey, for instance, used the manuscripts of the Conservation Library extensively for his research on the Echo Park controversy. Harvey is one of the few historians to delve deeply into the CLC archive in the last twenty years. Mark Harvey, *A Symbol of Wilderness: Echo Park and the American Conservation Movement* (Albuquerque: University of New Mexico Press, 1994).

8. Joy Hilliard, interview with author, March 17, 1997.

BIBLIOGRAPHY

Most of the primary research for this study was completed in the manuscript collections and archives of the Conservation Library of the Denver Public Library. It is important to note that, at this writing, the Conservation Library is in the midst of an extensive inventory and reprocessing. I have made every effort, however, to ensure that my citations reflect the locations and designations least likely to be significantly affected over the years. The core documents of the "CLC Archives" will not change location. This is also true for the crucial "DPL Archives" that contain the "DPL Head Librarian's" files pertaining to the management of the DPL and the CLC. The Carhart papers have been processed, and some items may have changed location by the time this book is published. Anyone attempting to locate specific archival sources referenced in this book should consult with DPL prior to requesting materials.

Additionally, the Carhart listings in the following bibliography represent only a small fraction of his voluminous publications. By the end of his career, Carhart had published twenty-two books and over four thousand articles. For this bibliography I have limited the selection to the books and articles that best represent his work in conservation and his evolving environmental philosophy. The full bibliography of Carhart's astonishing output awaits his biographer.

MANUSCRIPT COLLECTIONS

American Forestry Association Papers, Denver Public Library, Western History Collection, Denver, Colorado.

American Motors Conservation Awards Collection, Denver Public Library, Western History Collection, Denver, Colorado.

David Brower Papers, Sierra Club Records, Bancroft Library, Berkeley, California.

Arthur H. Carhart Papers, Colorado Historical Society, Denver, Colorado.

Arthur H. Carhart Papers, Iowa State University Library, Ames, Iowa.

Arthur H. Carhart Collections, University of Iowa, Special Collections Department, Iowa City, Iowa.

Arthur H. Carhart Papers, Denver Public Library, Western History Collection, Denver, Colorado.

Colorado Environmental Coalition Papers, Colorado Environmental Coalition Headquarters, Denver, Colorado.

Colorado Mountain Club Archives, CMC Headquarters, Denver, Colorado.

Colorado Open Space Council (COSC) papers, Denver Public Library, Western History Collection, Denver, Colorado.

Colorado Wildlife Federation papers, Denver Public Library, Western History Collection, Denver, Colorado.

Conservation Collection, Denver Public Library, Western History Collection, Denver, Colorado.

Conservation Library Collection Archive, boxes 1–14, Denver Public Library, Western History Collection, Denver, Colorado.

Conservation Library Oral History Collection, Denver Public Library, Western History Collection, Denver, Colorado.

Denver Public Library Archive, boxes 98–99, Denver Public Library, Western History Collection, Denver, Colorado.

Environmental Conservation Library (ECOL) Records, Minneapolis Public Library, Minneapolis, Minnesota.

Peter Farb Papers, Denver Public Library, Western History Collection, Denver, Colorado.

Ralph Hill Papers, Denver Public Library, Western History Collection, Denver, Colorado.

Edward Hobbs Hilliard Papers, Denver Public Library, Western History Collection, Denver, Colorado.

Alfred A. Knopf Records, Harry Ransom Humanities Research Center, University of Texas, Austin.

Aldo Leopold Collection, Denver Public Library, Western History Collection, Denver, Colorado.

Outdoor Writers Association of America Papers, Denver Public Library, Western History Collection, Denver, Colorado.

Rocky Mountain Center on Environment Papers, Denver Public Library, Western History Collection, Denver, Colorado.

Sierra Club Records, Bancroft Library, Berkeley, California.

Walter P. Taylor Papers, Denver Public Library, Western History Collection, Denver, Colorado.

William Vogt Papers, Denver Public Library, Western History Collection, Denver, Colorado.

Wilderness Society Papers, Denver Public Library, Western History Collection, Denver, Colorado.

Stanley P. Young Papers, Denver Public Library, Western History Collection, Denver, Colorado.

Howard Zahniser items, Denver Public Library, Western History Collection, Denver, Colorado.

THESES AND DISSERTATIONS

Backes, David. "The Communication-Mediated Roles of Perceptual, Political, and Environmental Boundaries on Management of the Quetico-Superior Wilderness of Ontario and Minnesota, 1920–1965." Ph.D. diss., University of Wisconsin–Madison, 1988.

Baldwin, Donald. "Historical Study of the Western Origin, Application and Development of the Wilderness Concept." Ph.D. diss., University of Denver, 1965.

Collins, Kay. "The Transmountain Diversion of Water from the Colorado River: A Legal Historical Study." M.A. thesis, University of New Mexico, 1965.

Doron, William D. "RARE II and Wilderness in California National Forests: The Politics of an Enduring Issue." Ph.D. diss., Claremont Graduate School, 1983.

Gilligan, James P. "The Development of Policy and Administration of Forest Service Primitive and Wilderness Areas in the Western United States." Ph.D. diss., University of Michigan, 1954.

Hesson, Jack M. "The Legislative History of the Wilderness Act." M.A. thesis, San Diego State University, 1967.
Kirk, Andrew G. "Conservationists and Wilderness Preservation in Colorado." M.A. thesis, University of Colorado at Denver, 1992.
Knight, Teri Ann. "Nevada Wilderness: A Case Study of Special Interest Groups." Ph.D. diss., University of Colorado, Boulder, 1989.
Neel, Susan Rhoades. "Irreconcilable Differences: Reclamation, Preservation, and the Origins of the Echo Park Dam Controversy." Ph.D. diss., University of California–Los Angeles, 1990.
Parham, Robert B. "The Civilian Conservation Corps in Colorado, 1933–1942." M.A. thesis, University of Colorado, Boulder, 1981
Voss, Walter Andrew. "Colorado and Forest Conservation." M.A. thesis, University of Colorado Boulder, 1931.
Zeff, Robin Lee. "Not in My Backyard/Not in Anyone's Backyard: A Folkloristic Examination of the American Grassroots Movement for Environmental Justice." Ph.D. diss., Indiana University, 1990.

INTERVIEWS

Carr, Lee. Interview with author. Denver, Colorado, March 26, 1992.
Collins, Kay. Series of phone interviews with author, June 1995.
Collins, Kay. Interview with author, Las Vegas, Nevada, November 1999.
Cumming, Linda. Interview with author. Denver, Colorado, July 10, 1995.
Finstick, Eric. Interview with author. Denver, Colorado, March 26, 1992.
Fuehrer, Roger. Interview with author. Denver, Colorado, July 6, 1992.
Hilliard, Joy. Interview with author. Denver, Colorado, July 13, 1992, and June 1995.
Kingery, Hugh E. Interview with author. Denver, Colorado, July 13, 1992.
Lamm, Richard D. Phone interview with author. Denver, Colorado, July 16, 1992.
Mounsey, Bill. Interview with author. Denver, Colorado, July 6, 1992.
Robertson, Todd. Interview with author. Denver, Colorado, March 11, 1992.
Swem, Ted. Series of interviews with author. Denver, Colorado, June–July, 1995.

ARTICLES

Backes, David. "Wilderness Visions: Arthur Carhart's Proposal for the Quetico-Superior Wilderness." *Forest and Conservation History* 35 (July 1991): 128–37.
Baker, Richard A. "The Conservation Congress of Anderson and Aspinall, 1963–64." *Journal of Forest History* 29 (1985): 104–19.
Baldwin, Donald. "Wilderness: Concept and Challenge." *Colorado Magazine* 44 (summer 1967): 226–40.
Beaton, Timothy J. "For Which the Bell Should Toll: The Doctrine of Federal Reserved Water Rights Has Run Its Course." *ELS Dialogue: University of Colorado Law School Environmental Law Society Journal*, March 1987, 1–8.
Biggs, Mary. "Librarians and the 'Woman Question': An Inquiry into Conservatism." *Journal of Library History* 17 (fall 1982): 409–28.
Booth, W. W. "Forest Conservation." *Trail and Timberline* 87 (December 1925): 1–2.
Borden, Harold L., and Fred R. Johnson. "Plan for the Recreational Development of Mount of the Holy Cross Region." *Journal of Forest History* 28 (October 1930): 813–16.

Brooks, Paul. "Congressman Aspinall vs. the People of the United States." *Harper's Magazine*, March 1963: 60–63.

Brunquist, E. H. "The Point of View of the Conservation Committee." *Trail and Timberline*, no. 339 (March 1947): 44.

———. "Wilderness Areas—Pros and Cons." *Trail and Timberline*, no. 480 (December 1958): 169–75.

———. "Wilderness Legislation: Last Lap?" *Trail and Timberline*, no. 517 (January 1962): 13.

Bush, Monroe. "Denver's Conservation Library." *American Forests* 77, no. 4 (April 1971): 12–15.

Carhart, Arthur. "Recreation in the Forests." *American Forestry* 26 (May 1920): 268–72.

———. "Going to the Glaciers: New Road Planned to Arapaho Peaks to Bring Ice Rivers Within Sixty Miles of Denver by Automobile—This Region, Part of Denver's Recreation Fan, to Be Developed as a Mountaineering Playground." *Municipal Facts*, March–April 1922, 7–9.

———. "What Is Conservation?" *Parks and Recreation*, August 1924.

———. "Two-Fisted Administration." *Blue Book Magazine*, February 1925, 150–82.

———. "Through the Red Dusk." *Blue Book Magazine*, March 1925, 7–33.

———. "The Race of the Forest Men." *Blue Book Magazine*, May 1925.

———. "The Sacrifice of Centipede Ranch." *Five Novels Monthly*, June 1931, 393–424.

———. "Down Went Communism." *Family Circle*, November 3, 1944, 10–11, 15–16.

———. "Raiders on the Range." *Trail and Timberline*, no. 339 (March 1947): 39–43.

———. "This Is Your Land!" *Sports Afield*, April 1947.

———. "Who Says—Sell Our Public Lands in the West?" *American Forests* 53 (April 1947): 152–157.

———. "Don't Fence Us In!" *Pacific Spectator* 1 (summer 1947): 251–264.

———. "Our Public Lands in Jeopardy." *Journal of Forestry* 46 (June 1948): 409–16.

———. "Forest in the Rockies." *American Forests* 54 (July 1948): 296–72.

———. "Land Grab: Who Gets Our Public Lands?" *Atlantic Monthly*, July 1948, 57–62.

———. "Trees and Game—Twin Crops." Washington, D.C.: American Forest Products Industries, c. 1950.

———. "The Menaced Dinosaur Monument." *National Parks Magazine* 26 (January/March 1952): 19–30.

———. "Bad-Man's Last Hangout." *Denver Westerner's Brand Book* 8, no. 10 (October 1952): 8–13.

———. "They Still Covet Our Lands." *American Forests* (April 1953): 11–12, 34.

———. "Poisons: The Creeping Killer." *Sports Afield*, November 1959.

———. "Historical Development of Outdoor Recreation." In *Outdoor Recreation Literature: A Survey*. ORRRC Study Report 27. Washington, D.C.: U.S. Government Printing Office, 1962.

———. "New Conservation Center." *Izaak Walton Magazine* 27, no. 11 (November 1962): 6–7.

———. "The Lore and Learning of Conservation." *American Forests* (January 1963).

———. "The Conservation Library Center of North America." *Green Thumb*, January 1964, 12–13.

Cayton, Colleen. "The Denver Public Library's Regional Energy/Environment Information Center: An Uncommon Cooperative Venture." *Library Journal* 106 (January 1, 1981): 21–25.

Cermak, Robert W. "In the Beginning: The First National Forest Recreation Plan." *Parks and Recreation* 9 (November 1974): 27–33.

Cronon, William. "A Place for Stories: Nature, History, and Narrative." *Journal of American History* 79 (March 1992): 1347–76.

Dain, Phyllis. "Ambivalence and Paradox: The Social Bonds of the Public Library." *Library Journal* 100 (1975): 261–66.

———. "Women's Studies in American Library History: Some Critical Reflections." *Journal of Library History* 18 (fall 1983): 450–63.

Eastlick, John. "The Conservation Library Center of North America." *Special Libraries* 54 (December 1963): 637–38.

Eckaus, R. S. "Appropriate Technology: The Movement Has Only a Few Clothes On." *Issues in Science and Technology* 3 (winter 1987): 62–71.

Elliott, Bert S. "Forest Conservation." *Trail and Timberline*, no. 129 (July 1929): 8.

Evans, Gladys C. "Association Defends National Forests." *Green Thumb* 5 (January 1948): 20–21.

Frome, Michael. "Wilderness: 25 Years and Far from Finished." *National Parks Magazine* 63, nos. 7/8 (July 1989): 35–41.

Fuehrer, Roger. "CMC Conservation: The History Unfolded." *Trail and Timberline*, no. 759 (April 1982): 87–90.

Graf, Harvey J. "Literacy, Libraries, Lives: New Social and Cultural Histories." *Libraries and Culture* 26 (winter 1991): 24–45.

Grey, Dorothy A. "Voices for Wilderness: Conservation Society Serials." *Serials Review* 15, no. 2 (summer 1989): 23–33.

Grotzinger, Laurel. "The Proto-feminist Librarian at the Turn of the Century: Two Studies." *Journal of Library History* 10 (July 1975): 195–213.

Ham, Vaughn E. "The President's Message." *Trail and Timberline*, no. 423 (March 1954): 38.

Harvey, Mark W. T. "Echo Park, Glen Canyon, and the Postwar Wilderness Movement." *Pacific Historical Review* 60 (1991): 43–67.

Hays, Samuel P. "From Conservation to Environment: Environmental Politics in the United States Since World War II." *Environmental Review* 6:2 (fall 1982): 14–41.

Hielte, Charles. "Outdoor Viewpoint: Less Griping, More Action!" *Colorado Outdoors* 7, no. 3 (May/June 1958): 33.

———. "Outdoor Viewpoint: We Need Free Access to Public Lands." *Colorado Outdoors* 7, no. 6 (December 1958): 33.

Hinkemeyer, Joan. "Energy/Environment Information Center." *Colorado Libraries*, March 1979, 18–19.

Huffman, Thomas R. "Defining the Origins of Environmentalism in Wisconsin: A Study in Politics and Culture." *Environmental Review* 16 (fall 1992): 47–69.

Jacobson, C. B. "Why Echo Park?" *Trail and Timberline*, no. 423 (March 1954): 31–34.

Jenkins, David. "Object Lessons and Ethnographic Displays: Museum Exhibitions and the Making of American Anthropology." *Comparative Studies in Society and History* 36 (April 1994): 242–70.

Johnson, Fred R. "Primitive Areas in the National Forests." *Trail and Timberline*, no. 140 (June 1930): 10–11.

———. "The National Forests and the Mountain Club." *Trail and Timberline*, no. 245 (May 1939): 55–56.

———. "The Denver Chamber of Commerce Believed in Conservation in 1909." *Green Thumb* 10, no. 8 (August 1953): 34.

Kelly, George. "Is Our Colorado Landscape in Danger?" *Green Thumb* 1, no. 4 (July 1944): 10–15.

———. "Trail Riders Explore Maroon Bells-Snowmass Wilderness Area." *The Green Thumb* 7:11 (November 1950): 18–19.

———. "Freedom of the Wilderness." *Green Thumb* 7, no. 11 (November 1950): 16–17.

———. "What Does Colorado Need?" *Green Thumb* 6, no. 8 (August 1949).

Krieger, George W. "Four Brown Fingers and a Green Thumb." *Denver Westerners Roundup* 47, no. 1 (January–February 1992): 3–18.

Kutzleb, C. A. "Gore Range-Eagles Nest Wild Area." *Green Thumb* 5, no. 7 (July 1948): 8–9.

Leibhardt, Barbara. "Interpretation and Causal Analysis: Theories in Environmental History." *Environmental Review* 12 (spring 1988): 23–36.

Lovins, Amory B. "Energy Strategy: The Road Not Taken?" *Foreign Affairs* 55 (October 1976): 65–96.

Maack, Mary Niles. "Toward a History of Women in Librarianship: A Critical Analysis with Suggestions for Further Research." *Journal of Library History* 17 (spring 1982): 164–85.

Mahler, Herman F. "High Country: An Oldtimer Gives Us Some Watershed Wisdom . . ." *Colorado Outdoors* 7, no. 2 (March/April 1958): 24–25.

Martin, Erik J. "A Voice for the Wilderness: Arthur H. Carhart." *Landscape Architecture* 76, no. 4 (July/August 1986): 71–75.

McCloskey, Michael. "The Wilderness Act of 1964: Its Background and Meaning." *Oregon Law Review* 45 (1966): 288–321.

———. "Wilderness Movement at the Crossroads, 1945–1970." *Pacific Historical Review* 53 (1984): 346–61.

McComb, John, and Douglas Scott. "Update: RARE II." *Sierra Club Magazine,* October 1977.

Melville, McClellan. "A Conservationist Conserves Learning." *American Forests* 79 (January, 1973): 15, 60–63.

Merchant, Carolyn. "The Women of the Progressive Conservation Crusade: 1900–1915." In *Environmental History: Critical Issues in Comparative Perspective,* ed. Kendall E. Bailes, 153–73. New York: University Press of America, 1985.

———. "Gender and Environmental History." *Journal of American History* 77 (March 1990): 117–21.

Miller, Mrs. Charles O. "Echo Park Dam in Dinosaur National Monument Is Not Needed." *Green Thumb,* no. 6 (June 1951): 16–18.

Myatt, William. "The Colorado Mountain Club." *Colorado Magazine* 39, no. 4 (October 1962): 271–88.

Naddy, Raymond. "They Are Not New Words." *Outdoor America* 35 (April 1970): 12.

Nash, Roderick. "A Home for the Spirit: A Brief History of the Wilderness Preservation Movement." *American West* 8, no. 1 (January 1971): 41–47.

———. "Arthur Carhart: Wildland Advocate." *Living Wilderness* 44 (December 1980): 32–34.

Norwood, Vera. "Western Women and the Environment." *New Mexico Historical Review* 65 (1990): 267–75.

Olson, Sigurd. "We Need Wilderness." *Green Thumb* 4, no. 3 (May–June 1947): 20–21.

———. "The Value of Wilderness." *Green Thumb* 7, no. 5 (May 1950): 28.

Passet, Joanne E. "The Literature of American Library History, 1991–1992." *Libraries and Culture* 29 (fall 1994): 415–39.

Peel, Donald E. "Echo Park Dam—Yes or No?" *Trail and Timberline,* no. 423 (March 1954): 30.

Peregrine, Marjorie. "Our Mountain Club Must Protect the Public Lands." *Trail and Timberline,* no. 340 (April 1947): 64–66.

Pesman, M. Walter. "Nature Protection Possibilities." *Trail and Timberline,* no. 140 (June 1930): 2, 12.

———. "Announcing the Formation of the Colorado Forestry and Horticulture Association." *Green Thumb* 1, no. 1 (February 1944): 1–6.

———. "Let's Not Jump in the Dinosaur Lake." *Trail and Timberline,* no. 423 (March 1954): 35–37.

Potter, Lori. "Federal Water Rights and Wilderness Preservation: Escaping the Confines of Consumptive Use." *ELS Dialogue,* March 1987, 1–8.

Rakestraw, Lawrence. "Conservation Historiography: An Assessment." *Pacific Historical Review* 41 (August 1972): 271–88.

Ramaley, Francis. "The Preservation of Natural Areas." *Trail and Timberline,* no. 200 (June 1935): 69.

Rockwell, Robert B. "Conservation Conference a Big Success." *Trail and Timberline,* no. 61 (October 1923): 7.

Rule, Betty Jo. "Can Man Survive? A Unique Library-Within-a-Library Is Doing Its Best to See That He Does." *Library Journal* (April 1970): 1448–49.

Scharff, Virginia. "Are Earth Girls Easy? Ecofeminism, Women's History and Environmental History," *Journal of Women's History* 7 (summer 1995): 164–75.

Schuff, Sally. "Water Wars in the Wilderness." *Colorado Rancher and Farmer* 43 (November 1989): 16–18.

Schwan, H. E. "Forest Conservation." *Trail and Timberline,* no. 213 (July 1936): 77–78.

Sewell, William H., Jr. "A Theory of Structure: Duality, Agency, and Transformation." *American Journal of Sociology* 98 (July 1992): 1–29.

Shoemaker, L. C. "National Forest Wilderness Areas." *Green Thumb* 4, no. 3 (May–June 1947): 12–27.

Stahl, Carl J. "The Recreation Policy of the Forest Service." *Trail and Timberline,* no. 17 (January 1920): 7–8.

Stewart, Francis. "The Case for Appropriate Technology." *Issues in Science and Technology* 3, no. 4 (summer 1987): 101–9.

Sutter, Paul S. "'A Blank Spot on the Map': Aldo Leopold, Wilderness, and U.S. Forest Service Recreational Policy, 1909–1924." *Western Historical Quarterly* 29 (summer 1988): 187–214.

Taylor, Alan. "Unnatural Inequalities: Social and Environmental Histories." *Environmental History* 1, no. 4 (October 1996): 6–19.

Toombs, Kenneth E. "The Evolution of Academic Library Architecture: A Summary." *Journal of Library Administration* 17 (1992): 532–39.

Vaille, Lucretia. "Colorado Mountain Club Scrapbook: The First 10 Years." *Trail and Timberline,* no. 43 (April 1922): 1–10.

Welch, Todd. " 'Green' Archivism: The Archival Response to Environmental Research." *American Archivist* 62 (spring 1999): 74–94.

White, Richard. "Environmental History: The Development of a New Historical Field." *Pacific Historical Review* 54 (August 1985): 297–335.

———. "Environmental History, Ecology, and Meaning." *Journal of American History* 77 (March 1990): 1111–16.

———. "Discovering Nature in North America." *Journal of American History* 79 (December 1992): 874–91.

Williams, Ted. "Natural Allies: If Only Hunters, Anglers, and Environmentalists Would Stop Taking Potshots at Each Other, They'd Be an Invincible Force for Wildlands Protection." *Sierra* 81, no. 5 (September/October 1996): 46–53.

Worster, Donald. "History as Natural History: An Essay on Theory and Method." *Pacific Historical Review* 53 (1984): 1–19.

———. "Transformations of the Earth: Toward an Agroecological Perspective in History." *Journal of American History* 77 (March 1990): 1087–1166.

———. "The Ecology of Chaos and Order." *Environmental History Review* 14:1–2 (spring/summer 1990): 1–18.

Worth, Conrad L. "Working with Conservationists: Reflections of a National Park Service Director." *Journal of Forest History* 24 (1980): 152–55.

BOOKS

Abbey, Edward. *Desert Solitaire: A Season in the Wilderness.* New York: Ballantine, 1968.

———. *The Monkey Wrench Gang.* New York: Avon, 1975.

Abdullahi, Ismail, ed. *E. J. Josey: An Activist Librarian.* Metuchen, N.J.: Scarecrow Press, 1992.

Adams, Henry. *The Education of Henry Adams.* Boston: Houghton Mifflin, Riverside Editions, 1946.

Akeley, Mary L. Jobe. *The Wilderness Lives Again: Carl Akeley and the Great Adventure.* New York: Dodd, Mead, 1940.

Albright, Horace M., and Frank J. Taylor. *Oh, Ranger! A Book About the National Parks.* New York: Dodd, Mead, 1937.

Alexander, Edward P. *Museums in Motion: An Introduction to the History and Function of Museums.* Nashville, Tenn.: American Association for State and Local History, 1979.

Allin, Craig W. *The Politics of Wilderness Preservation.* Westport, Conn.: Greenwood Press, 1982.

Armstrong, Susan J., and Richard G. Botzler. *Environmental Ethics: Divergence and Convergence.* New York: McGraw-Hill, 1993.

Backes, David. *A Wilderness Within: The Life of Sigurd F. Olson.* Minneapolis: University of Minnesota Press, 1997.

Bailes, Kendall, ed. *Environmental History: Critical Issues in Comparative Perspective.* Lanham, Md.: University Press of America, 1985.

Baker, James H., and LeRoy R. Hafen. *History of Colorado.* Vol. 2. Denver: Linderman, 1927.

Baldwin, Donald N. *The Quiet Revolution: The Grass Roots of Today's Wilderness Preservation Movement.* Boulder, Colo.: Pruett, 1972.

Baldwin, J., and Stewart Brand, eds. *Soft-Tech.* New York: Penguin, 1978.

Barth, Gunther. *Fleeting Moments: Nature and Culture in American History.* New York: Oxford University Press, 1990.

Bederman, Gail. *Manliness and Civilization: A Cultural History of Gender and Race in the United States, 1880–1917.* Chicago: University of Chicago Press, 1995.

Berger, Maurice, Brian Wallis, and Simon Watson, eds. *Constructing Masculinity.* New York: Routledge, 1995.

Berman, Marshall. *America in the Sixties: An Intellectual History.* New York: Free Press, 1968.

———. *All That Is Solid Melts into Air: The Experience of Modernity*. New York: Simon and Schuster, 1982.

Berry, Wendell. *The Unsettling of America: Culture and Agriculture*. San Francisco: Sierra Club Books, 1977.

Best, Steven, and Douglas Kellner. *Postmodern Theory: Critical Interrogations*. New York: Guilford, 1991.

Betz, Mathew J., Pat McGowan, and Rolf T. Wigand. *Appropriate Technology: Choice and Development*. Durham, N.C.: Duke University Press Policy Studies, 1984.

Bigwood, Carol. *Earth Muse: Feminism, Nature, and Art*. Philadelphia: Temple University Press, 1993.

Blair, Karen J. *The Clubwoman as Feminist: True Womanhood Redefined, 1868–1914*. New York: Holmes and Meier, 1980.

Blatti, Jo. *Presenting the Past: Essays on History and the Public*. Philadelphia: Temple University Press, 1986.

Blee, Kathleen M. *Women of the Klan: Racism and Gender in the 1920s*. Berkeley: University of California Press, 1991.

Bookchin, Murray. *Post-scarcity Anarchism*. Berkeley: Ramparts Press, 1971.

———. *The Philosophy of Social Ecology: Essays on Dialectical Naturalism*. Montreal: Black Rose Press, 1990.

Botkin, Daniel. *Discordant Harmonies*. New York: Oxford University Press, 1990.

Brand, Stewart. *The Media Lab: Inventing the Future at MIT*. New York: Penguin, 1988.

———. *How Buildings Learn: What Happens After They're Built*. New York: Penguin, 1994.

———. *The Clock of the Long Now: Time and Responsibility*. New York: Basic Books, 1999.

———, ed. *The Whole Earth Catalog: Access to Tools*. Menlo Park, Calif.: Portola Institute, 1968.

———. *The Next Whole Earth Catalog: Access to Tools*. San Rafael, Calif.: Point Foundation, 1980.

Braunstein, Peter, and Michael Doyle, eds. *Imagine Nation: The American Counterculture of the 1960s and 1970s*. New York: Routledge, 2001.

Bronner, Simon J., ed. *Consuming Visions: Accumulation and Display of Goods in America, 1880–1920*. New York: Norton, 1989.

Brooks, Paul. *Roadless Area*. New York: Knopf, 1964.

Brower, David, ed. *Wilderness: America's Living Heritage*. San Francisco: Sierra Club, 1961.

Browning, James. *103 Wilderness Laws: Milestones and Management Direction in Wilderness Legislation, 1964–1987*. Moscow: University of Idaho Press, 1988.

Buell, Lawrence. *The Environmental Imagination*. Cambridge, Mass.: Belknap Press of Harvard University Press, 1995.

Bundy, Mary Lee, and Frederick J. Stielow. *Activism in American Librarianship, 1962–1973*. New York: Greenwood Press, 1987.

Burke, Edmund. *A Philosophical Enquiry into the Origin of Our Ideas of the Sublime and the Beautiful*. Notre Dame, Ind.: University of Notre Dame Press, 1968.

Butler, Ovid, ed. *American Conservation in Picture and Story*. Washington, D.C.: American Forestry Association, 1941.

Callenbach, Ernest. *Ecotopia*. New York: Bantam, 1975.

Callicott, J. Baird. *In Defense of the Land Ethic: Essays in Environmental Philosophy*. New York: State University of New York Press, 1989.

Carhart, Arthur H. *The Ordeal of Brad Ogden: A Romance of the Forest Rangers.* New York: J. H. Sears, 1929.

——. *Colorado.* New York: Coward-McCann, Inc., 1932.

——. *Trees and Shrubs for the Small Place.* Garden City, N.Y.: Doubleday, Doran, 1935.

——. *How to Plan the Home Landscape.* New York: Doubleday, Doran, 1936.

——. *Drum Up the Dawn.* New York: Dodd, Mead., 1937.

—— [Hart Thorne]. *Saddle Men of the C-Bit Brand.* New York: Dodd, Mead, 1937.

—— [Hart Thorne]. *Bronc Twister.* New York: Dodd, Mead, 1937.

—— [V. A. Van Sickle]. *The Wrong Body.* New York: Knopf, Inc., 1937.

——. *The Outdoorsman's Cookbook.* Macmillan, 1945.

——. *Hunting North American Deer.* New York: Macmillan, 1946.

——. *Fishing Is Fun.* New York: Macmillan, 1949.

——. *Fresh Water Fishing: Bait and Fly Casting, Spinning, Lures and Equipment.* New York: A. S. Barnes, 1949.

——. *Hi, Stranger! The Complete Guide to Dude Ranches.* Chicago: Ziff-Davis, 1949.

——. *Conservation, Please! Questions and Answers on Conservation Topics.* New York: Garden Club of America, 1950.

——. *Fishing in the West.* New York: Macmillan, 1950.

——. *Water or Your Life.* Philadelphia: Lippincott, 1951.

——. *The Adventures of Pinto the Cowboy Pony.* Denver: Nifty Novelties, 1952.

——. *Son of the Forest.* Philadelphia: Lippincott, 1952.

——. *Timber in Your Life.* Philadelphia: Lippincott, 1954.

——. "The Home-Town Conservationist." Unpublished manuscript, c. 1957.

——. *The National Forests.* New York: Knopf, 1959.

——. *Planning for America's Wildlands: A Handbook for Land-Use Planners, Managers and Executives, Committee and Commission Members, Conservation Leaders, and All Who Face Problems of Wildland Management.* Harrisburg, Pa.: Telegraph Press, 1961.

——. "This Way to Wilderness." Unpublished manuscript, 1974.

Carhart, Arthur H., and Stanley P. Young. *The Last Stand of the Pack.* New York: J. H. Sears, 1929.

Carr, Marilyn. *The AT Reader: Theory and Practice in Appropriate Technology.* New York: Intermediate Technology Development Group of North America, 1985.

Carson, Rachel. *Silent Spring.* Greenwich, Conn.: Fawcett, 1962.

Cartmill, Matt. *A View to a Death in the Morning: Hunting and Nature Through History.* Cambridge, Mass.: Harvard University Press, 1993.

Chapin, Frederick. *Mountaineering in Colorado: The Peaks About Estes Park.* Lincoln: University of Nebraska Press, 1987.

Chapman, Arthur. *The Story of Colorado.* Chicago: Rand McNally, 1924.

Chouinard, Yvon. *Climbing Ice.* San Francisco: Sierra Club Books, 1978.

Clawson, Marion, and Burnell Held. *The Federal Lands: Their Use and Management.* Baltimore: Johns Hopkins University Press, 1957.

Clifford, James. *The Predicament of Culture: Twentieth-Century Ethnography, Literature, and Art.* Cambridge, Mass.: Harvard University Press, 1988.

Clifford, James, and George E. Marcus. *Writing Culture: The Poetics and Politics of Ethnography.* Berkeley: University of California Press, 1986.

Clough, Wilson O. *The Necessary Earth: Nature and Solitude in American Literature.* Austin: University of Texas Press, 1964.

Cohen, Michael P. *The Pathless Way: John Muir and the American Wilderness.* Madison: University of Wisconsin Press, 1984.

————. *The History of the Sierra Club, 1892–1970.* San Francisco: Sierra Club Books, 1988.

Collingwood, R. G. *The Idea of Nature.* New York: Oxford University Press, 1945.

Commoner, Barry. *The Closing Circle: Nature, Man, and Technology.* New York: Alfred A. Knopf, 1971.

Conn, Steven. *Museums and American Intellectual Life, 1876–1926.* Chicago: University of Chicago Press, 1998.

Cronon, William. *Changes in the Land: Indians, Colonists, and the Ecology of New England.* New York: Hill and Wang, 1983.

————. *Nature's Metropolis: Chicago and the Great West.* New York: Norton, 1991.

————, ed. *Uncommon Ground: Toward Reinventing Nature.* New York: Norton, 1995.

Davies, David W. *Public Libraries as Cultural and Social Centers.* Metuchen, N.J.: Scarecrow Press, 1986.

Davis, Mike. *City of Quartz: Excavating the Future in Los Angeles.* New York: Vintage Books, 1992.

Davis, Richard C., ed. *Encyclopedia of American Forest and Conservation History.* 2 vols. New York: Macmillan, 1983.

deBuys, William. *Enchantment and Exploitation: The Life and Hard Times of a New Mexico Mountain Range.* Albuquerque: University of New Mexico Press, 1985.

deBuys, William, and Alex Harris. *River of Traps.* Albuquerque: University of New Mexico Press, 1990.

Diamond, Irene, and G. Ornstein, eds. *Reweaving the World: The Emergence of Ecofeminism.* San Francisco: Sierra Club Books, 1990.

Dickens, Peter. *Society and Nature: Towards a Green Social Theory.* Philadelphia: Temple University Press, 1992.

Dickson, David. *Alternative Technology and the Politics of Technical Change.* Glasgow: Fontana/Collins, 1974.

Dinan, John A. *The Pulp Fiction Western: A Popular History of the Western Fiction Magazine in America.* San Bernardino, Calif.: Borgo Press, 1983.

Divine, Robert A. *The Sputnik Challenge: Eisenhower's Response to the Soviet Satellite.* New York: Oxford University Press, 1993.

Douglas, Mary. *Purity and Danger: An Analysis of Concepts of Pollution and Taboo.* London: Routledge, 1980.

Douglas, Mary, and Aaron Wildavsky. *Risk and Culture: An Essay on the Selection of Technological and Environmental Dangers.* Berkeley: University of California Press, 1982.

Douglas, William O. *A Wilderness Bill of Rights.* Boston: Little, Brown., 1965.

Drummond, Alexander. *Enos Mills: Citizen of Nature.* Niwot: University of Colorado Press, 1995.

Duerr, Hans Peter. *Dreamtime: Concerning the Boundary Between Wilderness and Civilization.* New York: Basil Blackwell, 1985.

Eastlick, John T., ed. *The Changing Environment of Libraries: Papers Delivered at the 1970–71 Colloquium Series, Graduate School of Librarianship, University of Denver.* Chicago: American Library Association, 1971.

Eastlick, John, and Robert D. Stewart. *Library Management.* Littleton, Colo.: Libraries Unlimited, 1977.

Eastlick, John T., and Willard O. Youngs. *A Survey of the Pikes Peak Regional District Library.* Chicago: American Library Association, 1967.

Eco, Umberto. *The Name of the Rose.* New York: Warner Books, 1980.

Ehrlich, Paul R. *The Population Bomb.* New York: Ballantine, 1968.

Ehrlich Paul R., and Anne H. Ehrlich. *Population, Resources, Environment: Issues in Human Ecology.* San Francisco: Freeman, 1970.

Elliot, Robert, and Arran Gare. *Environmental Philosophy.* University Park: Pennsylvania State University Press, 1983.

Entikin, J. Nicholas. *The Betweenness of Place: Towards a Geography of Modernity.* Baltimore: Johns Hopkins University Press, 1991

Ellul, Jacques. *The Technological Society.* Trans. Joachim Neugroschel. New York: Continuum, 1980.

Etulain, Richard, and Wallace Stegner. *Conversations with Wallace Stegner on Western History and Literature.* Salt Lake City: University of Utah Press, 1983.

Etulain, Richard. *Re-imagining the Modern American West: A Century of Fiction, History, and Art.* Tucson: University of Arizona Press, 1996.

———. *Telling Western Stories: From Buffalo Bill to Larry McMurtry.* Albuquerque: University of New Mexico Press, 1999.

Evans, Sara M. *Born for Liberty: A History of Women in America.* New York: Free Press, 1989.

Evernden, Neil. *The Natural Alien: Humankind and Environment.* Toronto: University of Toronto Press, 1985.

———. *The Social Creation of Nature.* Baltimore: Johns Hopkins University Press, 1992.

Ezell, Margaret J. M., and Katherine O'Brien O'Keeffe. *Cultural Artifacts and the Problem of Meaning.* Ann Arbor: University of Michigan Press, 1994.

Farb, Peter. *Face of North America: The Natural History of a Continent.* New York: Harper and Row, 1963.

Farber, David R. *The Age of Great Dreams: America in the 1960s.* New York: Hill and Wang, 1994.

———. *The Sixties: From Memory to History.* Chapel Hill: University of North Carolina Press, 1994.

Ferkiss, Victor. *Nature, Technology, and Society: Cultural Roots of the Current Environmental Crisis.* New York: New York University Press, 1993.

Fielder, John. *Colorado Our Wilderness Future, Proposed Additions to the Wilderness System.* Englewood, Colo.: Westcliffe, 1990.

Findlay, John M. *Magic Lands: Western Cityscapes and American Culture After 1940.* Berkeley: University of California Press, 1992.

Flader, Susan. *Thinking Like a Mountain: Aldo Leopold and the Evolution of an Ecological Attitude Toward Deer, Wolves, and Forests.* Columbia: University of Missouri Press, 1974.

Flader, Susan, and J. Baird Callicott, eds. *The River of the Mother of God and Other Essays by Aldo Leopold.* Madison: University of Wisconsin Press, 1991.

Fox, Richard Wightman, and T. J. Jackson Lears. *The Culture of Consumption: Critical Essays in American History, 1880–1980.* New York: Pantheon, 1983.

Fox, Stephen. *The American Conservation Movement: John Muir and His Legacy.* Madison: University of Wisconsin Press, 1981.

Fradkin, Philip L. *Sagebrush Country: Land and the American West.* New York: Knopf, 1989.

Fromme, Michael. *Battle for the Wilderness.* New York: Praeger, 1974.

Frykman, Jonas, and Orvar Löfgren. *Culture Builders: A Historical Anthropology of Middle-Class Life.* Translated by Alan Crozier. New Brunswick, N.J.: Rutgers University Press, 1987.

Gaard, Greta, ed. *Ecofeminism: Women, Animals, Nature.* Philadelphia: Temple University Press, 1993.

Garrison, Dee. *Apostles of Culture: The Public Librarian and American Society, 1876–1920*. New York: Free Press, 1979.

Geertz, Clifford. *The Interpretation of Cultures*. New York: Basic Books, 1973.

Giddens, Anthony. *A Contemporary Critique of Historical Materialism*. Berkeley: University of California Press, 1981.

Gitlin, Todd. *The Sixties: Years of Hope, Days of Rage*. New York: Bantam, 1987.

Gladden, James N. *The Boundary Waters Canoe Area: Wilderness Values and Motorized Recreation*. Ames: Iowa State University Press, 1990.

Glaser, Jane R., and Artemis A. Zenetou, eds. *Gender Perspectives: Essays on Women in Museums*. Washington, D.C.: Smithsonian Institution Press, 1994.

Gleick, James. *Chaos: Making a New Science*. New York: Viking, 1987.

Godfrey, Bob, and Dudley Chelton. *Climb! Rock Climbing in Colorado*. Boulder, Colo.: Alpine House, 1977.

Goetsch, Lori A., and Sarah B. Watstein. *On Account of Sex: An Annotated Bibliography on the Status of Women in Librarianship, 1987–1992*. Metuchen, N.J.: Scarecrow Press, 1993.

Goldberg, Robert Alan. *Hooded Empire: The Ku Klux Klan in Colorado*. Urbana: University of Illinois Press, 1981.

Gordon, Linda. *Women's Body, Women's Right: Birth Control in America*. New York: Penguin, 1990.

Gottlieb, Robert. *Forcing the Spring: The Transformation of the American Environmental Movement*. Washington, D.C.: Island Press, 1993.

Graf, William L. *Wilderness Preservation and the Sagebrush Rebellions*. Savage, Md.: Rowman and Littlefield, 1990.

Green, Harvey. *Fit for America: Health, Fitness, Sport and American Society*. Baltimore: Johns Hopkins University Press, 1986.

Grotzinger, Laurel Ann. *The Power and the Dignity: Librarianship and Katherine Sharp*. New York: Scarecrow Press, 1966.

Haraway, Donna. *Primate Visions: Gender, Race, and Nature in the World of Modern Science*. New York: Routledge, 1989.

———. *Simians, Cyborgs, and Women: The Reinvention of Nature*. New York: Routledge, 1991.

Harding, Jim, ed. *Tools for the Soft Path*. San Francisco: Friends of the Earth, 1979.

Hartmann, Betsy. *Reproductive Rights and Wrongs*. New York: Harper and Row, 1987.

Harvey, David. *The Condition of Postmodernity*. Cambridge: Basil Blackwell, 1989.

Harvey, Mark W. T. *A Symbol of Wilderness: Echo Park and the American Conservation Movement*. Albuquerque: University of New Mexico Press, 1994.

Hayles, Katherine N. *The Cosmic Web: Scientific Field Models and Literary Strategies in the Twentieth Century*. Ithaca, N.Y.: Cornell University Press, 1984.

———. *Chaos Bound: Orderly Disorder in Contemporary Literature and Science*. Ithaca, N.Y.: Cornell University Press, 1990.

Hays, Samuel P. *Conservation and the Gospel of Efficiency: The Progressive Conservation Movement, 1890–1920*. Cambridge, Mass.: Harvard University Press, 1959.

———. *Beauty, Health, and Permanence: Environmental Politics in the United States, 1955–1985*. Cambridge: Cambridge University Press, 1987.

———. *Explorations in Environmental History: Essays by Samuel P. Hays*. Pittsburgh: University of Pittsburgh Press, 1998.

Heim, Kathleen M., and Dianne J. Ellsworth, eds. *The Status of Women in Librarianship: Historical, Sociological, and Economic Issues*. New York: Neal-Schuman, 1983.

Helvarg, David. *The War Against the Greens: The "Wise-Use" Movement, the New Right, and Anti-environmental Warfare.* San Francisco: Sierra Club Books, 1994.

Hendee, John C., George H. Stankey, and Robert C. Lucas. *Wilderness Management.* Washington, D.C.: U.S. Department of Agriculture, Forest Service, 1978.

Herber, Lewis [Murray Bookchin]. *Our Synthetic Environment.* New York: Knopf, 1962.

Herndon, Grace. *Cut and Run: Saying Goodbye to the Last Great Forests in the West.* Telluride, Colo.: Western Eye Press, 1991.

Herron, John, P., and Andrew G. Kirk, eds. *Human/Nature: Biology, Culture, and Environmental History.* Albuquerque: University of New Mexico Press, 1999.

Hildenbrand, Suzanne, ed. *Reclaiming the American Library Past: Writing the Women In.* Norwood, N.J.: Ablex, 1996.

Hogner, Dorothy Childs. *Conservation in America.* Philadelphia: Lippincott, 1958.

Hooper-Greenhill, Eileen, ed. *Museum, Media, Message.* London: Routledge, 1995.

Hoy, Suellen. *Chasing Dirt: The American Pursuit of Cleanliness.* New York: Oxford University Press, 1995.

Hughes, Thomas P. *American Genesis: A Century of Invention and Technological Enthusiasm.* New York: Penguin, 1989.

Hunt, Lynn, ed. *The New Cultural History.* Berkeley: University of California Press, 1989.

Jackson, Peter. *Maps of Meaning: An Introduction to Cultural Geography.* London: Unwin Hyman, 1989.

Jackson, Sidney L., Eleanor B. Herling, and E. J. Josey. *A Century of Service: Librarianship in the United States and Canada.* Chicago: American Library Association, 1976.

Jéquier, Nicolas, ed. *Appropriate Technology: Problems and Promises.* Paris: Development Centre Studies, 1976.

Johnson, Inez Lewis. *Colorado's Wealth: A Bulletin on Conservation of Natural Resources.* Denver: State of Colorado Department of Education, 1941.

Junkin, Elizabeth Darby. *Lands of Brighter Destiny: The Public Lands of the American West.* Golden, Colo.: Fulcrum, 1986.

Kammen, Michael. *Mystic Cords of Memory: The Transformation of Tradition in American Culture.* New York: Vintage, 1991.

Karp, Ivan, and Steven D. Lavine, eds. *Exhibiting Cultures: The Poetics and Politics of Museum Display.* Washington, D.C.: Smithsonian Institution Press, 1991.

Keller, Evelyn Fox. *Reflections on Gender and Science.* New Haven, Conn.: Yale University Press, 1978.

Kelly, Kevin, ed. *Signal: Communication Tools for the Information Age. A Whole Earth Catalog.* New York: Harmony Books, 1998.

Kern, Stephen. *The Culture of Time and Space, 1880–1918.* Cambridge, Mass.: Harvard University Press, 1983.

King, Judson. *The Conservation Fight: From Theodore Roosevelt to the Tennessee Valley Authority.* Washington, D.C.: Public Affairs Press, 1959.

Kingery, Hugh E., and Elinor Eppich Kingery. *The Colorado Mountain Club: The First Seventy-five Years of a Highly Individual Corporation, 1912–1987.* Evergreen, Colo.: Cordillera Press. 1988.

Kingsworth, M. Jimmie, and Jacqueline S. Palmer. *Ecospeak: Rhetoric and Environmental Politics in America.* Carbondale: Southern Illinois University Press, 1992.

Kirk, Andrew G. *The Gentle Science: A History of the Conservation Library.* Denver: Denver Public Library, 1995.

Kolodny, Annette. *The Lay of the Land: Metaphor as Experience and History in American Life and Letters.* Chapel Hill: University of North Carolina Press, 1975.

———. *The Land Before Her: Fantasy and Experience of the American Frontiers, 1630–1860.* Chapel Hill: University of North Carolina Press, 1984.

Kor, Layton. *Beyond the Vertical.* Boulder, Colo.: Alpine House, 1983.

Kuhn, Thomas S. *The Structure of Scientific Revolutions.* Chicago: University of Chicago Press, 1970.

Lamm, Richard D., and Michael McCarthy. *The Angry West: A Vulnerable Land and Its Future.* Boston: Houghton Mifflin, 1982.

Langston, Nancy. *Forest Dreams, Forest Nightmares: The Paradox of Old Growth in the Inland West.* Seattle: University of Washington Press, 1995.

Lasch, Christopher. *The True and Only Heaven: Progress and Its Critics.* New York: Norton, 1991.

Lears, T. J. Jackson. *No Place of Grace: Antimodernism and the Transformation of American Culture, 1880–1920.* New York: Pantheon, 1981.

———. *Fables of Abundance: A Cultural History of Advertising in America.* New York: Basic Books, 1994.

Leonard, Stephen J., and Thomas J. Noel. *Denver: From Mining Camp to Metropolis.* Niwot: University of Colorado Press, 1990.

Leopold, Aldo. *A Sand County Almanac and Sketches Here and There.* New York: Oxford University Press, 1987.

Levy, Steven. *Hackers: Heroes of the Computer Revolution.* New York: Penguin, 1994.

———. *Insanely Great: The Life and Times of Macintosh, the Computer That Changed Everything.* New York: Penguin, 1995.

Limerick, Patricia Nelson. *Desert Passages: Encounters with the American Deserts.* Albuquerque: University of New Mexico Press, 1985.

———. *The Legacy of Conquest: The Unbroken Past of the American West.* New York: Norton, 1987.

Long, Franklin A., and Alexandra Oleson, eds. *Appropriate Technology and Social Values: A Critical Appraisal.* Cambridge, Mass.: Ballinger, 1980.

Lorbiecki, Marybeth. *Aldo Leopold: A Fierce Green Fire.* Helena, Mont.: Falcon, 1996.

Lovins, Amory. *The Energy Controversy: Soft Path Questions and Answers.* San Francisco: Friends of the Earth, 1979.

Lowenthal, David. *The Past Is a Foreign Country.* Cambridge: Cambridge University Press, 1985.

———. *The Heritage Crusade and the Spoils of History.* Cambridge: Cambridge University Press, 1998.

Lutz, Tom. *American Nervousness.* Ithaca, N.Y.: Cornell University Press, 1991.

MacCormack, Carol P., and Marilyn Strathern. *Nature, Culture, and Gender.* Cambridge: Cambridge University Press, 1980.

Malin, James. *History and Ecology: Studies of the Grassland.* Edited by Robert P. Swierenga. Lincoln: University of Nebraska Press, 1984.

Marcus, George E., and Michael M. J. Fischer, eds. *Anthropology as Cultural Critique: An Experimental Moment in the Human Sciences.* Chicago: University of Chicago Press, 1986.

Marcuse, Herbert. *One Dimensional Man: Studies in the Ideology of Advanced Industrial Society.* Boston: Beacon, 1964.

Marx, Leo. *The Machine in the Garden: Technology and the Pastoral Ideal.* New York: Oxford University Press, 1964.

McCarthy, G. Michael. *Hour of Trial: The Conservation Conflict in Colorado and the West, 1891–1907.* Norman: University of Oklahoma Press, 1977.

McHenry, Robert, and Charles Van Doren, eds. *A Documentary History of Conservation in America.* New York: Praeger, 1972.

McKibben, Bill. *The End of Nature*. New York: Random House, 1989.

McPhee, John. *Encounters with the Archdruid*. New York: Farrar, Straus and Giroux, 1971.

Meine, Curt. *Aldo Leopold: His Life and Work*. Madison: University of Wisconsin Press, 1988.

Merchant, Carolyn. *The Death of Nature: Women, Ecology, and the Scientific Revolution*. San Francisco: Harper and Row, 1980.

———. *Ecological Revolutions: Nature, Gender, and Science in New England*. Chapel Hill: University of North Carolina Press, 1989.

Mills, Enos A. *The Spell of the Rockies*. Boston: Houghton Mifflin, 1911.

———. *The Rocky Mountain Wonderland*. Boston: Houghton Mifflin, 1915.

Mitman, Gregg. *The State of Nature: Ecology, Community, and American Social Thought, 1900–1950*. Chicago: University of Chicago Press, 1992.

Monnett, John, and Michael McCarthy. *Colorado Profiles: Men and Women Who Shaped the Centennial State*. Evergreen, Colo.: Cordillera Press, 1987.

Mukerji, Chandra, and Michael Schudson. *Rethinking Popular Culture: Contemporary Perspectives in Cultural Studies*. Berkeley: University of California Press, 1991.

Mumford, Lewis. *Technics and Civilization*. New York: Harcourt, Brace and World, 1962.

———. *The Myth of the Machine: The Pentagon of Power*. New York: Harcourt Brace Jovanovich, 1970.

Nash, Gerald D. *The American West in the Twentieth Century: A Short History of an Urban Oasis*. Albuquerque: University of New Mexico Press, 1973.

Nash, Roderick. *Wilderness and the American Mind*. Rev. ed. New Haven, Conn.: Yale University Press, 1974.

———. *The Rights of Nature: A History of Environmental Ethics*. Madison: University of Wisconsin Press, 1989.

———. *American Environmentalism: Readings in Conservation History*. New York: McGraw-Hill, 1990.

Newton, Norman T. *Design on the Land: The Development of Landscape Architecture*. Cambridge, Mass.: Harvard University Press, 1971.

Noel, Thomas J., et al. *Historical Atlas of Colorado*. Norman: University of Oklahoma Press, 1993.

Norwood, Vera. *Made from This Earth: American Women and Nature*. Chapel Hill: University of North Carolina Press, 1993.

Novak, Barbara. *Nature and Culture: American Landscape Painting, 1825–1875*. New York: Oxford University Press, 1980.

Nye, Russel. *The Unembarrassed Muse: The Popular Arts in America*. New York: Dial Press, 1970.

Oelschlaeger, Max. *The Idea of Wilderness: From Prehistory to the Age of Ecology*. New Haven, Conn.: Yale University Press, 1991.

———, ed. *The Wilderness Condition: Essays on Environment and Civilization*. San Francisco: Sierra Club Books, 1992.

Offen, Ron. *Cagney*. Chicago: Henry Regnery, 1972.

Ogden, Gerald. *The U.S. Forest Service: A Historical Bibliography, 1876–1972*. Davis: Agricultural History Center at the University of California, 1976.

Ormes, Robert M. *Guide to the Colorado Mountains*. Denver: Colorado Mountain Club, 1957.

Orr, David. *Earth in Mind*. Washington, D.C.: Island Press, 1994.

Osborn, Fairfield. *Our Plundered Planet*. Boston: Little, Brown, 1948.

Paehlke, Robert C. *Environmentalism and the Future of Progressive Politics.* New Haven, Conn.: Yale University Press, 1989.

Passet, Joanne E. *Cultural Crusaders: Women Librarians in the American West, 1900–1917.* Albuquerque: University of New Mexico Press, 1994.

Pearce, Susan M. *Museums, Objects, and Collections.* Washington, D.C.: Smithsonian Institution Press, 1992.

Petroski, Henry. *The Pencil: A History of Design and Circumstance.* New York: Knopf, 1992.

Petulla, Joseph M. *American Environmental History: The Exploitation and Conservation of Natural Resources.* San Francisco: Boyd and Fraser, 1977.

———. *American Environmentalism: Values, Tactics, Priorities.* College Station: Texas A&M University Press, 1980.

Pollan, Michael. *Second Nature: A Gardener's Education.* New York: Atlantic Monthly Press, 1991.

Potter, David M. *People of Plenty: Economic Abundance and the American Character.* Chicago: University of Chicago Press, 1954.

Reed, James. *The Birth Control Movement and American Society: From Private Vice to Public Virtue.* Princeton, N.J.: Princeton University Press, 1983.

Reich, Charles A. *The Greening of America: How the Youth Revolution Is Trying to Make America Livable.* New York: Random House, 1970.

Reiger, John F. *American Sportsmen and the Origins of Conservation.* Norman: University of Oklahoma Press, 1986.

Reisner, Marc. *Cadillac Desert: The American West and Its Disappearing Water.* New York: Penguin, 1986.

Rheingold, Howard, ed. *The Millennium Whole Earth Catalog.* San Francisco: HarperSanFrancisco, 1994.

Richardson, Elmo R. *The Politics of Conservation: Crusades and Controversies, 1897–1913.* Berkeley: University of California Press, 1962.

Ripley, Dillon. *The Sacred Grove: Essays on Museums.* London: Victor Gollancz, 1970.

Roach, Gerry. *Colorado's Fourteeners: From Hikes to Climbs.* Golden, Colo.: Fulcrum, 1992.

Robbins, Roy M. *Our Landed Heritage: The Public Domain, 1776–1936.* Gloucester, Mass.: Peter Smith, 1960.

Robbins, William G. *American Forestry: A History of National, State, and Private Cooperation.* Lincoln: University of Nebraska Press, 1985.

Robertson, Janet. *The Front Rangers: A History of the Boulder Group of the Colorado Mountain Club.* Boulder, Colo.: Colorado Mountain Club, 1971.

———. *The Magnificent Mountain Women: Adventures in the Colorado Rockies.* Lincoln: University of Nebraska Press, 1990.

Rolston, Holmes. *Environmental Ethics: Duties to and Values in the Natural World.* Philadelphia: Temple University Press, 1988.

———. *Conserving Natural Value.* New York: Columbia University Press, 1994.

Roszak, Theodore. *The Making of a Counter Culture: Reflections on the Technocratic Society and Its Youthful Opposition.* Garden City, N.Y.: Doubleday, 1969.

———. *Where the Wasteland Ends: Politics and Transcendence in Postindustrial Society.* Garden City, N.Y.: Anchor, 1973.

———. *The Voice of the Earth.* New York: Simon and Schuster, 1992.

Rothman, Hal. *The Greening of a Nation? Environmentalism in the United States Since 1945.* New York: Harbrace, 1997.

———. *Saving the Planet: The American Response to the Environment in the Twentieth Century.* Chicago: Ivan R. Dee, 2000.

Rotundo, Anthony. *American Manhood: Transformations in Masculinity from the Revolution to the Modern Era*. New York: Basic Books, 1993.

Runte, Alfred. *Yosemite: The Embattled Wilderness*. Lincoln: University of Nebraska Press, 1990.

Rybczynski, Witold. *Paper Heroes: A Review of Appropriate Technology*. Garden City, N.Y.: Anchor Books, 1980.

———. *Taming the Tiger: The Struggle to Control Technology*. New York: Penguin, 1985.

Sale, Kirkpatrick. *The Green Revolution: The American Environmental Movement, 1962–1992*. New York: Hill and Wang, 1993.

Schumacher, E. F. *Small Is Beautiful: Economics as If People Mattered*. New York: Harper and Row, 1973.

Schuman, Patricia Glass, ed. *Social Responsibilities and Libraries*. New York: Bowker, 1976.

Schwartz, William, ed. *Voices for the Wilderness*. New York: Ballantine, 1969.

Scott, Anne Firor. *Natural Allies: Women's Associations in American History*. Urbana: University of Illinois Press, 1993.

Seager, Joni. *Earth Follies: Coming to Feminist Terms with the Global Environmental Crisis*. New York: Routledge, 1993.

Searle, R. Newell. *Saving Quetico-Superior: A Land Set Apart*. St. Paul: Minnesota Historical Society Press, 1977.

Shabekoff, Philip. *A Fierce Green Fire: The American Environmental Movement*. New York: Hill and Wang, 1993.

Shauit, David. *The Politics of Public Librarianship*. New York: Greenwood Press, 1986.

Shepard, Paul. *Man in the Landscape: A Historic View of the Esthetics of Nature*. College Station: Texas A&M University Press, 1967.

Shi, David E. *The Simple Life: Plain Living and High Thinking in American Culture*. New York: Oxford University Press, 1985.

Shore, William H., ed. *The Nature of Nature: New Essays from America's Finest Writers on Nature*. New York: Harcourt Brace, 1994.

Sinclair, Pete. *We Aspired: The Last Innocent Americans*. Logan: Utah State University Press, 1993.

Slotkin, Richard. *Gunfighter Nation: The Myth of the Frontier in Twentieth-Century America*. Norman: University of Oklahoma Press, 1998.

Smith, Frank. *The Politics of Conservation*. New York: Pantheon, 1966.

Smith, Henry Nash. *Virgin Land: The American West as Symbol and Myth*. Cambridge, Mass.: Harvard University Press, 1950.

Smith, Michael L. *Pacific Visions: California Scientists and the Environment, 1850–1915*. New Haven, Conn.: Yale University Press, 1987.

Soja, Edward W. *Postmodern Geographies: The Reassertion of Space in Critical Social Theory*. London: Verso, 1989.

Sprin, Anne Whiston. *The Granite Garden: Urban Nature and Human Design*. New York: Basic Books, 1984.

Steen, Harold K. *The U.S. Forest Service: A History*. Seattle: University of Washington Press, 1976.

Stegner, Wallace. *Beyond the Hundredth Meridian*. Lincoln: University of Nebraska Press, 1953.

———. *The Letters of Bernard DeVoto*. Garden City, N.Y.: Doubleday, 1975.

———. *The American West as Living Space*. Ann Arbor: University of Michigan Press, 1987.

———, ed. *This Is Dinosaur: Echo Park Country and Its Magic Rivers*. New York: Knopf, 1955.

Stratton, Owen, and Phillip Sirotkin. *The Echo Park Controversy*. Indianapolis: Bobbs-Merrill, 1959.

Strong, Douglas Hillman. *The Conservationists*. Menlo Park, Calif.: Addison-Wesley, 1971.

———. *Dreamers and Defenders: American Conservationists*. Lincoln: University of Nebraska Press, 1988.

Taylor, Bob Pepperman. *Our Limits Transgressed: Environmental Political Thought in America*. Lawrence: University Press of Kansas, 1992.

Thoreau, Henry David. *Walden and Other Writings*. Toronto: Bantam, 1982.

Thorpe, James. *Henry Edwards Huntington: A Biography*. Berkeley: University of California Press, 1994.

Tuan, Yi-Fu. *Space and Place: The Perspective of Experience*. Minneapolis: University of Minnesota Press, 1977.

Turner, Frederick. *Beyond Geography: The Western Spirit Against the Wilderness*. New York: Viking, 1980.

Tweed, William C. *A History of Outdoor Recreation Development in National Forests, 1891–1942*. Clemson, S.C.: Clemson University, 1977.

———. *Recreation Site Planning and Improvement in National Forests, 1891–1942*. Washington, D.C.: U.S. Department of Agriculture, Forest Service, 1981.

Udall, Stewart. *The Quiet Crisis*. New York: Holt, Reinhart and Wilson, 1963.

Ullman, James Ramsey. *Americans on Everest: The Official Account of the Ascent Led by Norman G. Dyhrenfurth*. Philadelphia: Lippincott, 1964.

Unger, Irwin. *The Movement: A History of the American New Left, 1959–1972*.

Van Slyck, Abigail. *Gender and Space in American Public Libraries, 1880–1920*. Tucson: Southwest Institute for Research on Women, 1992.

———. *Free to All: Carnegie Libraries and American Culture, 1890–1920*. Chicago: University of Chicago Press, 1995.

Vogt, Uilliam. *Road to Survival*. New York: William Sloane, 1948.

Wagstaff, J. M., ed. *Landscape and Culture: Geographical and Archaeological Perspective*. New York: Basil Blackwell, 1987.

Wallace, Mike. *Mickey Mouse History and Other Essays on American Memory*. Philadelphia: Temple University Press, 1996.

Ward, Barbara, and René Dubos. *Only One Earth: The Care and Maintenance of a Small Planet*. New York: Norton, 1972.

Warhall, Peter, ed. *Thirtieth Anniversary Celebration: Whole Earth Catalog*. San Rafael, Calif.: Point Foundation, 1999.

Weibel, Kathleen, Kathleen M. Heim, and Dianne J. Ellsworth, eds. *The Role of Women in Librarianship, 1876–1976: The Entry, Advancement, and Struggle for Equalization in One Profession*. Phoenix, Ariz.: Oryx Press, 1979.

Weil, Stephen E. *A Cabinet of Curiosities: Inquiries into Museums and Their Prospects*. Washington, D.C.: Smithsonian Institution Press, 1995.

Weiner, Douglas R. *Models of Nature: Conservation, Ecology, and Cultural Revolution*. Bloomington: Indiana University Press, 1988.

Weingand, Darlene E., ed. *Women and Library Management: Theories, Skills, and Values*. Ann Arbor, Mich.: Pierian Press, 1982.

Westrum, Ron. *Technologies and Society: The Shaping of People and Things*. Belmont, Calif.: Wadsworth, 1991.

White, Richard. *Land Use, Environment and Social Change: The Shaping of Island County Washington*. Seattle: University of Washington Press, 1980.

———. *The Organic Machine*. New York: Hill and Wang, 1995.

Wild, Peter. *Pioneer Conservationists of Western America*. Missoula: Mountain Press, 1979.

Williams, Michael. *Americans and Their Forests: A Historical Geography*. Cambridge: Cambridge University Press, 1989.

Williams, Raymond. *Problems in Materialism and Culture*. London: Verso, 1980.

Williams, Terry Tempest. *Refuge*. New York: Scribner, 1984.

Winter, Michael F. *The Professionalization of Librarianship*. Champaign: University of Illinois Press, 1983.

Worster, Donald. *Rivers of Empire: Water, Aridity, and the Growth of the American West*. New York: Oxford University Press, 1985.

———. *Under Western Skies: Nature and History in the American West*. New York: Oxford University Press, 1992.

———. *The Wealth of Nature: Environmental History and the Ecological Imagination*. New York: Oxford University Press, 1993.

———. *Nature's Economy: A History of Ecological Ideas*. 2d ed. Cambridge: Cambridge University Press, 1994.

———, ed. *The Ends of the Earth: Perspectives on Modern Environmental History*. Cambridge: Cambridge University Press, 1988.

Wrede, Stuart, and William Howard Adams. *Denatured Visions: Landscape and Culture in the Twentieth Century*. New York: Museum of Modern Art, 1991.

Wyant, William K. *Westward in Eden: The Public Lands and the Conservation Movement*. Berkeley: University of California Press, 1982.

York, Robert. *Forest History*. Durango, Colo.: San Juan and Montezuma National Forests, 1984.

Young, Richard, ed. *Environmental Law Handbook*. Bethesda, Md.: Government Institutes, 1975.

Zaslowsky, Dylan, and the Wilderness Society. *These American Lands: Parks, Wilderness, and the Public Lands*. New York: Holt, 1986.

Zimmerman, Michael E. *Contesting Earth's Future: Radical Ecology and Postmodernity*. Berkeley: University of California Press, 1994.

INDEX